CW00927241

ANCIENT ALTERITY IN T

Ancient Alterity in the Andes is the first major treatment of ancient alterity: how people in the past regarded others. At least since the 1970s, alterity has been an influential concept in different fields, from art history, psychology and philosophy, to linguistics and ethnography. Having gained steam in concert with postmodernism's emphasis on self-reflection and discourse, it is especially significant now as a framework to understand the process of 'writing' and understanding the Other: groups, cultures and cosmologies. This book showcases this concept by illustrating how people visualized others in the past, and how it colored their engagements with them, both physically and cognitively.

Alterity has yet to see sustained treatment in archaeology due in great part to the fact that the archaeological record is not always equipped to inform on the subject. Like its kindred concepts, such as identity and ethnicity, alterity is difficult to observe also because it can be expressed at different times and scales, from the individual, family and village settings, to contexts such as nations and empires. It can also be said to 'reside' just as well in objects and individuals, as it may in a technique, action or performance. One requires a relevant, holistic data set and multiple lines of evidence. *Ancient Alterity in the Andes* provides just that by focusing on the great achievements of the ancient Andes during the first millennium AD, centered on a Precolumbian culture, known as Recuay (AD 1–700).

Using a new framework of alterity, one based on social others (e.g., kinsfolk, animals, predators, enemies, ancestral dead), the book rethinks cultural relationships with other groups, including the Moche and Nasca civilizations of Peru's coast, the Chavín cult, and the later Wari, the first Andean empire. In revealing little-known patterns in Andean prehistory the book illuminates the ways that archaeologists, in general, can examine alterity through the existing record. *Ancient Alterity in the Andes* is a substantial boon to the analysis and writing of past cultures, social systems and cosmologies and an important book for those wishing to understand this developing concept in archaeological theory.

George F. Lau is Senior Lecturer at the Sainsbury Research Unit, School of World Art Studies and Museology, University of East Anglia, UK.

ANCIENT ALTERITY IN THE ANDES

A recognition of others

George F. Lau

Routledge
Taylor & Francis Group

LONDON AND NEW YORK

First published 2013
by Routledge
2 Park Square, Milton Park, Abingdon, Oxon OX14 4RN

Simultaneously published in the USA and Canada
by Routledge
711 Third Avenue, New York, NY 10017

Routledge is an imprint of the Taylor & Francis Group, an informa business

© 2013 George F. Lau

The right of George F. Lau to be identified as author of this work has been asserted by him in accordance with sections 77 and 78 of the Copyright, Designs and Patents Act 1988.

All rights reserved. No part of this book may be reprinted or reproduced or utilized in any form or by any electronic, mechanical, or other means, now known or hereafter invented, including photocopying and recording, or in any information storage or retrieval system, without permission in writing from the publishers.

Trademark notice: Product or corporate names may be trademarks or registered trademarks, and are used only for identification and explanation without intent to infringe.

British Library Cataloguing in Publication Data
A catalogue record for this book is available from the British Library

Library of Congress Cataloging in Publication Data
Lau, George F., 1969-
Ancient alterity in the Andes : a recognition of others / by George F. Lau.
p. cm.
Includes bibliographical references and index.
1. Indian philosophy–Andes Region. 2. Other (Philosophy)–Andes Region.
3. Indians of South America–Andes Region–Psychology. 4. Indian
cosmology–Andes Region. I. Title.
F2230.1.P53L38 2012
980'.01–dc23
2012015681

ISBN: 978-0-415-51921-2 (hbk)
ISBN: 978-0-415-51922-9 (pbk)
ISBN: 978-0-203-08473-1 (ebk)

Typeset in Bembo
by Taylor & Francis Books

Printed and bound in Great Britain by
TJ International Ltd, Padstow, Cornwall

CONTENTS

FIGURES

PLATES

Plates can be found between pages 114 and 115.

ACKNOWLEDGMENTS

It seems only right that a book about others begins by showing appreciation to those who have enabled and enriched this work.

I would first like to thank the funding bodies who have made recent field and collections work in Peru and Europe possible. This includes the British Academy, the Heinz Foundation and National Geographic CRE. As always, the Sainsbury Research Unit for the Arts of Africa, Oceania and the Americas has been generous with time and support to get this publication prepared.

I appreciate very much the libraries and research institutions who have made researching and writing the various strands of this volume so delightful and productive. These include the Robert Sainsbury Library (Pat Hewitt, Jeremy Bartholomew and Matthew Sillence) at the University of East Anglia, Dumbarton Oaks (Joanne Pillsbury, Bridget Gazzo and Sheila Klos), the Centre for Anthropology at the British Museum, and the British Library.

Purposefully or not, various people have helped me to think through and visualize ideas found in these pages. In no particular order, these include Aristóteles Barcelos Neto, Bodil Olesen, Jeff Blomster, Scott Hutson, Jeff Quilter, Steve Hooper, Paolo Fortis, Michael Coe, Kevin Lane, Richard Burger, Fiona Sheales, Penny Dransart, Bill Sillar, Jim Bartle, Mary Miller, Donato Apolín, Rimika Solloway, Carolyn Tate, Mathieu Viau-Courville, José Oliver, Colin McEwan, Bill Sillar, Christopher Donnan, Steve Wegner and Ann Peters. I would like to thank Victor Ponte, Juan Paredes, Ann Peters, Helaine Silverman, Chris Donnan and Don Proulx for permission to reproduce photographs and/or illustrations. I would also like to recognize the helpful, critical commentary of the anonymous reviewers of the initial book proposal and the draft script for their trenchant comments. Of course, any errors of interpretation are mine alone.

Sections in Chapter 5 have been adapted and modified from 'The dead and longue durée' (edited by Izumi Shimada, *Living with the Dead in the Andes*, 2012). Similarly, some parts concerning predatorial relations (Chapter 4) have been adapted from work presented at Dumbarton Oaks. Routledge has been fantastic to work with; thanks are owed to Matthew Gibbons for showing interest in this volume very early on in its gestation and, equally, to Amy Davis-Poynter for shepherding it through to its publication phase.

I would like to dedicate this book to my parents, who have always supported my interests and endeavors, and happily continue to.

PROLOGUE

In great part, personal experiences gave rise to the outlook found in these pages. One was my upbringing in Southern California as an immigrant from Hong Kong. There was little more pivotal in my formation than the realization that my family and I were outsiders integrating into a new world. The difficulties of language and everyday lifestyle were revealed by the uprooting, but then also mitigated by initially settling in Los Angeles' Chinatown.

The recognition of my own Asian background did not really sink in, however, until we relocated into a predominantly Latino neighborhood in the northeast part of the city. Our domestic value system surfaced mainly when confronting those of others. Family doxa – e.g., 'work ethic', 'honor', 'responsibility' – did not always chime with the dispositions of my friends and my school cohort. These all had to do with 'face', broadly operationalized in my family as something like reputation and dignity, but with an agency to make me conform and strive to enhance it. It had a pervasive moral implication, judged by and affecting myself and those around me (see classic considerations in Goffman 1967; Hu 1944; Hwang 1987).

More clamorous but no less inculcating were my family's transplanted pagan practices, such as around Chinese New Year. I recall setting up the table to welcome the ancestors to return and dine with us, and impatiently waiting for them to leave so *we* could feast. My brothers and I would light incense and firecrackers, and burn fake paper money. The pyrotechnics wooed back esteemed forebears and scared unwanted spirits and irritated neighbors alike. Here, I reveled, unquestioningly, in the season of Chinese otherness. The lunar celebrations became just as second nature as the other cultural milestones during that part of the year. Christmas and Cinco de Mayo were all part of the 'melting pot', a popular term in the early 80s (but not used much today), of mindful bodily practice.

The other impetus for this book stems from my experience in Peru. This deals less with how others see me abroad, an ineffable mix of 'chino' and 'gringo', than with the process of doing research in the field. As any archaeologist will acknowledge, fieldwork often occasions moments of puzzlement. For me, they usually occur while looking at a pit profile, photographing excavation units, or talking about a scatter of artifacts, all leaving me scratching my head. Sorting out the situation usually requires coming to a plausible interpretation, a best estimate reconciling what I know, what people tell me and what seems reasonable in the given context. Inevitably, the querying and the hope of any successful resolution shift to me trying to situate myself in the perspective of my subjects to piece together some form of account.

This positioning, the taking on of another's perspective and empathetic reasoning through prior knowledge/experience, can be said to be at the heart of archaeology and its epistemology. In other words, a not inconsiderable proportion of our work is really about producing knowledge about others by locating ourselves and questions in a past made tractable through appeals to conditioned logics and comparison. The aim is to sense and appraise ancient contexts while alternating between our optics and those of others. This book proceeds with the hope of revealing something of those perspectives.

1

RECOGNIZING OTHERS

An introduction

If the lure of archaeology is a universal curiosity about the past, what hooks us, I would suggest, is the fascination to know its others – that is, those beings who are not us. We are constantly bemused by difference and not knowing. Why live there? They seem shorter. Why do it that way? They ate that? What an alien aesthetic.

If it was only a singular humanity, opinion or psychic unity that appealed, we need not search for this commonplace – for we already would know any outcome of that investigation. We need only look to ourselves or our biologies. It is because we trust in the inherent potential for difference, that we seek to find out more about them.

This book reveals how archaeologists might approach alterity in the past, here taken as the quality and imagination of otherness. It is perhaps axiomatic that in relating to others, both physically and cognitively, we come to comprehend and develop opinions about them. We sense and imagine others: we glorify and demonize them; we can like others but also liken them. They become monsters and paragons of beauty. They are sources of envy and appropriation, but are also desirable. In the process of understanding how alterity can work, we can also reveal something about ourselves.[1]

Several postulates frame my approach. The first is that recognition of and relations with unlike selves form the person (e.g., Fowler 2004; Gosden 2004; Harrison 1993; Strathern 1988; Viveiros de Castro 1992). That is, our status as individuals and self-hood are not predetermined at birth or even the course of our adult lives. Rather, we constantly develop personal statuses through engagements with others. These prompt recognition of selfhood, on the part of ego, but also from others.

A second postulate is that if alterity works as a basic human impulse now – at least in ethnographic reckoning – there is no reason to believe that it did not for past cultures. It would follow that it should be in the archaeological record that we can observe alterity. In fact, ancient art and other forms of cultural elaboration ('objects') tell us quite plainly that others mattered to people. Otherness manifested and was countenanced through various means, such as weapons, images, clothing and types of settlements. It is notable, then, that alterity to date has resisted sustained archaeological treatment. The lack of systematic study likely results from the limitations of the archaeological record and, perhaps just as important, scholarly doubts about the ability to deal with and recover aspects of prehistoric 'mind' or cognition (DeMarrais et al. 2004; Renfrew and Zubrow 1994). Archaeologists, especially those working in academic traditions, tend to stick close to empirical data. Interpretation tends toward the functional, and western understandings of the rational and adaptive.

In this book, I contend that archaeologists can profitably study alterity in prehistoric contexts that lack formal writing. In methodological terms, because of alterity's basis in social relations, it follows that it needs to be considered a fundamental dimension which effects archaeological variability. That is, alterity must enter into the net behavioral processes that affect the character and survivorship of the archaeological record (Schiffer 1995). In this volume, I comment on an increasingly reliable archaeological sample (ceramics, buildings, sites, settlement systems, etc.) from the Central Andes and, more specifically, of Peru.

While this book's approach is grounded in comparison of historical groups, it will foreground prehistoric things and contexts. Archaeological studies of alterity are generally informed by texts and text-based studies of historical sources within or about the society or culture in question (e.g., Gnecco 1999; Hay 2010; Oliver 2009; Pugh 2009; Torrence and Clarke 2000; Van de Guchte 1999); studies of colonial encounters between the west and non-west are especially prominent. This study, by obligation, cannot rely on formal written records that directly illuminate the groups and a time period. Rather, it must work mainly from the evidence of 'prehistoric' materials.

In an influential paper about the value of things, anthropologist Arjun Appadurai (1986: 5) pleaded for scholars to be more attentive to objects, their relative values, and how they matter to us, since 'things in general ... constitute the first principles and the last resort of archeologists'. The provocation remains powerful, but I would now partly disagree with it. The first principle and last resort of archaeology has to be ourselves, those who are charged with the analysis (cognizing and writing) of those things of the past that somehow make them intelligible, e.g., to students, colleagues, funding bodies, the general public, posterity. This is doubly entangled: knowledge is made through us about others, but it is also for others by us.

Writing overtly about the other might be considered part of the theoretical move toward a more reflexive archaeology (e.g., Bender et al. 2007; Hodder 2000). The move emphasizes drawing comparisons between contemporary and ancient experience. The move also concedes that any interpretation about the archaeological other, by obligation, draws in the views and background of the commentator.

My main question concerns how past others regarded their others. The rationale and outlook for the task are optimistic. Not only should alterity be 'located' in the prehistoric record, I contend that it should and can be investigated with some degree of rigor. My approach proceeds on the working premise that material things can instantiate and pilot forms of alterity. This is not merely a process of objectifying or materializing ideology, what archaeologists sometimes emphasize to explain why and how elites make and use things (e.g., luxury items, ornaments, monuments) to further their privileged position and authority. I aim to show that alterity, while certainly responsive to ideologies, is always embedded in multiple scales, and is prone to change. Sometimes, alterity, as reflected through elaborate objects and action, appears to be opposed to elite ideology altogether, or can be seen to resist and problematize it. By the same token, alterity frequently piggybacks on but can also be independent of the processes of social complexity.

For example, an enchilada or a Diego Rivera mural can serve equally well as signs of Mexican alterity, but, gladly, they rarely enter into the current furore about border exclusion, alien immigrants and deportation. A more prominent objectification of the heated social relations is the US–Mexico border. For many, it is the salvation of middle America: they want it higher and more fortified to stop the hordes. For others, it remains the gateway to opportunity, a chance to join the other. For others still, it is a measure of political stance, a drain on taxpayers' money, or merely a palliative for deeper, more chronic social ills. People are drawn to it: the border serves as, rather literally, an object of contention and a prism mirroring many facets of otherness.

The example also serves to introduce another general tenet of this book: the agency of objects. This holds that objects are effective, agentive things. They are not simply inert vehicles for materializing cultural preferences, styles or ideologies, but are often capable of actively mediating social relations. In effect, they do stuff in addition to being bearers of meaning. For this reason, they can be seen to have some properties of a social agent/person located within a network of relations with other social beings, in what anthropologist Alfred Gell (1998) dubbed the 'art nexus'. The utility of Gell's analysis, of course, extends beyond the examination of artworks, and contributes more generally to the theorization of things, for people.[2] Detailed more fully in previous work (Lau 2006b, 2010d, 2011), my perspective on agentive objects in the Andes stresses object–person relations, to the extent possible, in their original contexts. To examine alterity, understandings of objects in the archaeological record mediating selves and others in context are postulated and ultimately underwrite my conclusions. Thus, my aim with the analysis is to help begin to define, via archaeology, some of the coordinates and limits of alterity for an ancient culture.

The following chapters center on the ancient Andean cultural tradition known as Recuay, which flourished from approximately AD 1 to 700. The culture characterized a series of non-state societies in the intermontane valleys of the north-central Andes, in the region today comprised mainly of the Ancash Department, Peru (Plate 1). During the time, groups underwent a series of remarkable changes. Several more centralized, chiefly polities emerged later in its history and some groups showed remarkably greater wealth and ability to organize labor (Gero 1990; Grieder 1978; Lau 2011). As we shall see, many Recuay groups had intensive engagements, physical and cognitive, with their neighbors, most notably with the Moche people on Peru's north coast. The developments also happened after the fall of the Chavín civilization and before the rise of the Wari state, both of which had notable effects on the trajectory of the tradition. Dirt archaeology amply reflects this socio-cultural dynamism, especially in domestic, ceremonial and mortuary contexts. The Recuay themselves took pains to stress the new developments through the use and imagery of valuables – what I refer to periodically as artworks.[3] Their imagery almost always concerns the regard for the other.

A focus on Recuay also has the virtue of presenting new empirical data on a long recognized, but little studied culture. The culture is wonderfully vibrant and yet is undervalued in terms of its general contribution to the study of ancient world cultures. Recuay provides a convenient, more or less bounded totality (a 'culture') for my purposes because much of its material record shows a great attention to the recognition and engagement of others. The insights resulting from my analyses are bundled together to consolidate and enhance knowledge about this cultural tradition. Using Recuay culture as the laboratory for exposition is therefore at once an expedient and strategic choice.

Alterity: first principles

If it is essentially human or cultural to be social (that is, to relate to other sentient beings), then there's good reason to know the other. This is because those others can be helpful or instrumental for some purpose. An infant comes to know her mother through smell and touch. One comes to a conclusion that another is a friend because you can rely on him to buy you a beer or to be candid when it's difficult to do so. Of course it is common sometimes to be anti-social, and, even then, it is useful to know for what or whom one has this sentiment. Recognizing another, and acting accordingly, is sometimes a matter of life and death (Boyer 1996; Guthrie 1993). And finding a mate, way before Darwin coined the term natural selection, has long been known to be serious business – not least for dynastic purposes (e.g., Lévi-Strauss 1983; Martin and Grube 2000). How the recognition of others originates as a human faculty is a basic concern of those who study the emergence of humans and communicative intelligence (Dunbar 2004; Mithen 2005). Trusting unknown strangers in collaborative efforts has also been the basis for ancient and contemporary economic life (Seabright 2004). In short, over humanity's past, alterity has mattered in benign as well as agonistic situations, for sheerly adaptive reasons.

Perhaps of greater immediacy to my approach now is that there are different kinds of alterity, which can reside in multiple scales and at different times. The notion of others is rarely fixed or in the singular: it is always contested, perspectival and changing. Like its counterpart, identity, alterity can characterize the local and the regional, as well as the self and also the ethnic group. Alterity also features as social phenomena that can occur simultaneously and change over time. It is also positioned to affect different domains of social life and organization: gender, ritual, politics, kinship, etc. Just as identity has proven to be complex to operationalize systematically in archaeology (e.g., Insoll 2006; Jones 1997; Thomas 1996), there will be no easy recipe or diagnosis to reckon ancient alterity.

The study of alterity is enhanced by knowledge of its complementary notion, identity. It works dialectically with identity. And although we need not 'find' identity to recognize alterity, it needs to exist in some fashion for alterity to exist.

Curiously, alterity might, on occasion, be easier to identify than identity. Although I live and work in England, I hardly see myself as a Brit. I don't root for the Arsenal or Liverpool football clubs, but I certainly count myself as a fan of the game. A related point is true for baseball: a good many bear an aggressive aversion to Yankee or Red Sox fans, who form, incidentally, their own respective 'tribes' and 'nations'. In these cases, it is clearer to pinpoint what one is not, than what one is. The same is true for certain ethnographic cases, where identity[4] is shaped not only of stuff and interpersonal relations on the 'inside', but also what is deemed to be on the 'outside' (e.g., Harrison 1993: 47).

I follow the definition of alterity in the *Oxford English Dictionary* as 'The state of being other or different; diversity, "otherness"'. One notion of alterity comprises the imagination of that quality of otherness constructed to distinguish or oppose oneself and/or one's community. For heuristic purposes, I will use the noun form of 'other' as a general cover term, but with some finer distinctions. Where it might be possible to observe, I will employ 'alter' to distinguish the other in a specific dyadic pairing (e.g., partner in a marriage, or a specific enemy in combat).

Alterity has played a much greater role in other scholarly disciplines. This has been mainly due to postcolonial studies interested in disentangling forms of power relations, not least in representations of colonized peoples (e.g., Bhabha 1994; Said 1978; Taussig 1993; Todorov 1984). Anthropology and, more recently, archaeology have been targets of this critique. By now, it is acknowledged that much analysis in the anthropological tradition is rooted in highly contingent accounts of other peoples and their ways of life (Clifford 1988; Marcus and Fischer 1986). That contingent intervention in reporting is socially constituted – in large part the result of the author's experience and also the institutional and historical exigencies in which the scholar operates (Hodder 1999). In other words, interpretation of others can never be truly objective; it is always locally situated and the result is always a compromise.

Whether we like it or not, archaeologists are implicated in a related process of knowledge production by 'writing culture', a term used by scholars to highlight the process and difficulties of holistic, objective representations of ethnographic groups (Clifford and Marcus 1986). Yet writing in archaeology is situated even farther away from the unit of analysis, whether that be ancient culture, society or humanity. The distance is both temporal, being farther apart in time, and empirical, being more reliant on other, many would call more indirect, forms of evidence.

Traditionally, socio-cultural anthropologists study their subjects through face-to-face encounters and first-hand observations of a living group. Meanwhile, most archaeologists can only approach ancient peoples or cultures from mute, largely static artefacts. What gives them voice, as it were, is the work of the archaeologist (Hodder 1986; Shanks and Tilley 1987). Equipped with a motley array of powerful tools (e.g., excavation, classification, analogy, statistics, radiocarbon dating), technical rigor and scientific method add weight to conclusions. Our main outputs are also exercises in translation: models, texts, photos, line drawings, tables and charts, videos, vocabularies. The stakes of reconstituting and presenting the past are higher than ever before, given the crucial transformative roles that archaeology and archaeological remains have in shaping community histories, identity politics and new heritage economies (e.g., Dietler 1994; Meskell 2002; Politis 2007; Silverman 2002b).

We can also begin to acknowledge that reflection and knowledge production about the other – the physical manifestations which regard, size-up and countenance others – are not restricted to archaeology, ethnography or even post-Enlightenment scholarly thought. It is part of the human condition which obliges an articulation of sociality in diverse but also often very formulaic ways. Alterity frequently has to do with relations with kin and one's community, notions of family, leaders, enemies, the dead and divinities. At the same time, it intervenes, cognitively, at various levels, from the nation-state (e.g., Hobsbawm 1990) to the house (Carsten and Hugh-Jones 1995). These furnish some convenient milestones for organizing this volume, with each chapter detailing a kind of alterity, each with its own expressions of otherness in ancient social life.

Alterity | identity | alterity

Since the 1980s, the topic of social identity and its importance for ancient cultures has been of great interest to archaeologists (Meskell and Preucel 2004). By identity, I mean the understandings which frame a person's recognition of self and those shared understandings of belonging to a particular collective.

The archaeology of social identity studies many kinds of identity, often having to do with gender, ethnicity, postcoloniality, class and inequality, community, to name but a few (e.g., Emberling 1997; Gero and Conkey 1990; Gosden 2001; Joyce 2001b; Schele and Miller 1986). Archaeologies studying identity by way of sexuality, childhood, artisans, death/ancestrality, ritual and the body/experience have also emerged (e.g., Ardren and Hutson 2006; Gillespie and Joyce 2000; Houston et al. 2006; Meskell and Joyce 2003). Much work on identity piggybacks on ethnographic understandings, especially for those regions with cultural continuities and rich direct historical comparisons (e.g., Heckenberger 2005; Janusek 2004; Schele and Freidel 1990).

The diverse kinds of identity find commonality in approaching identity as socially constituted, that is to say, oriented by meanings that people give to 'it'. This might concern types of class such as 'commoner' and 'noble', or types of gender, such as 'male' and 'female'. Cultural dispositions and actions produce identity corporately. Yet if kinds of identity are socially constituted, they are individually experienced and understood, just like alterity.

Like alterity, identity and how it might 'work' come across as rather vague abstractions. What these might be is perhaps best revealed by some further personal reflections. So, for example, I recognize my belonging to a Chinese-American identity because, well, my Chinese physical appearance demands it, but also because I celebrate the lunar new year (not least for mooncakes, red packet money and firecrackers), lived in Los Angeles' Chinatown, and greatly enjoy Hong Kong-style dim sum. I grew up with brothers and sisters who kind of look like me. We went to the same schools and attended to our ancestors; we also speak a broken version of Cantonese. Yet I also recognize that I am a working-class person, because I go to work everyday where my labor and production are alienated from me and commoditized in the economy of knowledge transmission. The tools of my trade – books, paperwork, computers, red pens – are strewn about the place of my work, the office. These are what make me effective. Yet they are obsolete, or at best marginal, when I am out in the field as an archaeologist. This identity abroad occasions a very different assemblage of tools, idioms, social relations and bodily comportment. That identity would be impossible if I was not given, for ninety days at a time, the official status as tourist and visitor by the Republic of Peru.

We can see that identity resides in many sorts of social domains, and can be manifested and produced by many different elements of culture, not least language, cuisine, work, things and shared histories. There is also a crucial temporal axis to identity, especially for those who study it diachronically. Archaeology approaches identity by looking at the ways that material culture actively expresses and reinforces modes of identification, and very often comparing patterns of evidence by phase. This is often at multiple levels – self, family, faction, village, region, nation. Very often, identity is about resistance, about not fitting in or complying.

If identity is everywhere, identity process (e.g., belonging or encompassing) cannot be reduced to singularities, nor is it ever absolute or always in one's control. Any and every thing, action and experience can feasibly count toward identity. This is what is meant when scholars circum-define identities as flexible, fluid, changing and multi-constituted. Its wooliness is made more so in archaeology, where operationalizing the identity concept often either projects into the past contemporary categories or relies on teleological reasoning (Meskell and Preucel 2004: 127). Even language, that great marker of identity, is rarely cut and dried. My severely broken Chinese and occasionally broken English are signs of being 'in-between' categories. Categories for inclusion, if indexed by my proficiency, are more like sliding scales than tidily-bound units.[5]

Furthermore, people go through their lives having many kinds of identities – some which are more enduring (at least for me, Chineseness, gender, class), or which change occasionally (e.g., professional standing). Some might seem situationally more useful or preferable (e.g., archaeology, language), and some inexorably change (e.g., age, notion of community). Some identity markers, such as language, may be less emphatic than others, and show up less as material form, but it is surely no less important. Not having one single category of identity unfortunately means there is no one particular diagnostic or formula for studying it. One can argue persuasively that culture is above all about identity, and identity is nothing else but culture. But that doesn't get us very far for discriminating kinds of identity in the past, their scales or patterns of change.

Faced with this sea of identity, alterity comes to, figuratively, fill a gap or reveal a background in which identity emerges. It has been asserted:

> All human cultures articulate, situate themselves by categorizing the world. Such a predicative act necessarily involves a distinction between that which is allowed into the sphere of culture, and that which is excluded; the circumscription of cultural identity proceeds by silhouetting it against a contrastive background of Otherness.
>
> *(Corbey and Leerssen 1991: vi)*

This 'contrastive background' is key to identifying and understanding cultural identity on the one hand, but also the alterity which serves to frame it. This is especially important in archaeology, which specializes in detecting difference in patterned contexts of different scales. Alterity can be discerned as difference in patterned contexts (the contrastive background).

Just as identity process occurs at multiple scales, the processes of alterity may operate on similar dimensions. Anthropologist Anne-Christine Taylor (1996: 204) remarks on the scalar quality of outside relations for Jivaroan groups of lowland eastern Ecuador:

> being alive is to be perceived, and to perceive oneself, as a person, a notion locally covered by the term *shuar*. This expression refers to a multi-layered set of relations based on contrastive terms: thus, according to context, the term shuar refers to "my bilateral kindred" as opposed to others, "my local group" as opposed to other territorial groups, "Achuar" as opposed to other Jivaroan tribal units, "Jivaro" as opposed to Whites and other Indians, and so on. In short, the term functions as a generalized "we/they" classifier.

As will be described later, Andean groups organize and experience similar categories centered on the notion of community at various different scales (Allen 1988). The criteria of inclusivity might be profitably examined, at least partly, as exclusivity.

This scheme alludes to a perspective that sees alterity (with which one does not identify) as recognized, often purposeful, cultural contrast. If what produces identity are shared norms, things and practices we term 'culture' and the generative framework for learned dispositions, evaluation and change, which we term the *habitus* (Bourdieu 1977), these same frameworks ought to characterize the processes of alterity, as difference-making. Yet these also seem to have less to do with alterity because of lack of sharedness and lack of practice that one might have with others. Curiously, while the methodological interest has been to detect variability (differences in comparable fields), only the position of self-identifying has been of interest, and has undergone serious consideration. The record of the non-identifying or the background has not.

The alterities of some kinds of others revealed in this book (e.g., predators, enemies, the dead) seem to have a great degree of stability, both across cultures and through time. The recognition of otherness tends to be a little more fixed, stable or normative – partly because we tend not to know. Part of the definition of alterity implies an ambiguity, a gap in knowing. Alterity's job fills that gap with certain evaluations – cognitive assessments informed by knowledge, common opinion, images and rhetoric.

For Tzvetan Todorov (1984), prior knowledge always impinges in alterity process, because recognition of others is founded on comparison and the intervention of oneself. In what he calls the 'problematics of alterity', the self is crucial in relating to others:

> First of all, there is a value judgment (an axiological level): the other is good or bad, I love or do not love him, or, as was more likely to be said at the time, he is my equal or my inferior ... Secondly, there is the action of *rapprochement* or

distancing in relation to the other (a praxeological level): I embrace the other's values, I identify myself with him; or else I identify the other with myself, I impose my own image upon him; between submission to the other and the other's submission, there is also a third term, which is neutrality, or indifference. Thirdly, I know or am ignorant of the other's identity (this would be the epistemic level); of course, there is no absolute here, but an endless gradation between the lower or higher states of knowledge.

(Todorov 1984: 185)

The third axis, the epistemic level of the not knowing, helps, then, to make alterity more self-sustaining. Identity is perhaps more fluid than alterity because we know ourselves more readily – we experience things that affect our identity and self-identification. Perhaps the most obvious example of this might be age, and how we identify with it. As we mature, we *know* we get more adept at doing things; we *know* we might remember less or our skin wrinkles; we *know* we get less tolerant. Most of us have much less direct knowledge about what it is like to perform homicide or have biologically expired. For that reason, many kinds of alterity might be more normative, and perhaps tend to be less shifting and palpable, archaeologically, than 'identity' – which is inevitably discursive and multifaceted. Put another way, identity presumes some knowledge of the inside (self, community, gender, etc.), some experience with its dispositions. There is no such expectation with alterity. Some kinds of alterity, such as those fomenting stereotypes, are more integrated and enduring, such as national programmes of ethnic inferiorization (Bhabha 1994: Ch. 3). They're sticky, because believers have less to go on.

Alterity might also tend to change less because otherness is often held at arm's length, if not wholly expelled, from our core values and everyday life. Certain kinds of alterity surface and enter into the imaginary more rarely. But when it does, however, it can be explosive and highly-charged. Racial or sexual intolerance comes to mind, and so does ethnic strife. If the difference-making of alterity tends to be slow or tougher to change, might this be a boon for the archaeology of alterity, which is better suited to detect and study large-scale diachronic patterns than rapidly changing instances?

One interesting complication of trying to locate alterity and identity is precisely because we have set it in opposition, or have conceded *prima facie* that difference is 'made'. If it was only a methodological matter of detection, as in discriminating what isn't identity as alterity, there wouldn't necessarily be a problem.

The issue is that alterity, for some Amerindian communities, actually counts as their basis of being – what has sometimes been called 'ontological predation'. In a piece of 'grand unifying theory', Eduardo Viveiros de Castro's 'GUT feeling' (2001) sees alterity *as* the identity process for many lowland Amazonian groups. Partly this is because the framing of society at large and social relations, for many Amazonian groups, extends *beyond* the bounds of kinship and the village. The model holds that one cannot know oneself, be socialized or be sociable without the existence and input of a 'motley crowd of Others' (theorized variously as enemies, friends, traders, strangers, game animals, marriage partners, infants and efficacious spirits). These are supra-local beings who are, first and foremost, kinds of generic, affinal others. These beings are structurally on the outside, yet that outside is encompassed by the notion of potential or virtual affinity – that which is necessary for the production of self and sociability. Production of persons in this scheme is about fundamental contrasts, usually in bodily appearance, between ego and that affinity. Moreover, sociality and identity are predicated on the internalization of others in some form.

Put simply, the potential relations with that motley crowd serve not only to orient sociality, they 'construct' the local group and its identity. Viveiros de Castro (2001: 24–25) avers:

> What makes such communities [kin collectives] "local"? I suggest they are defined and constituted in relation, not to some global society, but to an infinite background of virtual sociality [with potential affines] … [T]hey are made local by the very process of extracting themselves from this background and making, in the most literal sense, their own bodies of kin … [If] difference precedes and encompasses identity … the cardinal rule of this ontology is: no relation without difference.

For some Amerindian groups, then, the recognition of others, alterity, is at the heart of social identity.

Social relations broadly envisioned

In considering ancient alterity, it is incumbent upon us not to exclude the roles that non-humans have in the workings within a given collectivity. For many societies, objects, animals and supernaturals are often key personnel in social relations and understandings of social order and change (Descola 2005; Gell 1998; Viveiros de Castro 2004). Wider recognition about native understandings – for instance about how other cultures go about knowing and doing 'society', 'economy', 'self', 'body' – may be crucial before archaeology can operate the methods to reveal them (see also Alberti and Marshall 2009).

The ethnographic record expands the range of cultural patterns that help us to understand, or bridge, archaeological evidence and interpretation. Studies of lowland South America, especially, have important insights for considering social relations in other Amerindian societies (Fausto and Heckenberger 2007; Viveiros de Castro 1998). Many Amazonian groups perceive certain types of non-humans, such as plants, snakes and felines, to be like humans. They are organized in similar ways, and perform similar activities (make children, hunt, work, drink beer, have houses, etc.) (see also Fortune 1963; Guenther 1988: 195; Walens 1981: 23). One anthropologist asserts: 'Cultivated plants may be conceived as blood relatives of the women who tend them, game animals may be approached by hunters as affines, shamans may relate to animal and plant spirits as associates or enemies'; this is because '[h]aving been people, animals and other species continue to be people behind their everyday appearance' (Viveiros de Castro 2004: 466). People recognize them as beings with needs, intentionalities and dispositions resembling those of humans.

In having comparable patterns of culture, the locus of differentiation between kinds of beings resides in their bodies, or bodily appearance, in the ways that their species-specific corporeal condition shape their perspective (Viveiros de Castro 1998: 478; also Vilaça 2005).[6] For this reason, a crucial aspect of Amerindian alterity is an emphasis on exteriorities, in terms of bodily affects, gestures, capacities and appearances. These form the basis of selfhood and, in related fashion, alterity. The emphasis on attire and body-centric decoration ('social skins') to denote forms of personhood and identity are, of course, important in this regard (Gow 1999; Turner 1980). For in defining oneself, there is the implication of a recognition of others, if only because there is an elementary contrast of what one is not, was before, will be, or by what or with whom one is complemented. This may have particular resonance where persons (human, non-human and certain objects) are privileged and made sociable and 'relational' through very elaborate exterior surfaces (Lau 2010d).

In the diverse literature of lowland South America, scholars find that social others (broadly of humans, non-humans and artifacts), and especially their bodies, are fundamental to notions of selfhood (Descola 2005; Fausto and Heckenberger 2007; Santos-Granero 2009b; Vilaça 2002, 2005). The parts of other beings and artifacts are mobile and can be appropriated or transitioned to other ontological types (Viveiros de Castro 2004), consensually or forcibly (Fausto 2000). In this 'constructional' view of persons, a shared 'Amerindian mode of relatedness' stands as the framework by which every being becomes a synthesis of the combined efforts of all the beings who have contributed, socially and bodily, to its existence (Lagrou 2009; Santos-Granero 2009a).

Many Amerindian groups therefore understand bodies as forms in perpetual change. They are needy, in life and in death, requiring the vitality of others (Allen 1988; López Austin 1988; Monaghan 1995; Weismantel 2004). They are made and reformed through serial actions (e.g., eating, sex, dance, decoration) and substances that act on the body and give 'chronically unstable bodies' shape and meaning (Vilaça 2002, 2005). These are seen to nourish, enculturate and socialize individuals, while also nurturing the body politic (Classen 1993; Lau 2010d; Ramírez 2005). Important diagnostics of being and identity work on exterior corpora, including the 'social skin' (e.g., DeBoer 1991; Gow 1999; Saunders 1999; Turner 1980).

At the same time, what is important about others is that they are vital beings, or have vital, desirable properties that can be alienated. For many Amerindian groups, one might distinguish two genres of writing about sociality that affect the flow of vitality. One is familiar, centered at the level of the house and village community, and emphasizes the 'moral economy of intimacy' (Viveiros de Castro 1996: 188–91) (see also, recently, Sahlins 2011). Practices in this modality stress social reproduction via the contributions of intimate others – namely, kin, relatives and partners; the sharing and circulation of food and fluids produce, indeed embody, society (e.g., Gow 1991; Overing 1989). While this sociality has been studied mainly from the standpoint of village-based ethnography to characterize household practices (see also Allen 1988; Weismantel 1988), its core significance may also operate at more centralized forms of social organization.[7] For example, the moral, nurturing basis of political authority has been seen to be key in the cosmologies of native Andean leadership, what historian Susan Ramírez (2005) has called 'to feed and be fed' in the Inca empire (for earlier polities, see Lau 2010c; Quilter 2010).

The second modality concerns humans acquiring vitality through predation, both physical and symbolic. It is from the forceful taking from the domain of the other that one can enrich and constitute the self, in a 'symbolic economy of alterity' (Viveiros de Castro 1996: 189–90). Appropriation from the other manifests often in varied expressions in the domain of warfare, hunting and affinal relations, not to mention shamanistic practices, anthropophagy and trophy taking (Arnold and Hastorf 2008; Fausto 2000; Viveiros de Castro 1992, 2004). Frequently, these constitute ordered social relations *between* villages and communities. In the exchange, viewpoints and perspectives are transacted, and alterities and outside things are, literally, incorporated. Fashioning oneself and being empowered are thus simultaneously enabled by the contributions from others.

Crucially, the external perspective and subjectivity are not obliterated, but rather are countenanced and often reworked. In killing and eating an enemy, for example, an Araweté warrior of eastern Brazil becomes the enemy, and sees as his enemy did (Viveiros de Castro 1992: 245, 270–71; 2004: 479). Direct comparisons are impossible, but some aspects of perspectivism and ontological predation certainly resonate with Andean patterns. As later chapters will detail, these treat the internalization of outsiders, the emphasis on body parts and trophies, and native theory about leadership (see Arnold and Hastorf 2008; Gose 2008; Ramírez 2005).

While the terms and structures of the process are very Andean, the incorporation of otherness and subjectivities can be seen as part of a more general pattern. To be sure, re-situating social relations with outsiders, via indigenous logics, is a key strategy of native peoples during pivotal historical junctures of intercultural encounter (e.g., Sahlins 1985; Vilaça 2010). Sometimes, this involves the 'stranger-king' pattern in which a new leadership or dynasty (or the institution of sovereignty) is established by an outsider from abroad – the new sovereign subordinates others by, in no uncertain terms, incorporating them, and is, in turn, internalized cosmologically (Sahlins 1985: 75).[8] Material things are crucial in the process of conquest and conversion, not least because they often embody and are used to manage and give meaning to the encounter (Phillips 1998; Taussig 1993; Thomas 1991).

Ancient Andeans also privileged social relations with the dead, what I will treat as another crucial form of alter. We might call this the 'social economy of ancestrality', where engagements with the ancestral dead fund other domains of social and cultural life. This kind of sociality is less prominent in the literature about lowland peoples, but increasingly significant (Chaumeil 2007; Oliver 2009). The dead are a special type of social being: they have presence and importance at certain times and contexts; they have agency even in their absence or when dormant.

The Central Andes has a long tradition of conceiving the dead as living entities who continue to affect the lives of their descendants long after their biological death (Isbell 1997; Salomon 1995). While their original humanity is expired, they continue as persons of a sort that mediate social relations, frequently at very fundamental levels. There was perhaps no greater organizing principle in the late prehispanic Andes than one's ancestor. Tracking descent from esteemed progenitors was the basis for social differentiation, just as their cults acted as the centrifugal force in bringing descendants together as ritual collectivities. This was one of the reasons why their physical presencing was so vital for many cultures of the prehispanic Andes through time (Lau 2008). People saw, heard, touched and interacted with mummified bodies and surrogate effigies as social others.

This book therefore employs a broad definition of the social, which includes divinities, animals and certain objects with which humans engaged. Transactions between them in stylized modes, the 'symbolic economies' itemized above, produced persons and reproduced society at large. The interactions can sometimes be evidenced through archaeological work and sometimes through the imagery of artworks. In other cases, analogies are made through historical comparisons to bridge the data and possible interpretations. The balance of the evidence, especially the case study of Recuay, emphasizes diverse modes of physical interaction with the other and which perpetuate social relations of differentiation. Indeed, the ancient systems I reconstruct can work only if inequality exists and is acknowledged by its participants. Socio-cultural difference is the default position.

Making Andean difference

With respect to alterity in the Andes, general introductory comments are warranted to outline the region as well as Recuay's place in Andean prehistory. Of the six world areas defined as having 'pristine civilization', those which developed autochthonously (without much input from others), the Andean case shows notable characteristics.

The Central Andes is often considered exceptional for certain reasons. Many of the traits used to identify early civilizations were apparently absent in the Andes or were of marginal importance. A writing system, based on a written script, was never developed; nor were intensive agriculture and transportation reliant on animals and wheeled vehicles. A standardized currency and formal markets never held general importance for economic transactions. Hence, key dimensions of civilization – namely record-keeping, taxes, redistribution and intensifying production – took other forms, usually having to do with legitimacy, prestige economies and 'wealth in people' (e.g., Burger 1992a; Jennings 2011; Ramírez 1996: 15; Ramírez 2005).

The Central Andes, as a setting for cultural achievements, has also been considered different because of its unique environment (Fig 1.1). The world's longest continental

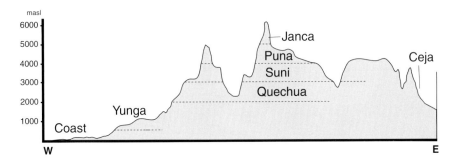

FIGURE 1.1 Schematic cross-section of the Central Andes, showing different ecological zones (masl = meters above sea level). Resources and land-use in each are based on temperatures, precipitation and geography.

mountain range results in tremendous ecological diversity within a tightly bounded and compressed geographic zone.

At the western edge of South America is Peru's arid desert coastline. Its proximity to rich maritime resources, fed by the cold upwelling waters of the Pacific Ocean, made this region habitable and productive for the earliest Peruvians (Moseley 1975). Life-sustaining rivers descend from the mountains to support valley flora and wildlife; the water also irrigates otherwise barren terrain. Moving eastward, one advances rapidly into the western flanks of the Andes, a rocky and desertic area outside the verdant riverine belts. One then ascends into high mountainous areas; just underneath the icecaps and glacial lakes lie zones highly suitable for the intensive agro-pastoralism that supported major populations and the great civilizations of the Andes. Further east, one encounters lushly forested slopes which lead down into the jungle lowlands of Amazonia. The diversity of resources and production zones, all within relatively close proximity, has always been an important variable in Andean lifeways and cosmology.

The vertical orientation of the Andes led the anthropologist John Murra (1972) to conceive of a model, known as 'vertical archipelago' (Brush 1977; Masuda et al. 1985; Mayer 2002).[9] Essentially, the model holds that Andean peoples through time developed adaptive strategies for best coping with the compressed and stacked character of ecological zones, or 'floors' (Fig 1.2). Because most resources for economic self-sufficiency are not found in one zone or season, it is beneficial for a community to establish 'colonies' or 'islands' near multiple resource zones in the vertical landscape. Effective resourcing from the islands, called an 'archipelago', could be through seasonal

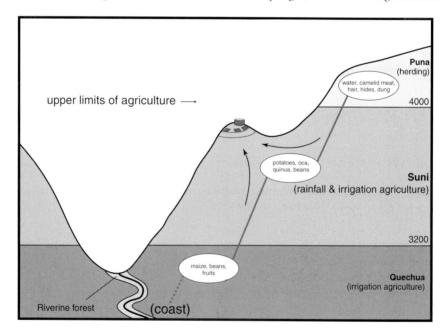

FIGURE 1.2 Acquisition of resources based on a vertical model. Resources from different zones complement each other to achieve community self-sufficiency.

mobility, exchange and other forms of interaction and allowed a given community to acquire the various items required for it to flourish. Verticality characterized groups of different scales, from hunter-gatherers to the largest New World states (Lynch 1980; Masuda et al. 1985; Morris 1985; Stanish 1992).

At the same time that the model has been influential in anthropology and archaeology, it has fueled notions of a particular Andeanness, or *lo andino* (Gade 1999: 31–41; Van Buren 1996). This consists of cultural traditions, dispositions and practices deemed to be distinct to the Andes and resistant to change and outside influence. Interestingly, it is precisely *lo andino*, the particularity of Andean history, lifeways and cosmovision, that is so guarded regarding its difference from other world regions and civilizations.

Since alterity is often pegged to ethnicity and collective identity, a critical problem will be the definition of social groups. The 'ayllu', another key notion in *lo andino*, has been of great importance in this respect. The term originates in the ethnographic and historical literature of native Andean groups, and appears to have had some antiquity (Isbell 1997; Moseley 1999). Ayllu, a Quechua term, basically describes social groups sharing a cosmological basis (usually belief in descent from common ancestors), ritual prerogatives and economic cooperation. This can range from a small lineage to its wider expression in ethnic groups, or even multinational polities such as the Inca empire; some scholars have discussed the notion of ayllu in its 'minimal' and 'maximal' forms (Platt 1986), and different scales of community and belonging (Allen 1981b, 1988).

The taxonomies need not detain us here, for detailed commentary on the term's operationalization in, but also opacity to, Andean archaeology already exists (Goldstein 2005; Isbell 1997; Janusek 2004). In general, I will refrain from using ayllu to describe pre-Inca developments in Ancash, mainly because we have little secure information about what language(s) were spoken at the time.

It should be noted, however, that when I make reference to ancient Recuay social collectivities, I will be making presumptions that they very likely shared some qualities of ayllu and their organization. In part, this is possible because segmented collectivities, styled 'ayllu' and similar units, were paramount in the organization of highland Ancash native society during late prehispanic and colonial times (e.g., Espinoza Soriano 1978; Hernández Príncipe 1923; León Gomez 2003; Masferrer Kan 1984; Zuidema 1973). In the north central highlands of Ancash, ayllu-like collectives very likely developed by the Middle Horizon, and there is additional evidence, mainly of chiefly ancestor veneration, that similar groups existed at least by the early first millennium AD (Lau 2000, 2002).

What is crucial here is that belonging to an ayllu-like group almost certainly predisposed social relations in certain ways. It prescribed relations with all manner of social others: with whom one could marry, ally and work, worship, make economic exchanges, or with whom one fought and participated in ritual activities (Allen 1981b; Duviols 2003; Rostworowski 1988). In other words, belonging to one group very likely formed an important vector for alterity at the level of the house, village community and regional social group.

Ayllu distinguished themselves on the basis of their position and status *vis-à-vis* other ayllu. They practiced marriage restrictions and were characterized by forms of rivalry and ranking against other ayllu. Ayllu organization therefore presupposes intensive interactions with similar groups and some organization and practice that reproduces the larger collectivity. This frequently took the form of a ranking or hierarchy of all the segments in a given community and/or region (Espinoza Soriano 1978). In effect, the status of an ayllu and its members was effected through relations with other ayllu with which it shared organizational being.

At the same time, highland Ancash ayllu organization appears to have been quite flexible, and able to absorb major social changes. The Incas, for example, managed to add a fifth ayllu, a community of potters, into a prior organization of four in the Recuay area (Zuidema 1973). Groups could split and establish their own lines, or dynasties, with new heroes minted as illustrious ancestors (Hernández Príncipe 1923). Group origin stories and connections to place formed an important theme recorded in colonial period oral traditions (e.g., Rostworowski 1988; Salomon and Urioste 1991; Zuidema 1990). These were histories of collectives (ayllu) showing how both collectivity and their resources were in flux during the turbulent centuries before and after the Spanish conquest (Gose 2008; Ramos 2010). Sacred places and the divinities who inhabited them were eminently protean and distributed.

At one level, we can understand this adaptability of Andean collectivities as a necessary strategy for survival during periods of tumult. On another level, the historical process of incorporation and new dynamics of social groups are patterned in strikingly similar, almost formulaic, ways. The patterns suggest dispositions toward ambivalent others framed uniquely within Andean ways of understanding their world as one of repeated social upheaval and re-organization through their internalization. The question then becomes how prehistorians can recognize this process over time.

Distinguishing ancient Andean social groups usually involves close study of variation in material style. Since the time of the German scholar Max Uhle, using style to discern cultural integrity and distributions has been of utmost priority in Andean archaeology; the trajectory of related but distinct cultures is what distinguishes the Central Andean area (Bennett 1948; Kroeber 1944; Lumbreras 1974b). Styles are presumed to co-vary with cultural groups and reflect socio-economic developments, and changes in group composition will, more or less, be reflected in stylistic choices.

Although ethnographically-oriented studies rightly problematize many of the foundations of the pots = people equation (Dietler and Herbich 1998; Gosselain 2002; Ramón 2008; Sillar 2000), pottery remains essential in the study of ancient social boundaries (Stark 1998). There is greater attention paid to the production, use and consumption of ceramics to enhance discussions of distributions at settlement, intra-community and regional levels (e.g., Bray 2003; Druc 1998; Janusek 2002; Lau 2006a; Owen 2007). By rejecting a simple one-to-one correspondence between ceramics and people, there's still acknowledgment of the utility of ceramics for informing social dynamics and, crucially, change through time. Frequently, these pivot on a more generous approach for constituting style, taking into account different techniques and materials in fabrication and use as part of collective practice, that is, how identity is constituted and reinforced through ceramics, such as in cuisine, ritual prerogatives, or the political economy. In some ways, I wish to alternate the direction of this perspective, to ask of the data how pottery not only builds community for some circles, but also how it may curtail community and create boundaries with others.

Architecture, metalwork and textiles have also informed studies of social boundaries (e.g., Aldenderfer 1993; Isbell 1997; Lechtman 1996; Oakland Rodman and Fernández 2001). These elucidate large regional technical traditions and cultural dispositions, but also, because of the nature of preservation of these materials, often need to cope with smaller samples and vagaries in dating/provenience. Bioarchaeological approaches have been increasingly important to characterize cultural differences among populations (e.g., Blom 2005; Williams 2005). Cranial modification, for example, may have been intentional marking of ethnic and status affiliations. Other corporate 'ways of doing things' are crucial in notions of self and alter, such as everyday dress and language, but these will be more difficult to find archaeologically (Topic 1998).

It is notable that the Recuay are characterized by considerable stylistic heterogeneity in all their major media: pottery, stone sculpture and architecture. The variation in material style forms the rationale for what I have called the Recuay 'commonwealth' (Lau 2011). I consider this a regional community of coeval collectivities, most small-scale chiefly polities, distinguished by their distinct, but by no means homogeneous, material culture, imagery and economic dispositions in their specific region of highland Ancash, during the first to eighth centuries AD. On the one hand, analysis of material style in these media lets us make distinctions between Recuay groups and neighboring groups (e.g., Moche, Cajamarca, Lima). On the other hand, stylistic analysis of pottery allows differentiation of groups within the region, for example, to contrast groups at ancient Yayno and Pashash – two major archaeological sites in northern Ancash. In other words, like alterity, there may be great utility in recognizing what Recuay is by understanding what it is not.

Representing and engaging the other

Any study of ancient alterity will need to shift some of the burden of evidence to the imagery and representation of the other. In part this is because social histories are bound up in period-based representational schemes (Baxandall 1972; Gruzinski 1992). In addition, for groups without written histories, this is about as close as scholars are going to be able to get at ancient narratives that construct alterity.

The task might be likened to studying ancient Greek art (e.g., pottery, sculpture) to reconstruct Trojan-ness and the story of the Trojan War. Of course, the task is made much harder without the Homeric epics, but it is not impossible. Names, reasons and the general plot may be missing but figural actions and formal features are often apparent. There needs to be emphasis on how representation emphasizes difference. We might observe differences in physical human features, attire, gestures, and actions between figures, or identify features in the formal qualities of the object (surfaces, color, position, etc.). Perhaps more important, they can be studied in comparison to ultimately provide a 'thick description' of synchronic patterns between objects and in context, as well as patterns through time and space (Geertz 1973).[10]

Some cultures actively depict others. Indeed, some would argue the emphasis on alterity is the basis of representation (Taussig 1993). Some might link the representation of others to more general nationalist programs, of making political alliances, and peoples into rivals, enemies, tribes and races (e.g., Bhabha 1994; Hobsbawm 1990; Pollitt 1979). Very commonly, it occurs in commemorative narratives and objectification of victory. Not only is this the subject of much Attic pottery focused on the Trojan War (Burgess 2001; Woodford 1993), the representation of triumph is common across many societies where leadership drew on agonistic/warfare ideology (e.g., Davis 1996; Lau 2004a; Martin and Grube 2000; Verano 2001), including inscription on the body (e.g., Borić and Robb 2008; Tung 2008). There are typical ways that victors and enemies are represented through size, positions and conditions (underfoot, stripped, splayed, etc.). The physical action makes no equivocation about the net result, however: a proclamation of conquest over the enemy. These exercises in the ideology of alterity contribute to the illusory belief in the idea of the state, of its legitimacy and dominion, what Abrams (1988) has called 'politically organized subjection' (see also Silverblatt 2004: 11–12).

The other is also depicted to contrast against local, proper customs. Sometimes foreigners are shown with crucial physical differences (e.g., facial hair, unusual noses) and wearing important, potentially 'ethnic' markers, such as hats and facial hair (Blackmun 1988; Blier 1993; Drew and Wilson 1980; Mullins and Paynter 2000; Schuler-Schömig 1979). Quite frequently, there is attention to how the other is misshapen and grotesque. They also engage in unorthodox behaviors more befitting of non-humans, such as animals and mythical beasts (Strickland 2003). During times of exploration and colonization, the new and unknown often become associated with the monstrous and hybrid. At the same time that this spawns fear and caution, the complex fuels resentment and acts to legitimize appropriation from the other. Scholars have postulated that an intensification in circulating new items and materials as strange, monstrous and cosmologically potent was a common solution in early complex societies across the world (Helms 1993; Wengrow 2011). The representations, of course, verge on the stereotypical, but they remain uncanny categories that connect humanity and cross-cultural encounters in significant ways (Bhabha 1994; Hall 1997).

Some two decades ago, anthropologist Michael Taussig (1993) observed how mimetic representation seeks to tap into something potent from that represented. According to the model, mimesis tries to capture the power or potency of the original. The reason we represent or replicate anything (e.g., an effigy, landscape painting, the written word) is because we want something from it, whether that imitation is an image of Christ or in the form of cargo cults. People emulate others, so the theory goes, in order to somehow internalize and to make sense of them. In doing so, the 'mimetic faculty' reveals something of the nature of the hierarchical, colonial relationship, but also provides some opportunity for traction and privileged engagement over the represented (colonial other). Taussig (1993: 237) writes,

> For the white man, to read this face [an African representation of a white man] means facing himself as others read him, and the "natives' point of view" can

never substitute for the fact that now the native is the white man himself, and that suddenly, woefully, it dawns that the natives' point of view is endless and myriad.

Thus self-reflection, a kind of internalization, becomes basic in inscribing other cultures.

I will attempt to show, however, that Andean alterity was more than only representation, an expression of the mimetic faculty. It pivoted on the engagement with the other as basic to social and cosmological order. This occurs at a number of levels which transcend mere representation or emulation.

First and foremost is the notion of complementary opposites, a striking feature of historical Andean groups (e.g., Duviols 1973, 1977; Gelles 1995; Urton 1993) as well as archaeological cultures (Burger and Salazar-Burger 1993; Dillehay 1998; Isbell 1977; Moore 1995). This organizing principle essentially centers on the notion that the world is made up of opposed forces, such as high–low, right–left, sun–moon and male–female. While each element is distinct, and while one might be privileged over the other, both are required for balance or completion in order to form a mutual whole. Not surprisingly, the juncture and meeting of the paired elements, often called *tinkuy* in Quechua, may be the loci of great semantic value. The joining of rivers, paths and people (on occasions such as marriages and ritual battles) are places for dynamic convergences. They often stand as and for significant places and times, where momentous, energetically productive things have happened or can happen.

The notion pervades forms of Andean social organization, such as moiety groups, paired ayllu, herder/cultivator groups, and upper and lower divisions of a community (Netherly 1993; Platt 1986; Urton 1993; Venturoli 2006). Based on this principle, sociality is organized literally in concert with the other. If so, we might consider the essence of dual organization to be grounded in alterity. When dealing with Andean dualism, most scholars have sought to address how the elements of the pair are similar, fit together or become harmonious as a unit. What I will emphasize in this discussion is the basis for contrast or opposition for the pair to exist in the first place. Subsequent chapters will discuss salient dyadic arrangements based on recognition of others as instantiations of union: male–female; predator and prey; high–low ranking members of society; and intra-settlement 'opposites'. These do not merely reconcile complementary forces, but are fundamental expressions of inequality; indeed, they basically attend to the recognition of the impossibility of social equality.

Intrinsic inequality is also basic to another type of alter in Andean cosmology: conquerors, a topic of recent ethnohistorical studies (Gose 2008; Ramírez 2005; Silverblatt 2004). Anthropologist Peter Gose (2008), in particular, has noted how there existed a persistent pattern of locals internalizing, physically and cosmologically, conquering outsiders using the intelligible idiom of 'invader as ancestor'. Thus, during the colonial period, some native Andean groups saw the Spanish as ancestors. This revelation follows a native way of historical and social integration, which had been practiced, apparently, long before Pizarro. The process entails the vanquished inserting their ancestral histories into the conquerors' histories, and creating a complementary system of organization and worldview which naturalized the new hierarchical pattern. This (re)produced many of the forms known as dual social organization, such as upper and lower divisions or moieties. The invaders' gods and sacred places would also be fitted, and ranked, in the existing local pantheon.

The complementary, if hierarchical, pattern might be said to fit into a general Andean ontology of livelihood based on alterity. There can be no well-being without productive work based on reciprocity and generosity to others (Mayer 2002). And it would be unusual to see Andean society without a certain institutionalization of the reciprocal essence of that work (Fonseca 1974: 108). The historical ruptures which supplanted certain persons with others only changed the actors; the ontology of production enmeshing superiors and commoners remained the same. Treating the Inquisition and ancient Andean leadership respectively, both Ramírez (2005) and Silverblatt focus on their moral dimensions as '"projects of normalizing" – taking for granted and internalizing the social categories that organize power by making them appear to be intrinsic to life' (Silverblatt 2004: 12).

In sum, the representation of the other constitutes an important way of studying the past. This is because cultural production (e.g., knowledge, artworks, etc.) about the other is not limited to modern scholarship, but formed an important manner in which people and groups imagined and interacted with others throughout human history.

Chapter organization: scale and kinds of alterity

Having detailed the general problem and framework, the remainder of this work concentrates on four domains of ancient social life centered on the recognition and social economies with others. The domains are related and not mutually exclusive, but are considered separately in their own chapters. In each, alterity resides at different scales. Thus the organization serves at once as a device necessary for presentation but also as categories emerging out of different kinds of data which, by obligation, frame the scope of interpretation.

The next chapter, Chapter 2 – 'Region, Art and Society', provides the geographic and cultural bearings for my arguments and case studies. This chapter first examines the geography of the Central Andes. Each macro-region (coast, highlands, eastern slopes) has its own distinctive characteristics which instill cultural difference. Then I describe the archaeological background to understand the developments of the Early Intermediate Period, especially the general social and cultural differentiation of the first millennium AD that arose after the decline of the Chavín culture. I emphasize the rise of regional art traditions, and their role in reflecting and making social boundaries. The developments of each regional tradition are crucial because they are the source of representations for recognizing many kinds of other. The chapter then focuses on two neighboring art traditions as a case study which shows, despite their entangled histories of interaction, overt regional scale 'alterity'.

Chapter 3, 'Familiar Others', examines how others are crucial in the world of the house and settlement – what is described as the 'inside'. It begins by examining the interpersonal level of others of the same collectivity, glossed as a group of people who share commonplaces in identity and affiliation, as manifested in descent, co-residence and place. Data on Recuay domestic practices, settlement layouts and figural imagery provide key lines of evidence for everyday social interactions.

The character of domestic practices coincides with activities and imagery of nurture, growth and exchange. Particularly important are those deliberate interchanges with others (e.g., feeding, sex, body ornament) that transform the body. In this 'moral economy of intimacy' (Viveiros de Castro 1996: 189), the exchange of nourishment and vitality between others is crucial (e.g., Harris 1981; Vilaça 2002, 2005; Weismantel 1989). Artworks are especially important here for distinguishing the various actions that embed the roles and activities of specific persons on the inside.

The chapter then describes social relations deemed important in the making of chiefly persons. Certain types of finely made objects, glossed as 'artworks', facilitate chiefly subjectivity, especially during ritual practices. Among the most important activities were public ceremonies, feasting and chiefly/ancestral veneration *with* others, which sought their engagement and public acknowledgement.

Chapter 4, 'Predatorial Relations', examines the perception of outsiders and enemies. An emphasis is given to the role of architecture in making physical and symbolic difference. Like the previous chapter, this section draws on art imagery, but focuses on how it can express inter-community relations through material style and evidence of fortifications. The latter point concerns the physical community (the village, town, fortress), and its relations with other communities. Defensive buildings and settlement features indicate that Recuay groups, more often than not, found their neighbors to be warlike, and limited exposure to them.

The remarkable figural imagery of Early Intermediate Period cultures also enables a complementary discussion of how humans represented interaction with other beings, human and animal. Here predation and the appropriation of vitality from others are at once explicit (e.g., killing, trophy taking) and expressed through metaphor. The imagery of a 'symbolic economy of alterity' stresses predatorial relations of difference; these were privilege taking and eating others, and the making of subordinates. This section also covers how one powerful coastal group, the Moche, found the Recuay to be warlike others: Moche artists emulated highland chiefly tropes and depicted the Recuay as potent subordinates taken in combat. Early Intermediate Period art and ritual practices frequently optimized predatorial relations.

I discuss the final kind of other, the dead, in Chapter 5, 'The Dead and the Living'. The potency of the dead, namely expired progenitors, resides in the alterity of their social relations with the living (Helms 1998). Archaeological evidence is presented in both the context of ancestor ceremony and the materiality of physical effigies of ancestors. Spatial arrangements of tomb and funerary contexts will be described to approximate the alterity as social beings and agents of fertility and well-being. The forms, activities, contents and reuse of the burial spaces show how the ancestral dead have their own habits and dispositions. In the Central Andes, interactions with the living and the dead were regular affairs. While the dead maintain relations with humans and can be said to form their own community (modeled on living types), the dead are useful precisely because they are *not* human and no longer like us. Yet from the Andean viewpoint, they still want and live like humans. While they see their descendants as children, the descendants see them as elders: the relationship of interdependence cascades into many different domains, especially post-burial funerary practices and their life–death symbolism.

Chapter 6, 'Conclusions', provides a synopsis of the different sections. Alterity at the level of the collectivity, elites, enemies and divinities will be summarized to review the book's basic proposal: the perception of and the engagement with the other was crucial for Andean societies of the Early Intermediate Period, in general. What relates these domains are analogical relationships that articulate, in hierarchical fashion, the various social beings (Descola 2005, 2006; Heckenberger 2005).

Alterity process often centered on the transaction and internalizing of something crucial from the other. It is concluded that what made Recuay persons relied on the recognition and actions of others. In thinking about and recognizing others, social relations and order are, in a sense, reified, even if they are partially destabilized or turned inside out. Others were sources of nourishment and vitality – and the constant emphasis on alterity was precisely to capitalize on what could be gotten out of it. The desire of alterity, if you will, centers on how to live with and benefit through the other.

Overall, the book considers little-known developments in Andean prehistory and, in revealing the patterns, illuminates the ways that archaeologists, in general, can examine alterity through the archaeological record. The study begins to elucidate the time-depth and variability of past processes of alterity, which are for the most part known through the historical and ethnographic literature. Finally, what a study of ancient alterity contributes is a critical look at the contingency, the social constitutedness of meanings, which intervenes in the interpretation of past cultures. This will be a substantial boon to the consideration of past belief systems and writing about the past.

2

REGION, ART AND SOCIETY DURING THE EARLY INTERMEDIATE PERIOD

This chapter provides the geographic and socio-historical bearings to contextualize the regional developments of the Early Intermediate Period, approximately AD 1–700 (Fig 2.1). It focuses first on the Central Andes as a composite environment and culture area by describing the major geographic regions. They were places for different sources of human–environment interactions that create economic and cultural difference.

I then introduce the major cultures under study – namely the Moche, Nasca and Recuay – with special emphasis on their arts and social arrangements. These resulted from the demise of the Central Andes' first major pan-Andean culture, Chavín. Yet they were hardly the inheritors of its traditions. Besides the alterity produced by regional and local geographic features, alterity at large scale is examined at two levels, first, as a global rejection of Chavín's principles, and then secondly by characterizing a long sequence of regional interaction between two major cultures of the period, Recuay and Cajamarca.

Andean environments

One of the greatest sources of alterity in Peru today is the profound cultural differentiation attributed to peoples of the highlands, coast and forested Andean slopes and lowlands. When one comments on any of these regions, elements of alterity are known and referenced in contrast to those perceived of others. There are many vectors for differentiation. To name a few: what and how languages are spoken, the crops people grow, available foods/resources, the vegetation, geographical features, landscape, the clothes worn by people, the different faiths, urban versus rural life. The varied environments and knowledge about local ways of life affect the opinions of others.

The Central Andean environment has profoundly influenced the lifeways, history and experience of each region (Pulgar Vidal 1972; Tosi 1960). Let us briefly examine

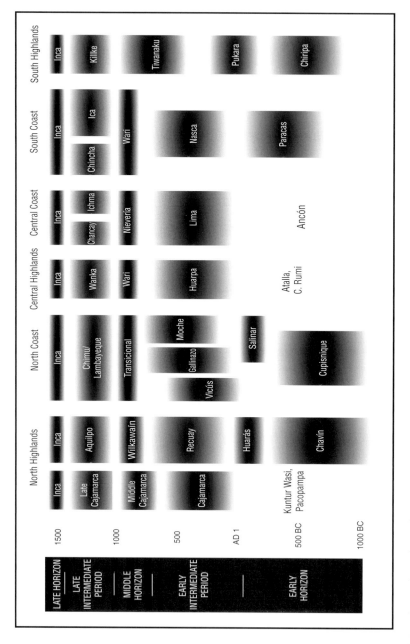

FIGURE 2.1 Relative chronology of the periods discussed in the text. Periods of cultural integration (horizons) contrast with periods of regional developments (intermediate periods).

the main salient characteristics of the three major topographic and climatic zones: the coast, the highlands and the forested slopes of the eastern Andes (or *montaña*).

The principal geographic feature of the Peruvian coast is the Pacific Ocean. Its cold upwelling Peru (or Humboldt) Current makes the waters off the coast of Peru one of the richest fisheries in the world. For coastal communities, the nutrient-rich waters nourish a host of important marine resources: fish, birds, marine invertebrates and mammals. The cool waters also prevent precipitation from developing in the region, leaving the Central Andean coast one of the driest deserts on earth. The climatic system has extreme consequences during El Niño–Southern Oscillation phenomena, when the Pacific's system of currents changes. Warmer currents displace the colder waters off the coast of Peru, bringing with them heavy rainfall, inundation of floodplain fields, and devastation of marine species who depend on cold nutrient-rich waters.

In an otherwise desertic environment, agriculture on the coast is made possible by waters flowing down from the Andes cordillera to the east. The narrow ribbons of land on either side of the rivercourses can be used for farming (Plate 2). The wide plains of the lower valleys, especially, were valuable because they could be reclaimed through irrigation. Major ancient settlements of coastal Peru are often found in or near arable, floodplain areas. Coastal peoples flourished through cultivation of maize, cotton, beans, squash, manioc, peanuts and a host of other vegetables and fruits. Many of these were domesticated by the second millennium BC and intensively farmed later in prehistory. Major crops in recent times also include rice and sugarcane.

Further into the humid mid-valley areas of the Pacific Andean flanks, important crops included chili pepper, fruits and coca leaf. While never staples, these crops were crucial in cuisine and social relations in general. For example, coca was so important as a crucial stimulant for work, ritual offerings and as a social lubricant that lands for its cultivation were fought over, both by the force of arms and through litigation (Rostworowski 1988). Throughout northern Peru, groups also valued middle valley areas for their access to key trunk canals that facilitated the irrigation of lower lands (e.g., Moseley 1983; Shimada 1994).

The highland portion of the Central Andes, meanwhile, is perhaps best known for its spectacular mountains, especially the snowcaps called *nevados*. Many of the largest glaciers rise over 6000 meters above sea level. Human life, however, flourished in those vast rugged tracts of land below the ice (Plate 3). Rivers originating in the high Andes carve into the lush, intermontane valleys that have long formed the breadbasket for Andean peoples. Not well suited for agriculture using draft animals or machinery, the steep slopes continue to be farmed efficiently through human power.

Like other densely inhabited mountainous regions across the world, people relied on innovation and resourceful techniques to flourish. For example, freeze-drying potatoes and meat exploited sharply dropping night temperatures to preserve them for transport and consumption when needed (e.g., Mamani 1981). Another important strategy was the domestication and intensive use of camelids, the llama and alpaca. Native to the highland Andes, they flourish on montane vegetation, are surefooted on tough slopes, are used as pack animals, and provide a host of resources (hair fiber, meat, bone, dung and sinew).

Another critical technology was social. Andean people specialized in the cooperation of large groups to perform tasks that otherwise were beyond the ken and capacity
of smaller numbers. 'Verticality' optimized the acquisition of resources found or
produced effectively in different ecological zones, which in the highland Andes are
often stacked, and therefore called 'floors' (Masuda et al. 1985; Murra 1972).[1] For
most highland groups, the key strategy of self-sufficiency emphasized complementary
work in two main zones: the extensive steppic tablelands for herding camelids, and
the steep slopes immediately below for tuber cultivation and high-altitude cereals. If
coastal diets are known for their marine resources, highland foodways are best known for
their variety of potatoes, as well as their traditional sources of meat, guinea pig and the
domestic camelids. Domestication of tubers and animals occurred much earlier, but
intensive production of them became more prominent only by the end of the second
millennium BC. Most groups across the Andean highlands organized their livelihood
around agro-pastoralism, complemented by many resources obtained through trade
from other zones, both locally and from different regions.

East of the continental divide, the Andes descend rapidly into tropical montane
forests (Young and León 1999), known as the *ceja de selva* or *montaña*. Unlike the
grassy or thorny vegetation characterizing most other parts of the Central Andes,
these humid cloud forests on the eastern slopes are rich in plants and tropical woodlands, and associated animal life (Fig 2.2). Rainfall is abundant, produced by warm,
rain-laden air welling up from the Amazon basin. Where there is adequate drainage

FIGURE 2.2 Photo of *ceja de selva*, Pájaten region, Río Abiseo National Park, Peru. Regular
precipitation and humidity produce densely vegetated cloud forests along the steep
eastern slopes. Photo courtesy E. Flores.

and good soils, cultivation can be very productive, with common crops today being maize, fruits, nuts, coca and coffee.

Compared to the coast and highlands, the prehistory of cultures in the forested eastern slopes is little understood, mainly due to limited scholarly research and poor preservation. Transport in the region remains very difficult. The present record suggests that ancient groups in this region were critical, not least as intermediaries between various highland, coastal and lowland groups – with much evidence of stylistic interaction (Church 1996; Lathrap 1973a; Tello 1960). Exchange almost certainly focused on certain food resources and unusual materials, such as rarities from tropical animals (feathers, teeth, pelts, etc.) and plants (hallucinogens, hardwoods, etc.), not to mention certain imageries and beliefs, apparently with tropical forest origins.

In sum, the distinctive triumvirate of macro-environments in the Central Andes conditioned very different human lifeways (Bennett 1948; Steward 1946). The compression of environments may have favored the processes for the rise of complex societies and civilizations in the Central Andes. Yet rarely do environmental zones begin and end neatly in the Central Andes. For Andean groups, the tidy categories of environmental floors are perhaps less useful than how they are used as 'production zones' (Mayer 1985). Farming and herding work are based on what is effective in the given environment; local strategies key in its physical qualities and resources. Characterized by what different zones are like, or not like, they become the basis for cultural associations: 'It is the contrasts (which really interest campesinos [farmer-peasants]) that can be applied to geographical areas, things, people, food, music, or whatever, in various orders of magnitude' (Mayer (1985: 50). Production zones – at once cultural and economic – are a source of alterity.

One kind of production, regional foodways, based on local resources, is one of the greatest measures of Andean cultural identity and differentiation. It is a source of pride, heritage and belonging. It is also what distinguishes geographical regions and their respective peoples from others. Highland food is characterized by meat stews and potatoes, while the coastal diet often centers on seafood and fresh vegetables, and the lowland areas on riverine creatures and manioc products. Partly, this is environmentally determined, for many of the foodstuffs are limited to the specific geographical region and, in some cases, to only certain spots. The rise of rapid and mass transport has blurred some of this resource regionalism today.[2] In sum, the stuff of regional identity (e.g., food, dress, language, lifeways) is often recognized in comparison to those of others. The expectation for regional differentiation, a background of difference, is a key way to approach alterity in the past.

Something as basic as the availability of trees and wood provides a useful concluding example to this section, for it has a profound effect on the livelihoods and identity of human groups. Wood is certainly the most plentiful on the forested eastern slopes. In the montane areas of the Andes, woodlands today are mainly limited to high areas that are outside the foraging areas of humans interested in firewood and animals looking to graze. And to the west further still, trees are limited to riparian zones of the desertic coast. Logs for building purposes may have been brought in from long distances. Not surprisingly, architecture, especially monumental architecture, in the highlands very often focused on stone and mud clay, while adobe was most common along the coast. The availability of wood also affected kinds of food preparation as well as the use of fuel for cooking, staying warm and for making crafts.

In short, because of the heterogeneity of the Andean physical landscape and climate, how people go about everyday living in their landscapes creates cultural difference in each region: how they travel, build houses, make and eat food, herd animals, how people work, etc. This is the basic stuff of cultural history and cultural ecology, but also the basic stuff of Andean alterity. It would be surprising if people in the past did not recognize their neighbors as different because of their different ways of doing things in these different regions.

After Chavín

The first move toward great cultural integration in the Central Andes – during the Chavín horizon – involved synthesizing various cultural dispositions originating from coast, highlands and jungle lowland areas (Burger 1992a). The preceding section provided the environmental context for considering regional developments during the first millennium AD. We now turn to Chavín, the first instance of an Andean 'horizon' overcoming, culturally, the challenges of the Andes' heterogeneity and coming to have a strong hold on developments across the Central Andes (Rowe and Menzel 1967). The following Early Intermediate Period cannot be fully understood without contextualizing Chavín's demise.

Emerging in the north highlands, with its great center at Chavín de Huántar (Ancash), the civilization prospered through proselytizing a cult of fertility and pilgrimage, and a far-flung exchange network that trafficked in forms of special knowledge pegged to special portable rarities. The items included semiprecious stones and minerals, obsidian, *Spondylus* shell, metalwork and fine ceramics. The intensification of camelid-based production as well as exchange also were critical in Chavín's success (Miller and Burger 1995).

Chavín objects frequently bore imagery and were used in ritual practices founded upon a shamanic belief system. The imagery highlighted mythical anthropomorphic (Fig 2.3) and zoomorphic figures (Burger 1992a; Conklin and Quilter 2008). Many of the materials and objects were vehicles to convey the otherworldly knowledge and religious practice of the cult. Portable and visually captivating, the Chavín art style spread across the Andes in unprecedented fashion and comprised the crucial media in the first of the Central Andes' great periods, or 'horizons', of cultural integration (Rice 1993; Rowe and Menzel 1967; Willey 1948).

It was the Peruvianist, Julio C. Tello, who forged an intellectual current in which Chavín's influence was palpable throughout Andean prehistory (Burger 2009). Not only was Chavín viewed as the earliest Peruvian civilization, it laid the foundations on which all later Andean developments would build (also Lathrap 1974). His writings likened the trajectory of Andean prehistory to the growth of a tree, in which the trunk, Chavín, ramified to nurture civilization elsewhere, leaving a legacy in art, social organization and cosmology (Tello 1942, 1960).

FIGURE 2.3 Carved sculpture, showing the principal fanged anthropomorphic deity of the Chavín culture, first millennium BC. Later Recuay imagery of highland Ancash relied much less on fanged anthropomorphs and lowland predatorial animal prototypes, such as jaguars and caymans.

John Rowe's influential essay (1962: 21) perpetuated Tello's image of a profound Chavín legacy: 'there followed a period characterized by the development of many distinctive local styles in the area where the Chavín style had once dominated. The Chavín style must have left some sort of tradition, however, as Roman art left a tradition in the Middle Ages, because several attempts were made to revive aspects of it in later times.' Rowe identified several ways to examine this tradition (also Rowe 1971). One concerned archaism, such as of later styles that emulated the vessel shapes and imagery of Cupisnique culture (Chavín-contemporary). The other treated the reemergence of religious or stylistic ideas, such as the revival of motifs in later highland cultures. For Rowe (1962: 21), these 'seem to mean that Chavín art and Chavín religion cast a long shadow in ancient Peru'.

Despite popular sentiment, it is evident that the *cultura matríz* (mother culture) model is no longer tenable (Burger 1992a). Chavín period groups at once received and synthesized a host of foreign influences, which they recast for their own ends. Furthermore, by the early centuries AD most Andean regions had developed their own cultural patterns largely independent of Chavín content. Most prominently, each zone featured its own art systems that no longer overtly followed Chavín preferences in imagery, techniques, or, by extension, cosmology. Various groups across the Central Andes began to flourish, each with its own very distinctive material styles and practices. In highland zones, the most prominent styles coalesced around the Titicaca region (Pukara), Ayacucho (Huarpa), Cajamarca (Cajamarca) and Ancash (Recuay). Along the Peruvian seaboard, the major cultures emerged in the south coast (Nasca), central coast (Lima) and the north coast (Moche, Vicús and Gallinazo).

The cultural patterns, during the terminal Early Horizon and early Early Inter-mediate Period, constituted the first large-scale *rejection* of pan-Andean things and ideas that we understand as the Chavín phenomenon. All throughout Chavín's former domain, groups no longer traded for or had access to formerly much sought after objects and materials. The exchange of Quispisisa-type obsidian, the principal source exploited during the Early Horizon, slowed to a trickle (Burger et al. 2006; Burger et al. 2000). And ceramics, metal artifacts, and probably textiles, quickly stopped circulating (Burger 1992a; Druc 1998). In terms of materials acquisition and stylistic interaction, at least, groups became increasingly insular.

There was evidence also of greater social unrest. In particular, the swift appearance of abundant fortifications indicates increasing levels of internecine conflict and warfare. In many areas of northern Peru, especially, people began to erect fortifications in their settlements and situate their communities in higher, more defensible areas (Plate 4), a pattern that becomes important especially in the later and terminal Early Horizon (e.g., Brown Vega 2009; Daggett 1985, 1986; Ghezzi 2006; Lau 2011; J. R. Topic and T. L. Topic 1987; Topic and Topic 1982; Wilson 1987). These aimed, mainly, to cope with the perpetual uncertainties of ambivalent neighbors and incursions from outsiders.

In some middle valley areas of the north coast, however, settlement arrangements also helped buffer large areas from territories occupied by other ethnicities (Millaire 2008; Proulx 1982). The religious integration characteristic of Chavín's height seems to have given way to greater political tumult and territorialization during the centuries just before and after the time of Christ. The community built during Chavín times became more fragmented.

This time period is also known for the emergence and popularization of different styles of pottery. In the north, there was widespread adoption of 'white-on-red' pottery.[3] These vessels were made out of a simple red terracotta clay, sometimes red-slipped, on which were painted white designs, usually repetitive and geometric in form. The style was pervasive across the Peruvian coast, from north to the central coast, and in many parts of the highlands. It was so prominent that some scholars proposed a white-on-red 'horizon' (Bennett 1944; Kroeber 1944: 110; Willey 1945, 1948).[4]

While a pan-Andean 'horizon' seems unlikely, archaeologist Gordon Willey's account of white-on-red remains remains useful to acknowledge, '[The] lack of symbolic art in the White-on-Red horizon may, in itself, reflect a weakening of the old Chavín cult of the jaguar. If so, this slackening of religious feeling seems more likely to have been the result of internal trends than of foreign impact.' His comments have seen little subsequent consideration, but are remarkable because those 'internal trends' characterized many groups at about the same time (early Nasca, Pukara, Huarpa, Cajamarca), not just those who used white-on-red pottery. Almost all local styles emerging after the cessation of Chavín's sway quickly evacuated symbolic associations to the Chavín complex and its complex imagery. Rather than being passive or epiphenomenal to the events of the Early Intermediate Period, then, one could argue that the 'slackening', what I see as a common alterity (a cross-cultural disposition of being *not-Chavín*), was at the core of its formation.

Other patterns also indicate a major change in religious belief and practice. Ritual and monumental buildings, for example, began to be built for very different purposes. Many highland peoples no longer suscribed to the Chavín-period predilection for platform pyramids with wide open plazas, exemplified at places such as Chavín de Huántar, Kuntur Wasi and Pacopampa.

In fact, parts of the ceremonial center at Chavín de Huántar were destroyed, dismantled or reused for more prosaic functions after Chavín's zenith (Lumbreras 1977; Rick 2008). Most notably, Chavín's sunken circular plaza was razed and then repurposed as a makeshift area, sheltered from winds and mudslides, for a series of common dwellings over many generations.

People buried their dead into the sides of Chavín's main temple as well as in common dwellings in parts of the monumental sector. Although there must have been some recognition of the antiquity of the ruins, the interventions were not so much reverential as much as expedient treatments. The burials were probably of local inhabitants who may have resided at the Chavín site not long after its abandonment; some burials were in cists located underneath house floors and between walls, suggesting perhaps an ongoing relationship between the living and the deceased.

In the north highlands after Chavín, the building projects which garnered the most labor investment and high-quality work stressed small funerary buildings, fortifications and, especially later on the Early Intermediate Period, large residential complexes (Lau 2010c: 346). Monumental construction, in other words, became less important for pilgrimage and public performance.

Changes in imagery provide another line of evidence for more localized, smaller-scale ritual prerogatives. Chavín art and imagery stressed major divinities, probably weather gods and cosmogonic figures, responsible for the well-being of their venerating communities (see Fig 2.3). The divinities were adopted across a wide spectrum of societies on the coast and highlands (Burger 1992a; Conklin and Quilter 2008; Rowe 1962). By the Early Intermediate Period, groups quickly supplanted them with very different supernaturals (Lyon 1978), often having to do with local ancestors (Recuay), ritual personages (Nasca) and regional divinities (early Moche, early Lima, Recuay).

There is reason, therefore, to interpret the variable responses to the demise of Chavín as the first large-scale irruption of alterity in the Andes. There was a concerted, fairly simultaneous reaction against Chavín. Many groups all over the Central Andes actively wanted something different, something that was emphatically *not Chavín*, and found means to transcend the previous affiliation.

There was no prescription for how this rupture was achieved, and there were many different local expressions. Some areas stopped exchange of long-distance goods; some areas began to depict new deities; some areas developed expressive media involving new techniques and imageries; other areas began to fight with their neighbors more. The patterned rejection of previous foreign-inspired cultural dispositions would also characterize the end of the Wari state and religion, around AD 900–1000 (Lau 2011). This was second major irruption of pan-Andean alterity, which was also cross-ethnic, cross-regional and occurred largely synchronically.

Large scale in effect and palpable throughout the Central Andes, it is impossible at present to pinpoint reasons why people everywhere no longer saw Chavín as beneficial or favorable. It is certain, however, that the retreat of Chavín influence invited new locally-driven changes. We know the cultural heterogeneity after Chavín's time of integration as the Early Intermediate Period (Lanning 1967; Rowe and Menzel 1967).

Regional cosmologies and art traditions

Having given a brief introduction to the major environmental regions of the Central Andes and the antecedent culture of Chavín, I want to focus now on how these regions, broadly-speaking, played a role in alterity-making.

All across the Andes, during the Early Intermediate Period, people paid great attention to the major features and happenings of their respective lands and territories. Whether the Pacific Ocean, high-altitude lakes, giant rocks or snowcaps, people claimed features of their landscapes as embodiments of local divinity, and places of origins and mythic histories. Water was an important life-giving substance and its flow animated these places. Also, their actions – lightning and thunder, rains, floods, avalanches, quakes, El Niño – were at once signs of their potency and unpredictability.

The Early Intermediate Period was marked by a great tethering between ritual, collectivities and local landscapes. To be sure, this occurred earlier during Formative times (Burger 1992b; Reinhard 1985), but greater population densities, new proclivities in defensive settlements and settlement patterns, and the growth of regional cultures indicate a move toward people increasingly marking local places. More than that, they invested great effort in enhancing places that already had cosmological significance. The huaca temple mounds of Moche culture (Alva and Donnan 1993; Castillo et al. 2008; Donnan 2007; Franco Jordán et al. 2005; Uceda and Tufinio 2003), the ancestor mausolea of the Recuay (e.g., Lau 2011), or Nasca cemeteries (Carmichael 1995; Silverman and Proulx 2002) all show groups of the Early Intermediate Period marking unique landscapes, especially burial grounds for their esteemed dead. People returned again and again to their ritual places over many centuries, often adding and modifying the built environment. Not only did evidence of major public ritual accumulate and become increasingly sedimented in these places, it is probable for Nasca, Moche and Recuay that the basis of identity – authority, place, descent – emerged through these places. This was at once unprecedented in terms of diversity as well as in terms of number.

If identity is pegged to the recognition of cultural difference, the rise of alterity during the Early Intermediate Period makes more sense during this time of great socio-political dynamism. The cultural integration during the Chavín horizon fragmented into a mosaic of regional, ethnic groups (Plate 1). No longer having a common cosmological bond, groups became increasingly differentiated. Ritual also became increasingly different, more varied across the Central Andes. We can only surmise through the art and contexts of ritual that the mythical narratives and the major divinities also diverged, grafted to local places. Just as important, people increasingly anchored to physical features unique to their respective place – mountains, caves, rocks, lakes, springs, islands, etc. This was through building, venerating and burying in key spots. All the regional cultures of the Early Intermediate Period have this basic emphasis on local sacred landscapes.

The regional patterns of the Early Intermediate Period are often attributed to the emergence of competing polities or large-scale ethnic groups. This can really only be part of the story, however, since ethnogenesis and social heterogeneity need not be accompanied by great material diversification. The regionalism was, at least in part, underwritten by conscious choices to maintain stylistic boundaries. What was given emphasis was not necessarily only what one was. We might also theorize the Early Intermediate Period as emphasizing what one was not, or different from.

The time before the Incas, the Late Intermediate Period (ca. AD 1000–1450), provides a sobering example of the complex relationships between material culture and social differentiation. We know from ethnohistorical sources that there was great social and ethnic differentiation in the Central Andean highlands (Rowe 1946). Generally speaking, however, the archaeological record only evinces fairly minor stylistic differences, especially for groups in adjacent highland regions (D'Altroy and Hastorf 2001; Parsons et al. 2000). For example, it remains very difficult to distinguish the major ethnic groups of highland Ancash on the basis of material style. The groups (e.g., Pincos, Huari, Huaylas, Conchucos, Piscobamba nations) all feature very similar ceramics, architecture and dwelling and economic patterns (Druc 2009; Ibarra 2009; León Gomez 2003).

Knowledge about the languages spoken by ancient groups would help to more clearly define local ethnic differences. Unfortunately, there are few robust data connecting language and archaeological cultures for the time period before the Incas and the early chronicles (Adelaar and Muysken 2004; Heggarty and Beresford-Jones 2012). What seems possible, however, given the present archaeological evidence, is that there was substantial linguistic diversity during the Early Intermediate Period. In part this is reflected in the linguistic diversity, seen especially in northern Peru, during proto- and early historical times (Adelaar and Muysken 2004; Lau 2012; Quilter et al. 2010; Schaedel 1985; Topic 1998).

A more salient vector for alterity was the great pattern of indigenous nobles using material culture to actively manage their privilege (e.g., Bawden 1996; Lau 2004b; Woloszyn 2008). The great innovation of the Early Intermediate Period was not so much the social differentiation, for strong variability in wealth and social inequalities had long existed in one form or another. Rather, it was the regional diversity and formal distinctiveness in which these inequalities manifested. This is discernible through the growth of large centers, new kinds of burial practices and economic infrastructure, but especially in the emergence of regional art traditions.

By this term, I mean a time-space unit (Bennett 1948; Rowe and Menzel 1967; Willey 1945) based on a 'corporate art style' (Moseley 1992: 73; Silverman 1996: 21) which has time-depth, a long trajectory of internal transformation and durable stylistic dispositions. Improved sequences have allowed coeval patterns to come into sharper focus. For instance, each of the major traditions (e.g., Cajamarca, Lima, Moche, Nasca, Recuay) featured a unique repertoire of favored techniques and media that emerged following the receding of Chavín (Castillo et al. 2008; Donnan and McClelland 1999; Goldhausen 2001; Lau 2004b; Matsumoto 1994; Proulx 2006; Segura Llanos 2006; Silverman and Proulx 2002; Watanabe 2009).

It is useful to describe Moche as an example of a regional art tradition, not least because it is the best studied; and recent decades of work have resulted in an unparalleled sample for the period. Moche was the most renowned of the regional art traditions of the Early Intermediate Period (Benson 1972; Bourget 2006; Bourget and Jones 2008; Donnan 1978; Jackson 2008). Although the culture had long been recognized in studies of ancient America, it surged into global prominence with the discovery of the Sipán tombs, among the richest ever found in the New World. A series of large-scale, long-term research projects on *huaca* platform pyramids and civic-ceremonial complexes have now complemented the archaeological emphasis on funerary sites and settlement patterns (Alva and Donnan 1993; Castillo et al. 2008; Pillsbury 2001; Shimada 1994; Uceda and Mujica 1994, 2003). The synergy between field research and iconographic studies has revolutionized the understanding of Moche culture and society (Bourget and Jones 2008; Donnan 2004, 2007; Donnan and McClelland 1999; Golte 2009; Makowski 2008; Quilter and Castillo 2010). Because syntheses about the Moche record exist already, I will limit my discussion to developments that are most pertinent to this study, namely general patterns of social differentiation and their relationship to alterity process.

First, what is generally understood as Moche art – mainly decorative ceramics, lapidary and metal work, sculpted murals and wood, and monuments – was essentially elite prerogative.[5] The major media of Moche art arose in the service of elite lifestyles, ritual practice and political ideology, frequently in conjunction with monumental buildings (Fig 2.4). They were used by the living but also accompanied the esteemed dead as offerings in their tombs. The relationships between commoners and elites remain far from clear; however, commoners were much less party to intensive engagements (e.g., acquisition, use, consumption, disposal) with Moche fancy materials, in life or death.

Second, it is increasingly evident that there were many regional variants of the Moche art style, especially in ceramics. The notion of a single militaristic expansion state (Larco Hoyle 1938; Topic 1982; Wilson 1988) has been generally supplanted by a model of multiple polities with fairly considerable heterogeneity in political arrangements. These are associated with valley-based pottery styles, presumably made by local potters for political elites and high-status peoples (Castillo and Donnan 1994; Donnan and McClelland 1999; Quilter and Castillo 2010). The polity based in the Moche valley may have established power over several valleys to the south (Chapdelaine 2011).

FIGURE 2.4 Moche stirrup-spout vessel, showing a modeled deer and fineline painted scene of deer hunting with spearthrower, darts and latticed net. UK collection.

What linked the different valley-based lordships was a common religious system that emphasized sacrificial ritual that nourished divinities. Many elements of the art tradition were key to the religion and can be linked to what Christopher Donnan termed the 'Warrior Narrative', which follows the narrative arc of enemy capture and sacrifice for the nourishment of divine beings (Donnan 2004). It begins with warriors preparing for combat (Plate 5), the defeat of enemies in combat, their parading as captives, and their ensuing presentation and sacrifice for the supernaturals. We know that the personas of the main supernaturals were assumed, at least sometimes, by certain key nobles, who wore their symbolic regalia at death. For some scholars, the religion is the source of Moche identity (Quilter 2010); for others it is the ideological apparatus of Moche political organization (Bawden 1996; Donnan 2010). How the theocratic ideology articulated with domestic practices remains difficult to determine, but at this stage it seems that commoner ritual did not engage much with the 'Warrior Narrative'. What is clearer, however, is that religious practices were those of renewal, and that Moche leaders cast themselves as divine mediators and influential in the flows of life-giving forces. As will be seen, this was also the case with Recuay, but their main divinities were ancestral progenitors.

Finally, the Moche record shows significant interactions with many other cultural groups that can be theorized as relations of alterity. Moche maintained significant cultural boundaries with other regional art traditions, namely Gallinazo, Vicús, Cajamarca and Recuay (Makowski 2008). Many of these coexisted from the early centuries AD until the eighth century AD. More chronological work is necessary on Vicús and Gallinazo. Gallinazo seems to have been a separate elite style that also endured for the greater part of the Early Intermediate Period (Millaire 2009). This is not to say there was no interaction. On the contrary, there is considerable evidence of shared cultural elements, particularly in pottery style (e.g., in forms, surface treatments, imagery). The main point remains that all these cultures followed very distinct trajectories *despite* their propinquity.

The stylistic coherence has usually been taken to mean the cultural insularity or integrity of the group – things and practices that emerge out of and express a corporate identity. And while this is almost certainly true, the logic mainly addresses why one group opted to be insular and stylistically coherent at a given time. It has less capacity for addressing why *many* groups or regional styles shared this same pattern or held the same disposition, at the same time (synchronically) and, crucially, over a long period (diachronically). Distance or lack of communication does not seem to be adequate either, since there is firm, if limited, evidence for trade between the groups. Decorative pots of other styles (e.g., Recuay, Wari, Gallinazo) are occasionally found in Moche-dominated areas, as are Cajamarca and Wari-period pots in Recuay areas. There was certainly also stylistic interaction, where knowledge and ideas from other areas were transacted.

Any explanation of northern Peru during the Early Intermediate Period must acknowledge an intentional *differentiation* from other groups, as manifested through local styles. That is to say, pottery manufacture and use can express a regional-scale alterity. The alterity effected material things that sought to confront or deny altogether the image of the other, especially in those border zones between major cultural groups. This happens in terms of pottery distribution and imports. The point is equally useful whether we consider groups using material style as boundary maintenance or physical emulation of prestige styles (Bankmann 1979; Bernuy and Bernal 2008; Castillo 2000; Lau 2006a; Makowski 2009; Montenegro 1993; Reichert 1982). Both genres of materials actively engage with a period-wide engagement of alterity; they regard production of 'what is not us'. It seems to have less to do with cultural identity, in the singular.

Many groups of the different cultures (e.g., Moche, Recuay, Cajamarca, Gallinazo) were in contact with each other over many centuries. That the styles maintained their integrity over this time indicates that each region's pottery-making dispositions were enduring and slow (even resistant) to change. Neither side could be said to have dominated the other.

For several key Early Intermediate Period traditions, such as Moche and Recuay, it is becoming clearer that the internal variability of each tradition was owed in great part to the cultural initiatives of local nobles and artisans in different regions (e.g., Castillo et al. 2008; Donnan and McClelland 1999; Lau 2006b). Craft production, best known for the Moche, grew increasingly vital for high-status groups in demographic centers (e.g., Bernier 2010; Shimada 1994; Uceda C. and Rengifo C. 2006; Vaughn 2005). Workshops were often located in the major settlements, and attached to or near elite buildings and their occupants. Moche potters also purposefully made ceramic substyles to distinguish one group, probably associated with individual power groups, from one another (Donnan and McClelland 1999). Emerging elites were therefore essential in the decision-making processes in production of what and what not to make and depict.

Across the Andes, like the Moche, the ceremonial practices of nobles, especially in funerary contexts, were central to the distinctiveness and resilience of each regional tradition. Besides being objects for public display, they were increasingly destined for burial and for accompanying the deceased (Alva and Donnan 1993; Carmichael 1995; Castillo et al. 2008; Grieder 1978). Such things as garments, headdresses, ornaments and weapons were all part of the increasing trend to mythologize and commemorate the esteemed deceased.

To be sure, not all material production has survived in the record, but there were distinct preferences for the production of personal adornments which enhanced the bodies of important persons and their performance. Beyond their celebrated ceramics, Moche craftspeople emphasized textiles, lapidary work (with stones and shell) and especially metalwork. They perfected techniques for alloying and elaborating the surfaces of metal ornaments, such as gilding, silvering and hammering (Lechtman 1984). The emphasis on decorated surfaces also manifested in tattooing.

Very different regional art traditions emerged along Peru's south coast. During the Early Intermediate Period, this region of the Central Andes was characterized by two important cultural traditions, Paracas and the later Nasca (Paul 1991; Proulx 2008; Silverman and Proulx 2002). Groups of these cultures inhabited the coastal and interior valleys, between the hilly flanks of the Pacific, and flourished through farming, complemented by fishing, herding and hunting. Paracas is best known for developments near the Paracas Peninsula and Ica drainages. Although the Nasca heartland centered in the Río Grande de Nazca and Ica drainages, its stylistic influence was much more extensive, reaching as far north as the Cañete valley and in the south around the Acarí valley (Proulx 2008; Vaughn 2009). Water was a key resource, and hydraulic management through use of irrigation and ingenious underground wells was crucial in the highly desertic environment (Schreiber and Lancho Rojas 2003).

Much of the art and ritual of both cultures appears to have been concerned with fertility, both of the landscape and its people (Proulx 2006; Townsend 1985). This holds also for the famous Nasca lines or geoglyphs. Polychrome pottery was especially elaborate and abundant in ceremonial places. Both south coast groups are also well-known for their luxurious textiles, which often wrapped or covered their burial interments (Rowe 1990; Sawyer 1997). These weavings were extremely labor intensive and included diverse construction techniques, such as embroidery, double and triple cloths, and tapestry. The media, often beautifully elaborated in polychrome fibers, emphasized images of humans, plants, creatures and other beings that embodied celestial and supernatural forces important for life, food and renewal.

The north highland Recuay had similar life concerns. Their arts, meanwhile, emphasized pottery and stone sculpture. Cloth and metalwork were important, but there is a much smaller sample, in part due to poorer conditions for preservation of organic materials in the seasonally rainy highlands. They also depicted their ancestors and personal ornament on carved monoliths (Lau 2006b). Resist painting was common on ceramics. The Recuay made shawl pins and other metal adornments using casting and molds, a practice much more common among the prehispanic groups of Ecuador and Colombia (Grieder 1978; Scott 1998; Velarde and Castro 2010). These and other sophisticated techniques emphasized 'negativized' surfaces across many kinds of media (sculpture, weaving, metalwork) as part of a noble aesthetic (Lau 2010d). In general, many of the major advances in craft technologies were intimately tied to the imperative of distinguishing people through circum-corporeal enhancements – enhancements in, on and around the body. These techniques had the effect of marking and strengthening individual and group identity (see Gow 1999; Turner 1995; Walens 1981).

Most of the major Early Intermediate Period traditions developed unprecedented emphasis on human representation (Bourget 2006; Castillo 1989; Donnan 1978; Gero 2001; Jackson 2008; Lau 2011; Makowski et al. 1994; Proulx 2006). There were a few styles, such as Lima, where human imagery was not as prominent as the others. But in most of the other traditions, both highland (Cajamarca, Recuay, Pukara, Huarpa) and coastal (Gallinazo, Moche, Nasca), human imagery was either introduced, transformed or intensified during the Early Intermediate Period. The changes are related to how certain individuals came to be regarded as special, transcendent beings for local groups. In particular, artisans made objects that both depicted and helped re-enact histories in documentary-participatory forms. Epigrapher Simon Martin (2006: 64) stresses the virtue of such forms: they 'make a viewer a spectator, a witness, even a participant in an unfolding drama'.

Those dramas often concerned the past and mythical origins, of people, places and things crucial in the social life of Amerindian groups. They comprise what Henry Nicholson (1971) called 'pattern history', and before him Mircea Eliade (1959) theorized as 'mythicization of historical personages' – which center on repeating cosmological cycles, in which humans intervene, in the position of or with associations to past persons, precisely to embody and mediate that past (a wide pattern, see also Heckenberger 2007; Houston and Stuart 1996; Walens 1981). Artworks were important elements, some would call props, for mythical narratives, because they performed as agents in expressing and presencing historical elements of them as retellings unfolded.

Many of the regional art traditions continued up until about the seventh and eighth centuries, when new patterns associated with Wari state expansion and influence began to proliferate (Plate 6). Before this rupture, each tradition developed relatively independently over some six to eight centuries with fairly little persistent input from exogenous sources (Donnan 2003; Lau 2006a).[6] That is not to say that there was no cultural interaction or innovation, but makers heavily favored existing dispositions in style and techniques. The long history of bounded regional styles of material culture is especially important because a number of these cultures were neighbors, shared borders and often interacted with each other (Lau 2006a; Makowski 2008; Proulx 1982).

Recuay culture and lifeways

We can now turn more closely to Recuay, the culture which provides the indicative case studies for this book (Grieder 1978; Lau 2011). Recuay groups had their heartland in Peru's north central highlands, more or less within the highland zone of Ancash department, above 1500 masl (meters above sea level).

The region features important geographical and cultural boundaries. To the west are the Pacific coastline and adjacent foothills of the Andes, which rise up quickly moving eastward. This was the home to Recuay's contemporaries, namely the Moche, Gallinazo and Lima. Recuay's northern frontier consisted of highland La Libertad, in present-day regions of Santiago de Chuco and Huamachuco. To the south was the impressive mountainous region of the Cordillera Huayhuash. The eastern frontier is probably the least known: the Río Marañon was certainly an important boundary, but Recuay-style materials have also been found further east descending toward Amazonia.

Language was a major source of distinction between different groups of northern Peru and it seems probable that the rise of the Early Intermediate Period's cultural diversity was matched in the proliferation of different languages (Schaedel 1985). At least in late prehistoric times, the various zones of northern Peru were populated by groups who spoke different languages. Toponymic evidence suggests that groups of pre-Inca Ancash may have employed forms of Quechua and Culle (Lau 2012). Quechua was and continues to be widely spoken throughout the Andes. Culle, meanwhile, was mainly limited to highland La Libertad, especially the Huamachuco and Santiago de Chuco areas just north of the Recuay heartland (Adelaar 1988; Andrade Ciudad 1995). To the south, in the Huayhuash region, were the people of Cajatambo, who may have spoken another dialect of Quechua.[7] Along the coast, late prehistoric groups along the north coast spoke Mochica, Quingnam and several other languages (Adelaar and Muysken 2004; Cerrón-Palomino 1995; Quilter et al. 2010; Schaedel 1985). Overall, the time depth for the linguistic heterogeneity remains uncertain, as is the identity of ancient Recuay language.

The majority of known Recuay sites are located fairly high up in the Andes, between 3000 and 4200 masl. This zone was optimal for agro-pastoral economies at different levels of political complexity, from small independent communities to multi-village chiefly polities.

Economic production closely follows the alternation of pronounced wet and dry seasons. The wet season, usually from about October to April, produces very strong rains and converts the Andean slopes, especially along belts of land between 2500–4000 masl, into verdant mosaics of agricultural fields, or *chakras*. Although direct paleobotanical evidence is lacking, Recuay groups very likely farmed tubers (potatoes, oca, ulluco), beans, squashes, quinua (a high-altitude grain), and, at suitable elevations, maize. They used irrigation works and other water-management features such as drains and reservoirs (Lau 2011). Grinding stones at archaeological sites show a reliance on fairly intensive processing of plant foodstuffs. The Recuay also prospered through the raising of camelids (Plate 13). Guinea pigs, viscachas, rabbits, birds and deer were eaten, but camelids were by far the primary meat source. Camelids also provided hair fiber for textiles, as well as sinew, skins and bone for a host of purposes (Lau 2007).

Not much certain can be said about climate or environmental change during the Early Intermediate Period in highland Ancash. Records from ice cores taken from Andean glaciers, including in the Cordillera Blanca (Ancash), suggest substantial fluctuation of temperature and precipitation over the Holocene. It seems likely that groups adapted to changing climates and production zones accordingly (Carey 2010). In general, temperatures appear to have been colder than today, which probably pushed down agricultural zones while expanding the high pasture and wetlands ideal for grazing camelids (see Lau 2011: 32–37). The fifth century AD was characterized by warmer and wetter weather, but was followed by a long period of decline in temperatures and increasing aridity during from the sixth century to the end of the millennium. The coast, meanwhile, may have been affected by warmer and drier conditions (Shimada 1994: 124) and El Niño episodes (Bourget 2001).

Recuay groups lived and worked in a variety of settlement types. But they almost always favored locating their residential communities in high, difficult-to-access areas. Because of the emphasis on high placement, sites often extended over long stretches of ridges or the topmost parts of hilltops. This applied equally to small villages as to large fortified centers. Sites regularly featured defensive walls and other fortifications, such as trenches, restricted access and lookouts. The constructions suggest a perpetual concern for protection against neighbors and outsiders. Residential buildings often had modular rooms and units that were clustered as needed. Large freestanding complexes of multiple such units, probably the house complexes of supra-family collectives, became more popular later in the Recuay tradition and in areas with defensive concerns.

Cemeteries were also common in the Recuay world. These can be found as distinct sites (e.g., Tello 1929), but most Recuay settlements featured mortuary areas for burials near and sometimes within residential sectors (e.g., Bennett 1944; Grieder 1978; Lau 2002, 2010a). As will be seen later, this was to provide living communities with regular access to dead ancestors, the focus of social identity and ritual life.

Recuay's distinctive material culture was intended, in great part, for use in funerary practices. The pottery style is well-recognized and comprises over a few thousand vessels.[8] Very few modeled vessels have provenience or contextual information, however. The most systematic ceramic studies classify the style's diverse shapes and patchy distribution (Hohmann 2010; Reichert 1977; Smith 1978), and some chronological seriation exists (Amat 2003; Grieder 1978; Lau 2011). The best-known forms are decorative serving and eating wares: bowls, jars, bottles and spoons. Each is handmade and favors fine light pastes, including a whitish kaolinite fired at high temperature. Unlike plainer terracottas, the technology allowed their walls to be very thin, while making the vessels light. The fine clay also allowed detailed modeling, which was then enhanced by polychrome painting.

The modeled vessels were mainly closed jars and likely functioned to contain and serve small amounts of liquids. Chicha, a maize beer commonly used as an offering and social lubricant among Andean peoples, was likely the preferred liquid (Gero 1992: 18ff.). While fineware bowl sherds occur abundantly in residential refuse, decorative jars and bottles are very uncommon (Lau 2010c: 341). Modeled ceramics were produced in fewer numbers, and they were probably treated with greater care and curation.

Most modeled vessels were offerings and, apparently, stored in tombs. The best known assemblages come from elite graves (Eisleb 1987; Gambini 1984; Grieder 1978; Ponte 2006). Recuay tombs were very often for multiple interments and show signs of re-entry, probably for additional burials, new offerings and regular cult practices. Given the diverse range and imagery of vessels, it is possible that they may have been arranged with other objects (e.g., pots, sculptures, interments) to form tableaus within the tomb spaces. As well as caches with specific arrangements, paired vessels, especially open bowls, have been documented (Grieder 1978; Wegner 1988, 2000).

In addition to stone sculpture, ceramics are important because of their imagery, which frequently represents others (Bankmann 1979; Gero 1999, 2004; Grieder 1978; Hohmann 2003, 2010; Lau 2000, 2004a, 2010d, 2011; Makowski and Rucabado Yong 2000; Reichert 1977; Smith 1978). There will be greater detail in later chapters but, briefly, the imagery stresses three related themes in Recuay cosmology – ancestors, divinities and high-status persons. As in Moche and Nasca imageries, Recuay art-works were key to cosmology about life, death and renewal.

Regionality through time: the case of Recuay and Cajamarca

Some of Recuay's most important contemporaries made their heartland to the north, associated with Cajamarca culture (Reichlen and Reichlen 1949; Terada and Matsumoto 1985; Topic 1985; Watanabe 2009). Recuay and Cajamarca groups interacted with each other in palpable ways, and I have examined the socio-political contexts of the interaction elsewhere (Lau 2005, 2006a). At the same time that the record manifests evidence of cultural boundaries, it also allows the charting of how these north highland groups recognized each other as neighbors over time. The Recuay–Cajamarca case forms a modest part of the much larger history of interregional interaction during the Early Intermediate Period. But their relations furnish a succinct, indicative example of approaching regional alterities through time.

At first glance, Recuay and Cajamarca material worlds were very similar. Both groups, for example, flourished in the north highlands through agriculture and camelid pastoralism in their respective intermontane valleys. Both groups made delicate open bowls (Plate 7), often with ring bases, using light kaolinite clays – on which they painted and modeled intricate imagery (Lau 2006a). They also excelled in building monumental architecture, often with elaborate stonemasonry, in hard-to-reach, defensible areas. There were a few large settlements, probably the seats of chiefdoms, but most communities were dispersed across the highland landscape.

Cajamarca and Recuay groups likely had many dealings with cultures of the forested slopes in northeastern Peru. Not only were their territories near to groups in the eastern slopes but, like Recuay and Cajamarca, many groups of the forested eastern slopes were also rather warlike. This is consistent with sporadic finds of weapons, and rather prominent imagery of warriors and militaristic head imagery (Fig 2.5), seen also in other Early Intermediate Period cultures. Historical accounts describe groups of this region as bellicose to the Spanish and the Incas. Perhaps most prominent of these ancient groups of Peru's north highlands was the emergence of monumental architecture at defensive locations and various features of the buildings stylized as working fortifications. In a context of chronic internecine conflict, the decorative stonework, it seems, had an aesthetic effect for internal groups, but also inspired fear and awe for outsiders.

Recuay shared many other elements we would associate more with the northern Andes and the forested eastern slopes. Elements such as resist (negative) painting, key motifs and lost-wax casting are probably the main diagnostics. Ancestor cult,

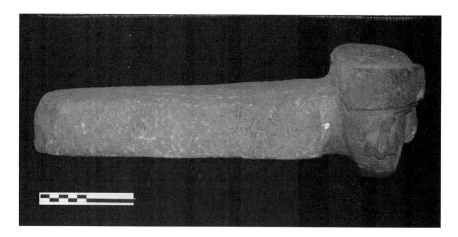

FIGURE 2.5 Tenon head sculpture, Pashash, Cabana. The long tenons would be inserted into walls to project the heads. Such sculptures link different regions of the north highlands. They depict helmeted warriors, often wearing banded helmet and ear ornaments, and were part of the increasing emphasis on militarism during the Early Intermediate Period. Cabana collection.

especially the celebration of chiefly figures, was another key commonality. These shared elements indicate that Recuay may have had fairly regular contact with cultures in the northern Andes and eastern slopes.

The long history of Recuay–Cajamarca interaction, meanwhile, is best shown through relations in material style and exchange of long-distance goods. This obtains despite the fact that highland La Libertad buffers Cajamarca from Ancash geographically. Cajamarca is especially interesting because the style had the uncanny ability to consistently transcend cultural and political boundaries in the Central Andes during the latter half of the first millennium AD (Bernuy and Bernal 2008; Lau 2006a; Matsumoto 1988; Menzel 1964; Shady 1988; Topic 1991). It is worth noting that for the time period in question, Cajamarca has seen much less archaeological investigation than highland Ancash – and future work may find greater evidence of Recuay in neighboring regions.

The record shows four major patterns of interaction (Fig 2.6), which furnish a first approximation of regional alterities – of interactions and recognitions of each other. Early on, there was marked stylistic interaction but not much interest in physical exchange of the decorative styles. Early Cajamarca–Recuay relationships appear to have consisted mainly of general stylistic similarities. Both traditions stressed simple open bowls, made of kaolinite clay, frequently with exterior positive-painted geometric and linear designs. In general, this early period, approximately the early centuries AD to AD 400, is characterized by fairly widespread stylistic interaction but low access to each other's prestige goods.

Later, from about AD 400–700, Cajamarca interaction in Ancash favored direct importation of small, portable kaolinite objects with 'cursive' painted designs (Fig 2.7). These are of quick, thin and repetitive dark strokes on light ground, which make linear as well as figural motifs (e.g., squiggles and flora). At the same time that there was a widening of access to luxury ceramics, there seems to have been a reduction in stylistic interaction, for both Recuay and Cajamarca styles grew increasingly different from one another. The technical and formal preferences of Cajamarca styles (e.g., tripod bowls, cursive painting, imagery) do not find much resemblance in Recuay (e.g., jars, bottles, modeled effigies, organic resist). Nevertheless, the ceramics of both traditions are almost always from burial contexts and places for ostentation, suggesting that local leaders from each side recognized and tried to acquire through prestige items the symbolic capital of highland neighbors.

By the seventh and eighth centuries AD, some increasingly successful groups across northern Peru began to look outward for new sources of prestige and symbolic links. Evidence indicates that leaders and status groups gained more interest in and, crucially, wider access to long-distance goods. This coincided with the expansion of Wari culture, by around AD 700, when the boundaries of many regional art traditions began to break down (Plate 6). The interaction networks of the Wari state intensified during the time, for Wari imports or related pottery styles consistently co-occurred with Cajamarca pottery at Ancash sites, in the highlands and the coast (Lau 2006a).[9] The Callejón de Huaylas was probably the primary north–south route for Ancash–Cajamarca exchange during the early Middle Horizon.

It is notable that when Cajamarca imports occurred in Ancash, they frequently appeared with other kinds of prestige materials. These include wares from identifiable

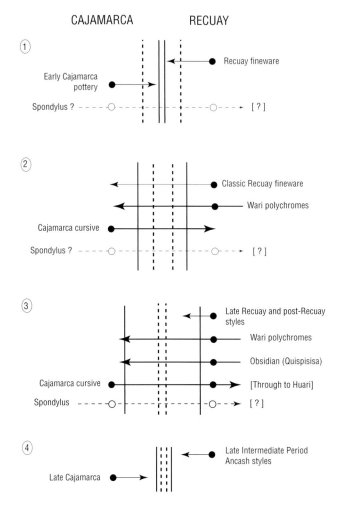

FIGURE 2.6 Schematic representation of interaction patterns between groups in Cajamarca and Ancash, first millennium AD. Solid vertical lines indicate access to long-distance goods, while dashed lines indicate degrees of stylistic interaction. Frame 1 (ca. AD?–400) is characterized by regular stylistic interaction but limited exchange of exotic items. Frame 2 (ca. AD 400–700) sees a widening of access but reduction in stylistic interaction, as the Recuay and Cajamarca styles grew increasingly different. Frame 3 (ca. AD 700–900) shows unprecedented access to prestige items, with limited, very specific stylistic interaction. Frame 4 (post AD 900) indicates very limited interregional interaction.

areas (i.e., Wari, Nievería, North Coast) and unknown production sources. Cajamarca pottery is, almost predictably, associated with contexts of status display, especially in mortuary contexts. This was a part of a broader pattern across the Central Andes, in which many local groups began to incorporate culturally diverse materials into their ritual offerings and paraphernalia. Later, instances of imported cursive pottery were frequently accompanied by instances of clear stylistic emulation.

FIGURE 2.7 Imported Cajamarca-style pottery in the Callejón de Huaylas, Ancash, Peru. The intermontane Santa valley (Callejón de Huaylas) was the main route for north–south interrregional exchange at the end of the Early Intermediate Period. Obsidian, *Spondylus* sp. shell, and decorative ceramics were among the valuables transacted. Cursive style pottery, especially bowls (left, from Antaraká) and spoons (right, from Wilkawaín, handle edge ground down) from Cajamarca, was also very popular. 'Cursive' refers to the quick thin strokes, often in repetitive linear and floral designs.

Unlike Cajamarca style, Recuay decorative pottery very rarely circulated outside of Ancash. It was uncommon for Cajamarca groups to import Recuay style pottery, although there are a few instances (e.g., Julien 1988: 218; Reichlen and Reichlen 1949: 145). Recuay-style pottery entered occasionally into highland La Libertad, the area in between present-day Cajamarca and Ancash departments (Church 1996; Pérez Calderón 1988, 1994; Topic and Topic 2001: 194; Topic and Topic 1987: 18), but by no means were they ever as popular as Cajamarca. This was probably because Recuay decorative, modeled ceramics were for specific kin groups and their collective rituals; they were heirlooms in a sense. Cajamarca pottery, abstracted and without overt imagery of such lineage histories, probably was not limited in this way. Put another way, Recuay ceramics held much less significance and agency outside its respective use group.

The final period of major Cajamarca interaction in Ancash (AD 700–900) occurred in the middle to late Middle Horizon (Krzanowski 1986; Krzanowski and Pawlikowski 1980; Shady and Rosas 1977; Thatcher 1972). Cursive pottery was still traded, but the most notable development was that highland Ancash groups began emulating specific attributes of Cajamarca cursive pottery. Local clays replaced kaolinite pastes, and certain shapes were adopted (tripod bowl) and derivative cursive designs and

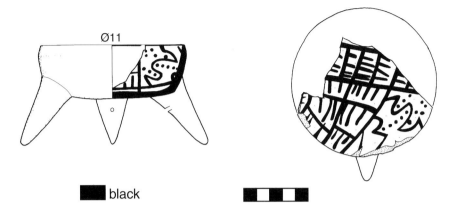

FIGURE 2.8 Local Cajamarca emulated pottery, from Chinchawas, Ancash. Shortly after the appearance of imported cursive wares, potters all across the Central Andes began to make local versions, apparently using local clays, pigments and brushing techniques for foreign forms and designs.

painting (ticking) using broad line weights featured, sometimes, in the local decorated wares (Fig 2.8). Thus, there was continued access to exotica, with very specific stylistic interaction (emulation).

After about AD 900, there was very limited overt contact between the Recuay and Cajamarca traditions. Groups in Ancash appear to have ceased importing and emulating Cajamarca style. In effect, local groups in each region stopped actively producing and recognizing the alterity of their highland counterparts. This was almost certainly related to the cessation of intensive Wari trade networks.

The regional art traditions of the Early Intermediate Period were distinguished by their stylistic coherence over a relatively long duration. This was important not only for Recuay and Cajamarca, but also Moche, Nasca, Lima and Gallinazo. Each showed relatively few drastic stylistic transformations that can be attributed to the influence of ethnic others, in spite of the fact that groups were aware of other cultures and, moreover, interacted with them in palpable, tangible ways. The art styles follow relatively customary patterns, with any changes and innovation often incorporated within established practices and dispositions for their respective regions. We might surmise that cultural boundaries, the stuff that frames alterity, grew more prominent for the very reason that there was persistent interaction.

The long trajectory of Recuay–Cajamarca interaction is important because it acknowledges a long history of recognition of an alter group, and tracks some of their material entanglements by way of trade and stylistic contact. Recuay tradition groups were cognizant of Cajamarca groups (and vice versa) from the earliest centuries AD, yet they participated in very distinct cultural traditions. Sometimes they wanted each other's luxury items; very often they did not. Recuay people were the more interested of the two in desiring the other style, especially for status display as offerings and grave goods. At one point in time, the desirability of Cajamarca pottery was so great in Ancash that people went to great lengths to acquire them or change their pottery production accordingly to copy them. To be sure, the relations of alterity here (desirability, emulation, conflict) were historically and politically situated. Relations of alterity can be studied at the regional level. The example has provided a broad-brush account of how it changed over nearly a millennium-long period.

Summary

This chapter sets the environmental and historical backdrop on which our case studies of alterity will be foregrounded. It first examined the three major geographic macro-regions of the Andes (coast, highlands and forested eastern slopes). It briefly described how each macro-region has its own set of resources, climatic regimes and landscape that affects lifeways and perceptions regarding the people from these regions.

The chapter then moved on to contextualize the complex social and cultural dyna-mism of the Early Intermediate Period, AD 1–700. It was seen that the earliest cultures emerged out of widely shared rejection – the first pan-Andean alterity – of Chavín horizon materials and ideas. The regionalism that ensued was borne out of local cultural initiatives which sought to differentiate from others who did not share the same landscapes, religion, language and material styles.

In Chavín's wake, a series of groups across the Central Andean coast and highlands filled the cultural vacuum. Each featured its own ways of doing and thinking about things. Unprecedented developments characterized each culture, but especially the various forms of luxury material items (artworks) that arose in the service of leaders and their close relations, broadly labeled as 'elites'.

The regional art traditions of the Early Intermediate Period were also distinguished by their long histories of relatively insular development. This occurred despite shared borders and regular interactions between the different cultural groups, who apparently wished to keep their identity and material styles largely distinct. In other words, they made difference based on their perception and engagement with others, developed over centuries.

3

FAMILIAR OTHERS

Kin, collectivity and authority

The previous chapter focused on a regional and long-term, diachronic perspective for approaching alterity. My discussion now turns to how otherness is crucial in the world of the house and the residential community. In particular, I will explore ways that Early Intermediate Period peoples emphasized and represented familiar others. By 'familiar', I mean those persons considered internal to and within a given collective – those on the inside, identified as kindred and local. This might be seen variably as family and partners, friends, children, co-residents and, in certain cases, leaders. It is an admittedly difficult category to define with great precision, but I would argue that this is precisely its virtue and logic – and the interpretative challenge for archaeology. Lacking means to study familiar others systematically, we can nevertheless discern, and surmise about, *some* revealing recognition of these kinds of others using the archaeological record of domestic contexts and art imagery.

Data on domestic practices, settlement layouts and figural imagery provide basic lines of evidence for everyday social interactions. Particularly important are those deliberate interchanges of materials and ideas with familiar others (e.g., feeding, eating, drinking, sex, gifts) that transform the body. In what some have called a 'moral economy of intimacy', the exchange of nourishment and vitality with social others is crucial. Artworks are especially important for prescribing the roles and actions of specific categories of persons. Crucially, the familiar becomes a key vector for political authority during the Early Intermediate Period – this is through insiders, potent familiars, becoming the heads of their respective collectivities.

A working narrative framework for this chapter follows. With the receding of the Chavín cult, increasingly regionalized cosmologies characterized the social and religious life of the various groups of the Early Intermediate Period. Such emphases in all the groups emerged alongside new kinds of residential practices and social arrangements. The developments often took the form of increasingly closed off and nucleated domestic complexes. These seem to indicate larger communities and residential groups on the one hand, and spatial divisions within complexes suggest greater divisions – internal segmentation – in the residential group on the other. New gendered roles also become prominent. This is paralleled by increasingly differentiated social groups within communities, where wealthier, larger and/or higher status factions emerge. For some groups, it was in the relations of kin and kin-based collectivities that leaders emerged during the Early Intermediate Period.

Familiar relations

In setting out the working thematic for this chapter, it is useful to return to ethno-graphic description of lowland South American groups which lays stress on a 'moral economy of intimacy'. This approach sees the social not being limited to or even primarily associated with the public or political. Rather, it emphasizes 'everyday sociability' defined by 'the sharing and caring between relatives' (Viveiros de Castro 1996: 189). The emphasis is on internal relationships of living with social others, at the domestic and communal level. It is also on how genders are complementary not only in domestic activities of production, but also production of people in communal contexts. What is often crucial is the circulation of substances (food, bodily fluids, internal potencies) through house practices and work, and how these flows effect social relations and society more generally. *Convivial* forms are also moral ones, stressing the contributions of close relations in feeding acts, knowledge transmission and nurture as part of good, proper living and making proper, sociable persons.[1] As a process, these actions value 'production over exchange, practices of mutuality over reciprocity structures, and morals of consanguinity over the symbolics of affinity' (Viveiros de Castro 1996: 189).

Another source of contrast regards the routinized daily character of convivial sociality, compared to the less frequent, but often highly punctuated and energetic, engagements with the outside. Hence there is emphasis on internal relations (within house and village) and the solidarity of 'living well' cultivated by co-residence and commensality. As would be expected, these forms of sociality, or idealized modes of 'communal living', characterize many groups; they are nevertheless organized and expressed in very different ways across Amazonia (Århem 1998; Gow 1991; Hugh-Jones 1995; Overing 1989; Overing and Passes 2000a). The behavior and symbolism of feeding, nurture and cor-poreal substances that create community also mark many other Amerindian cultures, not least of the Central Andes (Plate 8A, B); their importance for humans often articulates with understandings and practices of nonhumans (e.g., Allen 1988; Dransart 2002; López Austin 1988; Monaghan 1995; Walens 1981; Weismantel 2004). In part, this is because '[s]ocial relations, in this view, are the condensation and memory of the affective moods built up by daily interaction in nurturing, sharing and working' (Taylor 1996).

For some, the other pole of sociality regards predation and affinity, and interlocal relations with other groups and communities, typical of a 'symbolic economy of alterity' or 'ontological predation' (see next chapter, 'Predatorial Relations') (Taylor 1996; Viveiros de Castro 1996, 2001, 2004). Most scholars would agree that the two approaches to lowland South American societies are not necessarily antithetical, as much as they are partial (as ethnographic sampling) or complementary in overall sociality and social reproduction (e.g., Fausto 2000; Overing and Passes 2000b: 6; Rival 2001: 77; Santos-Granero 2007: 2). There is also the matter of the political – dubbed the 'political economy of control', one of the three tendencies in lowland South American ethnography (Viveiros de Castro 1996) – but often glossed over in debates about the 'moral economy of intimacy' versus the 'symbolic economy of alterity'.

Fernando Santos-Granero (2007) notes another kind of sociality – broadly, 'friendships' – that resides neither firmly within nor beyond the domains of kinship and affinity, but clearly articulates with them, socially and symbolically. Trading partners, shamanic allies and relations with other-worldly beings are kinds of friendship and opportunities for forging bonds with unrelated, ambiguous others. An 'antidote' to the burdens and prescriptions of kin and affinal relations, he argues that the formalization of amicable relations – based on friendship, trust and safety – with nonkin others in other tribes may have been a pathway to the establishment of macropolities in the ancient Amerindian world (Santos-Granero 2007: 15).

For my purposes, what is vital is not the polarization of kinship versus affinity, nor the interpretive reach of predation versus conviviality or amity. Rather, it is that these nominal, working categories of alterity – affines, predators, friends, allies, aliens, family, etc. – might find utility for detecting and bridging evidence of such patterns remnant in the ancient record. The various modes of sociality, marked by the recognition of others, offer some basic heuristic categories (and expectations) to apprehend the archaeological record and imagery of the Early Intermediate Period.

Sociality centered on a 'moral economy of intimacy' will emphasize spatial arrangements that articulate those people 'within' – what I shall call *familiar* others – especially in certain contexts and ways. Dwellings, as core places for the interaction of one with family and relatives, will certainly be of relevance; but also other kinds of communal structures indicative of shared living, activities and effort (e.g., compounds, longhouses, plazas, canals). Familiar others may be bounded by the domestic residence in minimal terms and, in most cases, village and community boundaries, in the maximal.

Within those settings, perhaps more than anything else, conviviality – as shared, communal living – presumes regular and sustained interactions with familiar others, perhaps over many generations. There should be great emphasis on feeding and directed flows of corporeal substances and fluids – namely, blood, semen, milk, food and beverages. Water and intangible vitalities associated with ancestral prototypes might also be included in this category.

We should also expect that the activities of familiar others are of certain genres as well. These include those activities of commensality and co-residence, of eating and dwelling together at different scales, and of certain kinds of cooperative work (Plate 9). We should not forget the integrative mechanism of the collective rituals for the dead and supernaturals – I treat these as kinds of other beings who are part familiar and external (see Chapter 5). The conjunction of these common interests, dispositions and actions may have the effect of producing 'community'.

Archaeology has much to offer here. If the ethnographic optic is not entirely suited to detect long-term social patterns and transformations, archaeology specializes in them. As we shall see, it is in the habits in the house – that domain of substance flow and reproduction among its denizens – that some Andean political economies emerged. Before we can approach these questions, it is important to discuss the status of art in Early Intermediate Period societies, and how it worked in the interests of collectivities.

Art, collectivity and memory during the Early Intermediate Period

Art and imagery are the backbone for this chapter, because they provide the fullest evidence of the growing concern for familiar others during the Early Intermediate Period. They also inform the sample of *in situ* contexts revealed through dirt archaeology. This section aims to contextualize my two examples (Moche and Recuay) – as indices of broader trends in residential variability and, ultimately, the social distinctions increasingly prominent in familiar, inside contexts.

The previous chapter discussed the emergence of regional art traditions during the Early Intermediate Period. Now I wish to generalize about their roles for local groups and, in particular, the function of their respective imageries for domestic and community-level collectivities.

The production and use of artifacts of fine manufacture (my main criterion for calling something an artwork) were crucial to the cultures of the Early Intermediate Period. In this chapter, I will be examining the social contexts in which certain objects circulated and the relationships that linked various forms. All the forms were functional in the sense of being used and performing for their makers and sponsors. If people in the proximity of the object were drawn into a 'nexus' of sociality (Gell 1998), the objects might be said to mediate – meaning to create, display, depict, reinforce and sever – kinds of social relations. In very general terms, images during the Early Intermediate Period very often served in three social domains, all interrelated to different degrees among its constituent cultures: death, memory and public display. Some background on these related topics are needed before we can return to the alterity of familiar others.

Death practices and cosmology are central to the arts of the Early Intermediate Period cultures (see Chapter 5). This is especially relevant given the funerary and offering roles of most fine pottery traditions in the Early Intermediate Period (e.g., Nasca, Recuay, Moche, Lima). More so than at any time before in Andean prehistory, a great range of funerary practices and their associated material culture proliferated among the regional cultures (Carmichael 1995; Donnan 1995; Lau 2000, 2002; Millaire 2002).

One could argue persuasively that the core differentiation in Early Intermediate Period groups stems from basic differences in funerary cultures and their attendant ideologies. For one thing, nearly all of the major pottery sequences are based on decorative wares that, more often than not, were parts of death ritual (Carmichael 1995; Donnan and McClelland 1999; Lau 2011; Proulx 2006). In all the cultures, the arts also enhanced the standing of special persons, alive or expired, within society.

Before Christianity, much Andean religiosity focused on ancestors embodied as mummified corpses, bundles and other effigies. These physical instantiations were not to distance and forget dead relations as much as to prolong their propinquity (Lau 2008). Death rituals fix a socio-cosmological order where those deceased deemed worthy and strategic became installed as durable object-persons: 'ancestors'. Early Intermediate Period patterns therefore contrast with practices focused more on dissolving, negating or forgetting aspects of the person at death (see Chaumeil 2007; Fitzsimmons 2009; Gillespie 2001; Küchler 2002).

For the ancient Andes, a range of evidence shows great interest in stabilizing the presence of esteemed forebears, such as periodic food offerings, visitations and rewrapping of ancestral bundles with new cloths; the cult image and its setting are perpetually re-formed outcomes of this desire (Lau 2008). This not only re-imagines the deceased person, for example as soul, corpse or ancestor. It also redefines the myriad statuses of the living in relation to his alterity.

Anthropologist Magnus Course (2007: 96) observes how Mapuche funeral oratory acts as a 'synthesis, a condensation of the diffuse relationships of which the Mapuche person is composed'. These, recounting significant acts and social relations in life, complete and stabilize the person in death, the person here objectified through accounts (also Comaroff and Comaroff 2001: 276). Colonial inquisitional testimonies remind us that regular corporate ceremonies entailed many other acts more resistant to archaeological detection: nighttime vigils, food taboos, playing of music, blood offerings, pouring libations, pilgrimage, dancing, etc. Crucially, the recounting of ancestral traditions through songs and stories was vital (e.g., Doyle 1988: 161–72). But how might ancient narratives which stabilize persons be discerned in societies without writing?

During the Early Intermediate Period, artworks became increasingly suitable forms.[2] By way of their representation, performance and as effective things, artworks showed how specific people were empowered in social networks of living and divine beings. In effect, the representations construct their alterity.

Much now has been said about 'how societies remember'. Paul Connerton's (1989) heuristic distinction continues to be useful in this respect: collective memory, those beliefs about the past preserved and propagated by a group, can be *incorporated* or *inscribed* (see also Bradley 2002; Mills and Walker 2008; Rowlands 1993; Van Dyke and Alcock 2003). The former is produced through bodily actions and physical performance. Incorporated by the senses, people remember as a result of doing and experiencing through the body, such as a posture, ritual or dance. 'Inscribed', meanwhile, describes memory that has been recorded graphically in some tangible form (a religious text, monument, photograph). Given their reproducibility, inscribed practices can be more standardized, spread more widely, and can be more efficient. 'Incorporated' practices, meanwhile, may be more improvised, less formal and situationally contingent.

Across the ancient Americas, the distinction between inscribed and incorporated practices is repeatedly circumvented, or transcended. Two of the most celebrated Precolumbian civilizations, for example, commemorated the historical and embodied qualities of their dynasts. Classic Maya lords celebrated their achievements (e.g., conquests, accessions, sacrifices, dedications) on stone uprights with accompanying inscriptions about the event and date. Likened to ancestors and maize divinities in look and comportment, these monuments became a 'forest of kings' (Schele and Freidel 1990). Around the same time, the Moche emphasized the performance of their narratives, in which nobles played the main protagonists (Donnan 2004). They reenacted a mytho-historical drama, portrayed also in pots and murals, in which a divine being incorporates the blood of sacrificed enemy warriors. Buried with the trappings of this role, the identity was forever bound with the lordly person. Many other Amerindian cultures joined the two forms of memory practice.

The image can commemorate past action – constructed, shared and passed on by a group. But mimetic imagery also facilitated certain kinds of subjectivity by repre-senting conventionalized social interactions (e.g., of sacrifice, subordination, giving). The depiction of others sought to differentiate people, to put generations of people, as it were, in their place. This chapter therefore views artworks as occupying key social roles in Early Intermediate Period developments. In this scheme, the logic of mimetic objects shifts to their representation, use and performance. I will argue that while some works are oriented to serve the present, they also forecast a later sociality, which is to emulate past events, actions and, often, the people who acted them in the past. Their effect was to perpetuate idealized arrangements and social relations with familiar others. Let us see this process at work first at the residential level (Moche), and then a contemporary process in representational format (Recuay).

Domestic worlds

This survey will first describe briefly the character of cultural changes in household and community life among Moche and Recuay groups. Then I will comment about the emergent forms of alterity in these contexts.

Archaeological work in Early Intermediate Period cultures has focused, in general, on funerary and monumental sites of high-status groups. Meanwhile, research into residential life and domestic production is really only in its infancy (Lau 2010c; Van Gijseghem and Vaughn 2008; Van Gijseghem 2001; Vaughn 2004, 2009). Much of the recent work operates broadly under the rubric of 'household archaeology'.

Approaches to household archaeology often proceed with several common premises (Nash 2009; Stanish 1989). First, the household is seen to constitute the basic economic unit of the society. And, as the locus of subsistence production and social reproduction, it is seen to be functional in adapting people effectively to their respective environment. Second, the household is seen to perform a crucial role in the resource redistribution of complex societies. When people are integrated into a larger system, they are said to come to manifest and reflect broader economic and political processes. These included long-distance trade and intensification of agricultural or craft production. Much of the seminal work done for the Central Andes demonstrates how domestic contexts changed alongside new forms of complexity (e.g., Aldenderfer 1993; Bermann 1994; D'Altroy and Hastorf 2001; Goldstein 1993; Janusek 2004; Stanish 1992).

More recently, there has been consideration about the experiential and symbolic dimensions of house life, about meanings of the house as a physical object and as a domain for everyday activities and domestic practices, including forms of ritual and socialization (DeMarrais 2004; Lau 2011; Ringberg 2008). What is produced is not only food, animals or households. Rather, there has been increasing emphasis on the production of persons associated with the 'moral economy of intimacy'.

Changing domestic practices

For a culture long researched in Andean archaeology, the residential practices of the ancient Moche are still relatively little-known. Most scientific investigations emphasize *huaca* temple pyramids, cemeteries and other high-status contexts, providing an unparalleled view of certain segments of this renowned ancient Andean culture, namely of nobles (Chapdelaine 2011; Jackson 2008; Quilter 2002, 2010).

In general, we know that Moche people lived in large settlements as well as in the surrounding countryside, in the nearby valleys and shorelines, where food was gathered and produced. Current knowledge about domestic practices relies on regional settlement descriptions (e.g., Billman 1996; Dillehay et al. 2009; Wilson 1988) and a handful of excavations, most from residential sectors of large nucleated 'urban' centers (Bawden 1990; Chapdelaine 2009; Prieto 2008; Shimada 1994; Topic 1977; Van Gijseghem 2001). The balance of the work highlights the role of the domestic sphere in indexing kinds of social organization (elites, non-elites, etc.) or tracking the effects of Moche political centralization. I want to outline here how changing cultural orientations in residential life, during the height of the Moche tradition, had an important effect on the ways that people engaged with familiar others.

Moche period residential compounds were part of north coast traditions of building agglutinated structures that had walls that abutted each other or that had rooms which shared walls. At least for the last millennia BC, these were especially prominent for important ceremonial buildings and commonly in monumental and quite extensive forms (e.g., Burger 1992a; Chicoine 2006; Moore 2005; Pozorski and Pozorski 2002). By Moche times, agglutinated architecture was very common also for residential buildings, both common and high status. These are often agglutinated rectangular rooms, often featuring large open patio spaces; the rooms evince a diversity of functions, including storage, food processing, sleeping and cooking. Direct antecedents to Moche-style compound architecture may be found at sites such as Cerro Arena and the Gallinazo Group (Brennan 1982; Millaire 2010). Recent investigations at the latter documented a diversity of residential architectural form and building quality, ranging from modest houses to large agglutinated compounds with interior courtyards, dating perhaps as early as the first centuries BC and up until about AD 600 (Millaire 2010: 6189).

The second half of the Early Intermediate Period (ca. AD 400–700) saw the proliferation of large Moche civic-ceremonial centers, as well as residential settlements in adjacent hinterlands. Farming and fishing villages were also linked to larger civic-ceremonial centers, very likely for defensive, economic/trade and ritual purposes. Many are located directly above the agricultural lands, and utilize expedient forms of construction and materials (adobe, stone, wattle/daub).

In the large centers, or towns, themselves, domestic housing shows great nucleation, often in the form of agglutinated enclosures, made of adobe bricks. These were probably the residential structures of corporate groups, perhaps multiple extended families, of different sizes and means. The complexes also show evidence of considerable artifact variability and this has been taken to indicate different strata of society, including an emerging 'middle class' at Moche itself (Van Gijseghem 2001: 264; see also Chapdelaine 2011: 202). Some of the enclosures feature evidence of storage. Some also show disparate access to high-status items, such as decorative ceramics, marine shells, lapidary work, metals, etc.

Other compounds actually feature evidence of intensive craft production (of similar prestige items). Items were probably for use by people in nearby high-status residential and ceremonial buildings (Bernier 2010; Shimada 1994, 2001; Uceda and Rengifo 2006). Unprecedented functional specialization thus characterized Moche communities. Certain crafts were probably organized through compound-based lineages and routed through workshops. Production of crafts was probably facilitated by feasting, gifts and other relations of reciprocity between makers and sponsors (Shimada 2001: 200–1).

What is surmised at Moche and other large centers is that wealthier groups (those better able to amass and display indices of wealth) had larger and better-quality residential complexes. These correspond to those groups who were able to best position themselves and their collectivities: they were bigger, more elaborate and more effectively organized (Van Gijseghem 2001: 270). In essence, residential architecture indexed the increasing segmentation of Moche groups and their respective communities.

One important aspect of Moche domestic ritual concerns the use of ceramic anthropomorphic figurines (Prieto 2008; Ringberg 2008). These are usually fairly small and portable mold-made figurines, hollow or solid, that depict a small range of anthropomorphic types. They often consist of women (clothed or nude), warriors/leaders, captives and other kinds of persons, denoted by special individual features, such as musical instruments, weapons and other personal ornamentation (e.g., labrets, headgear, attire). Some are perforated and may have been worn, carried or hung – perhaps as efficacious charms and tokens of identity, and almost certainly of special interest to people within Moche culture (Cordy-Collins 2001b; Jackson 2008: 43–45, 60–62).

Interestingly, the figurines occur fairly frequently in quotidian assemblages, in urban and rural, as well as high-status and more common domestic contexts. While some are found whole, most are broken, and dispersed throughout the residential space, but very often in hearths as well as in middens. The last use of some appear to have included procedures that 'killed' the image (e.g., breakage, dismemberment, puncturing) followed by purposeful deposition of the fragments in the termination ritual of buildings. Similar types of mutilation and closure activities characterize the captive effigies found broken with human sacrifices in the adjacent Huaca de la Luna temple (detailed in the next chapter) (Prieto 2008). The ritual termination procedures performed on the human effigies make an explicit analogy comparing the temporality and renewal of buildings and people. Renewal of the built spaces likely relied on the objecthood of the subjects.

The precise functions of the figurines remain unclear, but any interpretation must include their regular use at the residential level. It might be suggested that the figurines, as social agents of their bearers or indeed the residential space itself, served to mediate interactions with familiar others within the dwelling context. In one small rural settlement, mold-made anthropomorphic figurines were found abundantly across residential contexts; the distribution indicates their importance for widespread household rituals, and appear to have promoted, in the dwelling's occupants, group well-being as well as certain kinds of personal themes (child, male warrior and women). They focused on social status, 'on figures from their own social and religious sphere … Although all figurines … were probably used by individuals or on a household level, only whistles depicting warriors or musicians obviously represent social roles that extend beyond the household' (Ringberg 2008: 353). Probably made in workshops sponsored by Moche nobles (Russell and Jackson 2011), the figurines also almost certainly referred back to elite identity and networks.

It is not a coincidence that the growing differentiation of certain residential collectives, including higher-status families, coincided with other major changes. The transformations in Moche residential practices appear to have taken place by the middle centuries of the Early Intermediate Period, when the major centers, such as Moche, Huaca Cao, Dos Cabezas, Pacátnamu and Sipán were all growing in political and religious stature. Their dynamism manifested mainly in the construction of large temple pyramids, elite burial activities and the use of other elaborate art media for public display. But also during this time of social flux, anthropomorphic figurines – worn, held and in ritual use – helped to identify and stabilize the status of their bearers through their engagements with social others in residential contexts. It seems possible that the reliance on figurines in highly conventionalized and static gendered roles ('women', 'male warriors', 'children'), may have been to reinforce kinds of idealized persons during a time when the role and integration of the Moche household were increasingly unhinged by the pressures of urbanism and theocratic ideology.

A similar transformative process appears to have happened to Recuay domestic arrangements, but in a very different manner. Unlike most Moche population centers, Recuay groups established their communities in high, strategic places in mountainous terrain. The emergence of more nucleated town-like settlements, such as Pashash and Yayno, occurred later in Recuay history. During the first centuries AD, domestic architecture was for the most part dispersed and settlements were fairly modest in size. Villages consisted mainly of freestanding or part-agglutinated dwellings located strategically in high areas. These were usually two- or three-chambered rectangular structures, often measuring 4–5 meters across – perhaps the buildings for a nuclear family. They may have been arranged in an open space, but they were rarely fully circumscribed, or closed off, with walls.

A signal change occurred midway in Recuay's history, by the fourth century AD, at approximately the same time that the large Recuay centers emerged. Large multi-chambered house compounds began to be built (Fig 3.1). These continued the use of the earlier, modular domestic building, but combined many of them into one structural complex. In addition, the entire structure was closed off with an enclosure wall

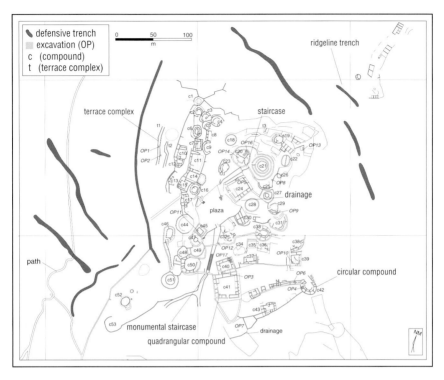

FIGURE 3.1 Plan of main sector, Yayno, Ancash. The monumental sector is characterized by a series of high-walled residential compounds, of both circular and quadrangular layouts. The entire sector is protected by a formidable trench system, segments of walls, and steep cliffs.

and given usually one or, at most, two entrances. The compounds could be of variable size, from about 10 meters across to as much as 35 meters across, and the largest had multiple stories. Apartment-like rooms were stacked around a central open space, or courtyard. Furthermore, there may be many compounds in any given site. Domestic refuse and activity areas, both in the rooms and courtyard spaces, indicate they were probably the dwellings and work spaces of different groups. They probably served extended families or multiple families and oriented around kinship lines.

Because this process has been described in greater detail elsewhere (Lau 2010c, 2011), I wish to limit my discussion to the implications for alterity. These concern how the changing architectural orientations might have effected new dispositions in domestic living and social relations with co-residents within the compound as well as people in the community at large. Clearly, the emphasis on the high location of communities for their defensive and economic virtues continued. Whereas before, there were many spatially discrete domestic structures, they were increasingly aggregated in the later centuries of Recuay history (AD 400–600). Given their variability in form, size and elaboration, we can suggest that the collectivities were also of different sizes and means. Whereas the basic units of living and production centered on smaller

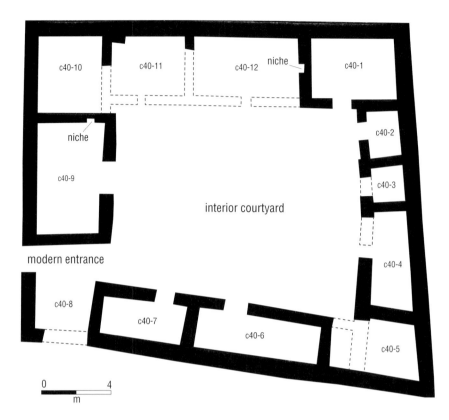

FIGURE 3.2 Plan of compound c40, one of the largest and most elaborate quadrangular compounds at Yayno. The outer rooms comprised multi-story residential spaces, and excavations revealed large amounts of domestic refuse inside the rooms, as well in the courtyard space just outside the doorways. The grandest room in the block is c40-9, which has at least one niche and employs massive black limestone boulders to frame the grand entranceway.

groups, probably small nuclear families, the later compounds demanded different kinds of social interaction – probably greater cooperation with co-resident families and less privacy between them (Figs 3.1, 3.2). Another important distinction seems to have been the co-existence of compounds that featured circular and quadrangular groundplans. Some were monumental and have elaborate features that most of the others do not, such as very decorative stonework, drainage and elaborate construction fills that leveled sloping areas.

The organization of work at large Recuay centers must have been quite different, if only because building large compounds could not be done easily without corporate labor, and because the large compounds are planned spaces that were much less flexible for casual renovations and expansions. Unlike small domestic structures, the compounds did not grow outward; rather, most compounds seem to have internal additions or renovations. An entire new compound might be added next to an existing one, but both were still freestanding closed-off buildings.

At the same time, the large settlements containing many compounds (e.g., Yayno, Honcopampa) must have been very different kinds of communities, compared to small, dispersed farmsteads. For instance, all activities centered within the high-walled compounds, rather than out in the open. There must have been increased insularity between those groups living in different compounds, so that what transpired in one was not necessarily seen by or recognized by any of the others.

In essence, living in closed-off enclosures occasioned new ways to engage one's co-residents and also the community at large. Access was very different, becoming much more limited and directed; if there were windows that looked outward, none have survived. Entire groups were therefore more shielded from others, limiting communications and interactions that hitherto were open to (insider) surveillance. The increasing social distance between residential collectives was increasingly tied into, if not basic to, the rise of increasingly differentiated collectivities and their respective leaders (Bawden 1990; Lau 2010c). The activities and objects that defined nobles became more private and only episodically visible, behind the tall walls of compound enclosures.

The transformations in residential architecture went hand-in-hand with increasing centralization in Recuay socio-political organization. Let us explore another coeval process: new ceramic imagery that stresses Recuay leaders as embodiments of the house, the physical and cognitive space in which they engage with familiar others.

Rise of chiefly alterities

This section highlights the alterity of special collectivities, as seen through repre-sentational artworks. In depicting a range of conventionalized human actions and practices, the figural imagery reinforces a model in which social transactions with others help to make persons. This is through mimetic, agentive objects which commemorated and facilitated certain kinds of power relations. At one level, the imagery becomes a material correlate of ranking. But it also allows a rare, if stylized, look at a native theory about the distinctive alterity of one common, if very distinctive, kind of insider other – namely, chiefs.

If archaeology studies past variability, one of the key developments in human history consists of when and where political inequality emerged, when people acceded to the value of chiefly leadership, and when the autonomy of villages was given over to larger political communities (see Carneiro 1981; Earle 1997; Service 1962). Chiefdom studies have seen substantial revision over the last few decades, as part of a general rethinking of the dominant functionalist, neo-evolutionary paradigm (Clifford 1988; Ferguson and Whitehead 2000; e.g., Patterson 1987; Pauketat 2007; see Yoffee 2005). While the term and its study remain heavily debated (Earle 1997; Redmond 1998a; Stanish 2003), the term 'chiefdom' remains useful precisely because it gives a succinct approximation of content (Drennan and Uribe 1987: xi; Spencer 1998: 105). But I would add that the principal value of this powerful, if freighted, term resides in 'chief', that is the notions of the leader as defining characteristic and as political agent, and less on a social adscription ossified through other criteria.

I will employ the following distinction: certain societies organized through chiefship (*chiefdoms*) and the conventionalized social relations taken locally as chiefly (*chiefship*).[3] A crucial objective should be to detect those collective practices that enable certain individuals to have differential access to sources of social power – especially, how others charge them with political authority. Put another way, my emphasis is on how they are made or perceived of as different, as 'chiefly'.

Archaeologists are good at identifying chiefly societies in several orthodox ways. The primary ways highlight material patterns which indicate ranking and differential access to resources (e.g., variability in sumptuaries, better diet, elite tombs, central places, monuments, etc.). This chapter attempts a complementary way for reckoning the alterity of chiefs – namely, through objects and their imagery. The premise is that ancient chiefly social relations, basic to societies we term chiefdoms, might be most readily discernible in representational artworks.

Documentary evidence tells us that great prominence is given to the cultural practices that allow certain individuals to be recognized as chiefly – as able warriors, community leaders, ancestors or otherwise privileged members of the group. Chiefs often consolidate and extend their influence in myriad domains – e.g., exchange, alliances, war, marriages, feasting – all of which articulate them with other beings, human and nonhuman, and special times and places. Through social interactions, they gather resources – material and immaterial – in ways that engender an 'organized acquiescence' (Sahlins 1972: 139).

If forms of personhood are shaped through the actions, contributions and perspectives of others (e.g., Fowler 2004; Strathern 1988; Vilaça 2005; Viveiros de Castro 1992), then chiefliness ought to be evidenced through social interactions with other beings. It is perhaps not coincidental that much Early Intermediate Period art begins to actively show and involve social relationships, where persons of certain kinds are overtly acknowledged through relationships to and interventions with other beings, including the viewer. In the case of Recuay imagery, transactions with a range of others can be said to make the chiefly person. More than merely a symbolic representation or materialization of ideology, the imagery helps to detect a formalized sociality of emerging chiefs.

Political organization in highland Ancash

We do not know what language(s) Recuay groups spoke, or the native terms they used for leaders. So what remains is a working, polythetic concept ('chief') drawn from a number of comparisons to reconcile with archaeological patterning. Crucial comparisons derive from sixteenth- to seventeenth-century census and inquisitional documents of highland Ancash, written long after the demise of Recuay groups (Cook 1977, 1981; Hernández Príncipe 1923; Masferrer Kan 1984; Millones 1979; Varón Gabai 1980; Zuidema 1973, 1978). These provide some sense of what indigenous leadership was like before the Europeans.

Curacas were the hereditary male leaders of multi-village polities, headed by a paramount lord and associated settlement. Census visits from 1558 observe these polities numbering in the upper hundreds to several thousand; there were six such groups comprising one moiety of the macro-ethnic group (Espinoza Soriano 1978: 21–40; Varón Gabai 1980). Subordinate headmen (e.g., in one group, seven) led subgroups of constituent villages or groups of villages. These formed descent-based collectivities, or *ayllu*, that were ranked internally and had politico-ritual functions. Chiefs obliged labor services from able-bodied tributaries, usually male heads of households. The documents noted their tremendous affluence, as reflected in lands, herds, valuables, kin and labor obligations.

It is notable that archaeology does not bear out the great inequalities in wealth and centralization credited to late prehispanic Ancash polities, AD 1000–1532 (also elsewhere, see Bauer and Kellett 2010; Parsons et al. 2000; Sandweiss 1992; Sturtevant 1998; Whitehead 1998). Although settlements can be extensive with large populations, the evidence for major tombs, public buildings and great wealth differences is meager. The discordance can be attributed to a range of problems introduced by archaeological sampling, colonial-era policies and historical writing. Curiously, the Recuay record is more consistent with orthodox material correlates of chiefdoms (Bennett 1944; Eisleb 1987; Grieder 1978; Lau 2010c; Orsini 2007; Ponte 2006; Wegner 1988). The largest best-known settlements, such as Yayno and Pashash, were major centers. Not only were these densely occupied, they networked smaller communities in their vicinity. They also feature monumental buildings of ceremonial and residential function, and noble interments were lavished with sumptuous ceramics, metalwork, stone sculpture and textiles.

The bellicose character of highland Ancash groups was noted by the Spanish (Espinoza Soriano 1964: 12–13; Varón Gabai 1980: 38–39). While ayllu groups were loosely confederated (coalescing, apparently, during times of ritual, exchange and war), they were also typified by infighting. Conflicts arose due to difficulties of succession and resource entitlements, especially labor (Espinoza Soriano 1978: 21, 38; Gose 2008: 149; Hernández Príncipe 1923; Millones 1979). Colonial accounts of neighboring areas complement the picture from highland Ancash (Julien 1993; Netherly 1977; Ramírez 1996, 2005; Topic 1998); descriptions from other regions are also important for comparative purposes (e.g., Clastres 1987, 2010; Heckenberger 2007; Oliver 2009; Redmond 1998a; Santos-Granero 1986; Skar 1982; Steward and Faron 1959; Trimborn 1949).

The sources highlight the essential position of chiefs in ritual-political orders. They were often stewards of traditional, often 'idolatrous', knowledge and practice (Arriaga 1968: 68; Millones 1979). But *curacas* were also considered special instantiations of ancestors, as part of a divine legacy and chiefly line (Duviols 2003; Lau 2010c; Zuidema 1973, 1978). According to Salomon (1986: 125–27), three salient emphases characterized northern Andean chiefs of highland Ecuador: 1) 'the lordly personality as harsh, fiery and strict', 2) 'the association of the native lord and abundance, especially of food and maize beer', and 3) 'the ideal of the house of the native lord as a symbolic center, not only of political activity, but of cosmic order' (Fig 3.3). They also mark themselves with the splendor of material things, especially rare preciosities and fine apparel fundamental for public ritual and ostentation (also Helms 1993).

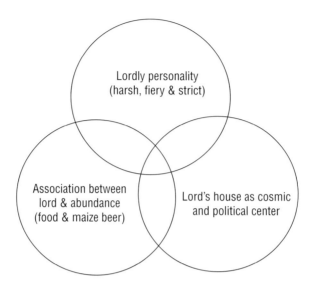

FIGURE 3.3 Schematic diagram showing recurrent themes in the chiefly ideology of highland Ecuador (based on Salomon 1986: 125).

The social imagery of Recuay artworks

It is notable that all these traits of chiefly alterity are emphasized in Recuay artworks. General points about the ceramics, imagery and contexts were summarized in the previous chapter. What is important now is to discuss those images that construct a chiefly alterity within collectives. The objective here is to make general observations on the range of figural imagery and certain categories of depicted social actions that distinguish the chiefly person.[4]

The modeled ceramics depict highly stylized figures, usually chiefly males in conventionalized forms of interaction with other beings; what I have referred to as 'genres of action' (Lau 2011: 213). Some show single figures, while some feature multiple figures. These genres sometimes overlapped, but three general categories are presented to organize this discussion.

Chiefly veneration

A common genre was the veneration or celebration of a well-attired male figure, located centrally while presiding over subsidiary figures. He is often standing, although seated, supine and prone positions also occur. Art historian Raphael Reichert (1977: 55–56) remarked that this imagery was essentially 'hierarchic in nature, emphasizing an individual [male] to which various subsidiary human and/or animal figures are subordinated'.

That the male figure was privileged is founded mainly on formal grounds: frequency of appearance; size differences and frontality; central position in group scenes; and their great elaboration in apparel and accoutrements (also Carrión Cachot

1955; Grieder 1992). He is distinguished by ear ornaments and an ornate headdress, and sometimes collars and neck pendants.

He often clutches a weapon: a shield and/or mace. He may also hold a cup or flute. The smaller, plainer figures (up to eleven), convene around the central figure and sometimes bear items, such as cups or bundles. Their postures, shared by all the ancillary figures, are of general reverent attention. Usually, they all face inward toward the chiefly figure (Plate 10); occasionally, they face the same direction as the chief, which is toward the viewer or receiver of liquid. The surrounding figures are probably kin and followers who make up the central figure's retinue. It is notable that some of the ancillary figures have warrior associations. These figures have military items (clubs, shields, trophy heads) and seem to reference occasions where subordinate warriors formally recognize a war leader (Redmond 1998b).

Chiefly males are also identified with a frontal bodiless head design (Fig 3.4), perhaps a principal divinity with feline and fiery solar associations (Hohmann 2003; Makowski and Rucabado Yong 2000; Tello 1923). Both males and females are adorned with painted zoomorphic creatures, apparently lesser mythical beings or supernaturals.

FIGURE 3.4 Recuay effigy vessel, showing a central male flanked by two females. The frontal head design (with four appendages) on the tunic is almost always associated with male chiefs and ancestors, and appears to have had feline and solar associations (adapted from Hohmann 2010: Abb. 125).

Some group representations show merriment and drinking. In these, small figures convene in festive embraces and dances, all around the chiefly individual (Plate 10, Plate 11). He is often standing or seated, or sometimes assumes the form of a mummy bundle. Occasionally, some of the ancillary figures play musical instruments. Some vessels show the chief presiding inside a structure. In other cases, he is embodied as the house structure, physically encased by the building but also taking on architectural features and qualities, in or on which ancillary figures stand (Lau 2010c).

Unlike their Moche neighbors, the Recuay did not render naturalistic facial features typical of individual 'portraits' (Donnan 2004). Several functional reasons may account for this. The regalia, which is highly distinctive, was perhaps sufficient to identify chiefly individuals (Grieder 1992: 184; Reichert 1978: 31). Also, the relatively small group sizes and familiarity of people may have obviated the need to identify them visually (Gero 2001: 28). I would add that the subdued emphasis on 'individuality' and the funerary mask-like facial features resonate with the logic of a continuing chiefly person, a position embodied by various individuals over the course of generations.

Overall, the differential treatment of human figures in scale and elaboration is one of the clearest indicators for ranking in Recuay society. These scenes recognize the main figure as central to the small groups depicted (e.g., women, attendants and warriors). The representations highlight the chief's position in various festive and solemn corporate events.

Actions with women

There are other kinds of conventionalized actions with women. In addition to multi-figure scenes, women are occasionally represented on their own. Most individual female figures are seated, carrying jars or holding items in gestures of presentation: headdresses, cups and bundles. Small figures, perhaps large figurines or infants, are held out as well. Women sometimes play handheld drums, an important instrument in public events and funerary ritual (Arriaga 1968: 19; Doyle 1988: 215).

The relationship between females and the large jars is notable because the vessels were likely for chicha. Both men and women hold cups/bowls, but the jars represent the principal domain of women – implicating them in the making and transport of maize beer (Plate 12). The vessel often doubles as the jar carried using a headstrap. Through the brewing and distribution of chicha maize beer, the women not only complemented specific male practices, but held 'autonomous' political power (Gero 1992: 23). A close association between women, chicha-making and collective ritual is also seen in Nasca art (Proulx 2006: 115).

Another genre of action with women was sexual intercourse. Copulation depictions always feature a man and woman. They wear elaborate regalia, including headdresses, or are blanketed in ornate cloths while together. Their attire and size indicate they are of commensurate high statuses and a noble pairing (Gero 1999, 2001, 2004; Reichert 1977). There were two typical positions: the male on top; and a dual sitting style with the female's legs wrapped around the male's waist. Crucially, in both, the partners are face to face and extend their arms to the other in mutual, visual acknowledgment. We understand the actions of noble women, therefore, to be increasingly important in the constitution of highland political authority.

Engagements with zoomorphs

Recuay imagery often featured animals and zoomorphic creatures. It focused on highland animals: camelids, mountain cats, dogs, deer, condors and owls. Not all creatures can be identified definitively to species, however, and some clearly have mythical dimensions.

Perhaps the best known Recuay depictions are those in which a man stands next to a camelid, leading it by a rope (Plate 13). The male figure sometimes holds weapons or a panpipe, but always wears elaborate attire and a headdress, as if for a ceremonial occasion. The images probably portray the moment before the man leads the camelid to its sacrifice (Carrión Cachot 1955: 69). Compared to the male figures, the camelids are depicted relatively plainly (Reichert 1977: 172–76). Camelids were sources of wealth and status, but they are not necessarily the focus; rather, it is the lord's act of presentation, perhaps in public contexts, such as feasting, sacrifice and offering in burial ceremony (Doyle 1988: 207–10). Notably, the camelid's 'offering' is accented by the fact that the camelid body, not the human's, is the physical receptacle.

The parts of animals are also critical to chiefly representation. Ornaments, for example, included body parts, and most often from the heads, of felines, birds, serpents and stags. These are especially prominent on headdresses, but are worn also around the neck or decorating bags. Human trophy heads also occur. Some vessels feature dogs and birds as perfunctory accessories of house scenes; they help to mark off a controlled, safe space. As part of noble apparel or the house, these depictions of 'incorporated' animals remind us about their important role in defining a chiefly domain (Lau 2010c).

Feline creatures are the most common animal images on Recuay pots and sculptures (see also next chapter). They are especially important in 'central figure' depictions, where a frontal human figure is flanked by two figures, a common theme also in stone sculpture (Figs 3.4, 3.5). The figures are usually feline, but there are also vessels which flank the male with large birds (raptors or condors), serpents, stags and women

FIGURE 3.5 Sculpture 26, central figure scene, Chinchawas. A humped, bicephalic creature is flanked by two profile male felines, and topped by a frontal head with appendages. The imagery emphasizes multiple transformations and complementary pairings.

(Hohmann 2010). Stone sculptures, meanwhile, sometimes show flanking mythical, bicephalic animals (e.g., Lau 2006b: Fig. 34). Recuay imagery also shows feline-like creatures engaging in violent, transformative actions on human bodies – eating at bodies (Makowski 2000). These depictions present the viewer with a dynamic, complementary relation: humans and zoomorphic creatures as masters of the other (see also next chapter).

Stylized, close relations

Examined together, the vessel imagery depicts a series of conventionalized relations that chiefly figures have with other beings, namely women, men and zoomorphs (Fig 3.6). They show scenes which constituted parts of a larger narrative, a type of image-based artmaking that became popularized during the Early Intermediate Period. But, unlike the mythic traditions of the Moche or Nasca, Recuay imagery emphasizes stylized biographical episodes of leaders and their close relations.

The group scenes appear to commemorate occasions of corporate recognition by followers (e.g., feasts, celebrations, war leadership, presentation and mourning). The main figure engages with a range of other beings. By doing so, the beings, along with the viewer(s), in effect acknowledge their respective statuses. It is notable that the

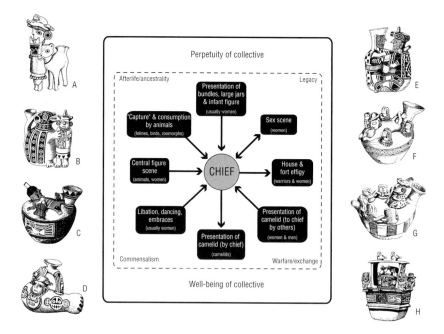

FIGURE 3.6 Schematic representation of chiefly sociality, showing the chiefly person's central pivotal relationship to a series of social others and conventionalized actions. The drawings illustrate the principal genres of action, where the chiefly personage receives, does or embodies (adapted from Carrion Cachot 1955: Lám XVf; XVIj; XVIIb,f,g,k; Fig. 1).

main figure does not ever interact with other males of the same stature or elaboration of attire – figures whom we might consider other chiefs or captains (cf. Attic pottery; Aztec or Moche combat depictions). Combat and conquest/seizure depictions are rare, yet size differences are categorical and rendered in the dimorphic manner.

Women clearly had significant roles in the chiefly ideology. These would include maize beer production, labor recruitment and procreation (Gero 1991, 1992, 1999, 2001). Important kinds of social reproduction centered on women and beverage-making occur throughout South America (see Allen 2002; Conklin 2001; Weismantel 2004). By presenting the male figures with drink and libations to ancestor effigies, women are seen as integral to their authority. Some of the group scenes also suggest the practice of polygyny (Disselhoff 1967: 118; Lumbreras 1974b: 112). Early colonial documents indicate that having multiple wives was a privilege among native Ancash nobility (Espinoza Soriano 1978: 38–39). This enhanced a chief's status, not least because it multiplied his capacity to garner labor obligations through regular hospitality (Gose 2008: 15–16, 133). Native women also held fame as wives of important curacas and as efficacious ritual specialists (e.g., Millones 1979; Mills 1994: 166–67). The depictions of sex appear to reference the consummation of a pairing and procreative action resulting in social reproduction.

Recuay sexual depictions are very different compared to those of the Moche. Moche sex depictions often celebrate female figures fellating males, females receiving anal sex, or male erections, all apparently to highlight 'male orgasm' (Gero 2004: 19). This may be related to the alterity of Moche women – one of segmentation and highly defined roles in the figurines – at least in art and also in the use of figurines discussed earlier. In contrast, Recuay representations are always between a male and female couple. For Gero (2004: 20), they express greater emphasis on gender complementarity, one where sex acts pleasure both partners and where the male is not privileged in the relationship. A crucial point in this regard is that the eyes of both partners are always trained on each other – in the act of mutual recognition. The copulating pair are sometimes accompanied by attendants or children, who serve perhaps to create an intergenerational temporality, collapsing events, outcomes and desires into one object.[5] Yet they are nonetheless also witnesses, just like the handler of the vessel, conferring acknowledgment of the union of chiefly figures and high-ranking women.

Animal or zoomorphic creatures can be said to be always interacting with human bodies. This is mainly depicted (human with animal figure), but is also implied through physical handling and reception of the vessel. Animals occur alone, but they are not studies of animals in a 'natural' habitat or daily life (e.g., Disselhoff 1967). More commonly, these animals occur in different contexts which allude to extraordinary human encounters or their appropriation as resources (see also Chapters 4 and 5).

Overall, it can be observed that there are different kinds of persons, most who are or become 'familiar others', being within the orbit of the chiefly figure. Chiefship entails both active and passive dispositions, which can be dichotomized as *actions to* and *actions from* the chief. *Actions from* consists of those engagements the chiefly figure directs at others, such as the presentation of camelids, playing a flute or exteriorization of ego as architecture. Some transactions, e.g., copulation, show reciprocating relations.

The wide majority, however, are constituted by actions received from others. The lordly figure is always at the center of activity. Stoic and monumental, he is the pivot and witness of action around him. In all cases, the transactions require multiple subjects, including the perspective of the viewer(s). If negotiating understandings of one's place with different individuals generates the self, and actualizes or enhances special capacities, then the actions can be understood as fundamental in constituting the 'chief'.

The social process of making chiefs therefore subjectivizes the object (as mimetic vessel), at the same time it objectifies the subject (chiefly person). Both movements are marked by equivalencies – in form and outer decorated surfaces – that connect the male chiefs/ancestors, representations of residences and archaeological ruins of house compounds (Lau 2010c, d). All these featured specially made, 'negativized' surfaces on corporate bodies that marked Recuay nobility and distinction. Actions and objects, then, served to enhance the alterity of certain individuals – who, in this case, are made more special, superior and effective than others.

One of the main purposes for subjectivizing such objects was to help periodically remember chiefly persons through repeated acts and contributions of others. The individual depictions inscribed episodes of an ancient biopic which acknowledged significant milestones of the person and pulled together past social relations. This must have been heightened in funerary rituals centered on a corporate tomb and its array of cult objects. It is not coincidental that the vessels implicate a network of beings, living and ancestral, obliged in the making and transaction of their special contents. Made by others *for* others, chicha helps activate the social relations based on sources of vitality that reside outside the individual (Conklin 2001: 167). Because ceramic figurines[6] are very rare, it was not simply the effigy that was important in Recuay practice; rather, it was the combination of figural forms that were *also* liquid containers.

If the appropriation of vitality from others is essential to religious experience (Bloch 1992), the objects were integral – for they immediately reciprocate that flow of vitality in the offering of liquid. Some vessels apparently served as receptacles, for holding and evacuating their contents using the same orifice.[7] Others, marked by an additional small tubular spout, are to redirect liquids through the chiefly body (Plate 14, Figs 3.4, 3.6). It follows that the pouring spout very commonly issues from the chief, action group or the building in which he forms the basis. The flows exemplify a kind of *embodied redistribution*.

The vessels therefore facilitate chiefly recognition through their use and viewership by the living. There may have also been the tacit prescription for future action within the collectivity, precisely to simulate previous postholders and bodily practice (e.g., positions, gestures, drink, libation, clothing). In this way, the miniature worlds of chiefs idealized the ritual-political life of the collective in perpetuity.

These imagined worlds of collectivities show people acceding to the political sway of the leader. The alterity of Recuay chiefs stressed their quality to provide and mediate between different sorts of others. In this way, there is certainly a convivial tenor to the imagery, not least because so many of them depict libations, dancing and feasting.

Some genres of actions are borne out through archaeology. Excavations have found dense food remains, ritual articles and offerings associated with special delimited spaces; these were contexts for feasting, ancestor veneration and very likely camelid sacrifice. Areas with large jars and colanders have been interpreted as the remains of women's activities and specialized production for feasts (Gero 1992). Studies have also revealed well-built tombs and houses that were decorated with stone sculptures, which resemble depictions showing chiefly veneration by women and the witnessing role of ancestral figures (Lau 2002, 2006). Yet the imagery also shows an array of other stylized practices, such as gifting, dance, noble pairings, animal interactions, while alluding to mourning, alliance-making and oratory. These may have been fundamental to the social life of Recuay groups, but will be difficult to recover based on current archaeological emphases and methods.

Summary

This chapter examined one significant and broad kind of alterity, centered on familiar others – those considered inside as part of the house and local community. Such others participate in 'moral economy of intimacy' – a framework for sociality based on producing kinspeople through everyday modes of conviviality and shared living. This kind of alterity was first examined at the level of domestic residences and intra-settlement collectivities. I then turned to art representations that portray actions associated with this sociality.

In general, the dynamics of identity and personhood in the 'house' or domestic sphere are becoming increasingly important in Precolumbian circumstances (e.g., Ardren and Hutson 2006; Joyce and Gillespie 2000), and my goal with this chapter has been to contribute to the question of how familiar relations perceive and engage with others *within* house and village settings.

I focused on Moche and Recuay because of their similarities and contrasts. I believe that further comparison with other regional cultures of the Early Intermediate Period, for which the record is increasingly rich, will enhance these understandings further. This is especially so if domestic arrangements are considered not only as a reflection of a broader political economy, but as a domain for the formation of crucial kinds of cultural production (socialization, value systems, gender) that also effect society.

I first summarized changing residential practices and identified how the Early Intermediate Period was a crucial time for new cultural dispositions about social others centered on households and dwellings. These coincided with other major developments: the emergence of monumental residences and more overt wealth accumulation and display. In particular, large nucleated settlements emerged during the later Early Intermediate Period, and rural communities became increasingly articulated with them. Collectivities, individuals within them, and their lifestyles became more differentiated. This provided, fairly schematically, a backdrop to contextualize the making and use of ancient depictions, mainly ceramic figures.

For both Recuay and Moche, art was at the service of new beliefs about authority, and was therefore a vector for social distinction. The cultures regularly imaged humans in the proximity of domestic contexts. Moche used small figurines in the household environment, I believe, to reinforce segmentation and certain kinds of conventionalized social roles that burgeoned during the late portion of the Early Intermediate Period. This is when civic-ceremonial centers increasingly dominated Moche social and religious life, and when dynamic changes characterized settlement patterns in the countryside. The figurines, not surprisingly, depict women, warriors, musicians and other special persons, all othernesses that were desirable as tropes for commoners. They were portable as keepsakes for their houses, and depositable as offerings and refuse during the transition to new spaces. Their making and acquisition connote some limited interaction between rural settlements and those town-based workshops/specialists responsible for the figurines. As objects of residential devotion, however, there were almost certainly ways that conveyed relations of difference between rural and urban domains.

Unlike the Moche use of domestic figurines, physically located inside residential contexts, Recuay domestic worlds viewed through the modeled ceramics were idealized – residing in the imaginary of artisans and the high-status people who commissioned them. Very few Recuay decorative pieces actually come from domestic circumstances; rather, they derive from places of funerary cult. This art celebrated a formulaic range of relations between many types of social beings, 'others' of human and nonhuman appearance, crucial in the social life of esteemed ancestors and their earthly representatives, chiefs. These include noble women carrying pots and holding infants and drinking cups, as well as animal beings. The scaling-down of the representation, stripping away unneeded detail, highlighted key personnel, events and practices during the 'pasts' of special people on the inside.

Thus Recuay depictions of figures worked differently from those of Moche. Rather than segment, these seemed to *integrate* by stressing social actions between unequal others. Their depictions of others were to construct and stabilize the alterity of high-status persons *internally* within these groups. As valuables basic in ancestor cults, the objects helped produce chiefly persons by portraying and enabling periodic exchanges with others. Even though the chiefly figures are celebrated as separate and marked as superordinate, it is also true that all the figures collaborate toward a similar function, which is ultimately the well-being and the subjectivity of that particular social body, embodied as the chief. That intersubjectivity concerns the circulation of flows – fluid and social – enabled and mediated by the chief. The pots, in expressing what others have done in the past, provide a time-honored formula, a 'pattern history', for what should happen in the future. Social relations, reduced in art to the recognition of a few special others and mutual nourishment between them, were therefore paramount in the constitution of Recuay social groups.

Some kinds of Andean chiefship have their origins in the house. Writ large, the symbolic economy of 'feeding' and 'parenthood' performs as a potent source of authority for much more centralized arrangements (Ramírez 2005, 2006).

By way of conclusion, it is useful to observe that a key objective of many Early Intermediate Period artworks and their attendant ritual centered on the recognition of the past, especially mythical or ancestral narratives, in relation to the political authority of the living. To say that many native Amerindian histories were special kinds of memory practice may be axiomatic, but it is also true that their material form or *how* they convey history may be a useful way to distinguish cultures. As commemorative instruments of multigenerational elite narratives, the circulation of elaborate Recuay figural ceramics did not move beyond the intersubjective world of residential groups defined by ancestors. They were rarely trade wares precisely because there was little interest (on the parts of other groups and cultures) for objects that oriented the memory practice of local descent groups. Recuay ceramics were forms for remembering – e.g., mobilizing and transmitting historical information, the 'past' – without the help of formal writing. And if the Recuay favored a tactile 'biopic' form focused on heavily abridged pictorial biographies, it plainly contrasts with the Moche scheme – with its core mythology and ceremony – centered on the 'Warrior Narrative', shared by lordships of this coastal civilization (Donnan 2004), but apparently by no others in Andean prehistory.

4

PREDATORIAL RELATIONS

Some three decades ago, Tzvetan Todorov (1984) wrote his influential work, *The Conquest of America*, on the first encounters between Europeans and Amerindians, the momentous events that would merge, and forever change, the Old World and the New: a combination of historical narrative and philosophical reflection on how each side reckoned the other. Todorov's study argued that the conquest was effected not so much by a clash of arms as much as by the clash of cultures, in communication, symbol systems and understandings of the other. The telling but rarely used subtitle of the book is, aptly, *The Question of the Other*.

In this chapter, I consider the question of the other, but recover the clash of arms, or warfare, as the framing device. In particular, I will examine the alterities of predation and violent interaction with outsiders (e.g., hunting, warfare, opposition, taking enemies) as important concepts in Andean cosmology. I first describe some principles of warfare and alterity in Amerindian contexts associated with a 'symbolic economy of alterity' and paired opposition. These emphasize the formation of self in relation to others; but, crucially, those others are of an unequal status and the relation is often predicated on confrontation, often of a violent or 'predatory' nature.

Then I present a range of evidence. The remarkable figural imagery of the first millennium AD cultures facilitates a discussion about human engagement with and appropriation from other beings, human and animal. The art imagery emphasizes the predation of vitality from others (e.g., killing, capturing, trophy-taking). The chapter will also describe additional forms of archaeological evidence, mainly settlement patterns and defensive features, that allow us to characterize inter-community relations. An emphasis is given to the role of defensive architecture in making physical and symbolic difference against ambivalent, bellicose neighbors. Finally, this section covers how Moche elites and artisans depicted the Recuay and their enemies to be potent outsiders and, ultimately, captive subordinates. Social life in the Andes during the first millennium AD was often fraught with conflict and warfare, and highlighted encounters with others based on predatorial dispositions.

Predation

An alterity based on predators and predation is stressed in this chapter. I employ loosely the general definition of 'predatorial' in the *Oxford English Dictionary*, '[synonym of "predatory"] Of a person: given to, or living by, plunder or marauding; ruthlessly exploitative, acquisitive, or rapacious … Of a manner, look, personal trait, etc.: characteristic or suggestive of such a person'. The latter detail, which concerns the 'manner' or 'look' of a person, is of particular relevance, since these concern the imagination and recognition of the predatorial other.

My use of 'predation' lays particular emphasis on physical or symbolic appropriation. Predation is used as a cover term for the process of deliberate acquisition from others for personal enhancement. The process inheres structural relationships that are often opposed: inside–outside, self–other, consanguines–affines, resemblance–difference (Viveiros de Castro 2001). As will be seen, the process can occur without an exclusive or particularly strong emphasis on violent engagements. No one needs to be killed, although, in certain circumstances, that is what happens.

Nor does my use of 'predatorial' connote a moral or depreciatory stance, as is often the case in contemporary Euro-American contexts (e.g., sexual 'predator' or 'predatorial' business takeovers). For many societies around the world, having predatorial qualities is respected, if not actively favorably looked upon. To be sure, indigenous Andeans also believe in loathesome predators that are much feared with little to offer in terms of virtue and valorization, such as *pishtacos*. These are predatorial beings, associated with Whites who kill, slice and steal fat from native Andeans (Bellier and Hocquenghem 1991; Canessa 2000; Weismantel 2001).[1] But, as will be seen, being judged a killer or hunter, having talent in combat, or being like other predators (jaguars, pumas, raptors, orcas) was probably more valued during the Early Intermediate Period. Being 'predatorial' was something special, a mark of distinction and social standing: a quality attributed to native warriors, chiefs and shamans, and structurally linked to other dimensions of cultural production.

My perspective on predation pivots on a set of premises. First and foremost, it is predicated on a taking from the other, or others. It is a process of acquisition, whether the thing taken is a physical object (treasure, booty, body part) or something less tangible (e.g., a name, victory, song, dream, right, spirit, etc.). Thus I will use predation to describe equally physical acts as well as symbolic acts and effects. Second, the acquisition process is deliberate and selective, and seems less opportunistic. What is gained through design is often an object of desire: it is gained by someone and lost by another.

Third, the being or personhood of the acquirer (i.e., predator) is enhanced by the predatory act, conferring status, prestige, social capital, etc. Although the acquired thing often does the enhancing, the act or the attempt of predation on others can be equally significant. Fourth, there is no expectation that predation needs to be species-specific, or limited to one species. Actions of predation can be conspecific (e.g., between humans) as well as by beings across species boundaries. A human can predate on animals, just as a hawk catches a rodent, or a god strikes down another god. Nor is the relationship a symbiosis, which presumes reciprocal or mutual benefits, and frequently over a period of time in two beings' lives.

Finally, what emerges is a relative subordination, or perhaps better a super-ordination. One being bests another. Perhaps more important than the result of someone 'losing' is that someone or something comes out on top, or comes to the fore. This is not simply a play on words; rather it can be seen as a characteristic form of Andean distinction and improvement. The relation might assume the form of master/attendant, hunter/prey or someone who simply has more food or resources than another. The relationship, ultimately, is an ordered pairing, at least for a time, and really exists because there is a pairing between the superordinate and subordinate element.

These premises are tethered to the different outcomes of predation, and their perception. In different situations in the Andean past, we can discern something about the concern for triumph and for defeat, for viewing others in certain ways. This is especially true for the record of ancient hunting and warfare, the two principal modes of Amerindian predation.

Sociality of Amerindian warfare

Warfare in ancient society leaves indelible marks on the archaeological record. Armaments, fortifications, skeletons and also the combat imagery of Precolumbian groups provide some indication of the frequency and economic impact of the practices. But not everything about ancient warfare survives the ravages of time and the elements.

Archaeologists are much less able to get at the many intangible, fleeting aspects common to warfare practice (e.g., techniques of combat, sounds and music, body painting and practice, songs, oral traditions, mourning, looting, etc.). These contribute heavily to the general rationale and doing of war. Lamentably for us, these less detectable, ephemeral expressions also have much to do with alterity.

For contextualizing an incomplete archaeological record, we need to turn to well-described forms of warfare practice and cosmology found in the historical and ethnographic literature. Not only do these often manifest aspects of the cultural background of ancient Andean groups, they also provide a much fuller reckoning of the representation and desirability of prey-like others, while also raising additional questions that archaeology can further address.

My consideration of ancient predation and the predatorial relies especially on ethnographic and historical work in the South American lowlands. But selective cases in Mexico as well as other areas are also important. Predation is especially important in recent explorations about the doing and cosmology of Amerindian warfare, particularly in the gigantic Amazonian watershed (Albert 1990; Carneiro da Cunha and Vivieros de Castro 1987; Clastres 2010; Conklin 2001; Descola 1993, 2001; Fausto 2000, 2007; Taylor 1996; Vilaça 2002; Viveiros de Castro 1992). This work complements an already substantial literature, focused on warfare's systemic role in political relations and social complexity (Carneiro 1970, 1981; Chagnon 1968; Clastres 1977; Ferguson and Whitehead 2000; Redmond 1994). Historically, the most influential studies for Andean prehistory have been from an ecological, functional position that theorizes warfare in social stratification and complexity.

Any sort of warfare is a paradox. At first glance, it would seem to subvert society by denying social cohesion. War atomizes and tends to eliminate others, thereby nullifying particular paths of social interaction. War creates enemies and conditions that lead to vengeance, putting at risk both the individual and communities who participate and making any *rapprochement* more difficult. It also destabilizes the fabric of social relations within the society. Societies who exist in perpetual conflict are frequently seen as fragile and incapable of cultural development or greater social complexity. Not only are members of society lost, people have divisive sentiments toward war ('for'/'against') and the very praxeological basis of warfare creates relations of inequality. War leaders ascend and there is often the matter of defeated, subjugated groups.

Acts of warfare, based on aggression and enmity, are nonetheless forms of social relation. Its recurrent practice between groups of different sorts comprises a palpable, if protean, form of social exchange. Rather than view societies (pejoratively) as making war, warfare can be understood under certain circumstances as making society, what forms collectivities (Clastres 2010; Harrison 1993; Viveiros de Castro 2004).

Ethnographer Simon Harrison (1993: 12) offers a sobering point about the rationale of war in Melanesia. What a group fights for is not necessarily 'to preserve their biological survival' but 'the existence of groups as distinct organizational and conceptual entities … the survival of its sociopolitical identity'. Warfare can be seen to work to maintain social boundaries (to keep identities apart) as it confronts opponents: exchange and war, therefore, 'make' groups. They 'can exist only in relations of opposition' because 'it is not the construction of relationships that preoccupies these actors but the construction, so to speak, of non-relationships: the building of social divisions, barriers and antagonisms' (Harrison 1993: 16–17). What western observers see as irrational behavior of an anarchic nature, e.g., 'primitive warfare', might make more sense as a highly distinct technology that defines social organization, rather than endanger it. As was discussed earlier about Andean organization, perceiving oneself and one's group identity through relations with others and their alterity may illuminate current ways to discern ancient ayllu-like arrangements, as well as prehispanic structures of dualism and complementary opposition.

If society is about integration, how did Amerindian groups go about reconciling the social and symbolic relations of inequality that warfare generates? This age-old paradox in social complexity has seen influential contributions, but in very different and still debated ways. Anthropologist Robert Carneiro (1970, 1981) saw the relations of inequality resulting from warfare as the prime mover in the rise of chiefdoms (via consolidation of multiple villages under central leadership) and states (via emergence of class system) (see also Redmond 1998b). Pierre Clastres (1977, 2010), meanwhile, also viewed warfare as a vector for leadership and hierarchy, but primarily as a mechanism that atomized societies and ensured their autonomy from the emergence of political centralization (see also Deleuze and Guattari 1987; Sztutman 2009; Viveiros de Castro 2010). Territorial dispersion and group autarky were political ends. For Clastres (2010: 272–73), warfare was not a kind of failed exchange, as Claude Lévi-Strauss (1969) proposed. Rather, Amerindian non-state societies were quintessentially warring societies. Groups defined themselves ('autonomous We') through conflict with others (also Harrison 1993). Time may not constantly be spent 'waging war', but groups were often permanently in a 'state of war', because their being consisted of 'we' versus 'foreigners'. We might surmise that Clastres' extreme views saw exchange and alliances as failed warfare.

More recent ethnography bridges approaches to warfare in Lévi-Strauss' structuralism and Clastres' political anthropology. It sees warfare as a particular kind of social and symbolic exchange – what Clastres (2010: 254ff.) characterized as Levi-Strauss' 'exchangist' perspective – one equally focused on predation but 'emphasizing the dialectics between identity and alterity that is thought to be at the root of Amazonian sociopolitical regimes' (Viveiros de Castro 1996: 189–90).[2] Studies have also considered violence and predation between many kinds of beings, not just human. On the one hand, they serve to problematize further the monads of exchange, hunting and warfare (Fausto 2001); on the other, they bring human–human relations into a much larger domain of social relations. Relations with an outside, including those styled as predation and affinity, are fundamental for lowland Amazonian sociality (Viveiros de Castro 2001).

Despite its richness, the overall literature on warfare in the South American lowlands, especially its emphasis on alterity, has seldom featured in informing the process and style of warfare for the Central Andes (Arnold and Hastorf 2008: 27). Although it is clear that European colonialism heightened tribe-making and their competition (Ferguson and Whitehead 2000), the record remains valuable for comparative purposes. To be sure, the circumstances are very different: the environmental setting, socio-demographic arrangements and historical contexts. Colonial initiatives included resettlement of Andeans, for example, as well as general pacification. But the indigenous rationale and accounting of warfare furnish many insights for the ancient Andes.

The next sections provide greater consideration of several interrelated themes: parallels between hunting and warfare; opposition and warriorhood; changing predator–prey subjectivities; and capture of outside people and things. Comparative Amerindian insights on these themes have great importance in understanding the archaeological record of the ancient Andes, and especially the ancient imagery.

Hunting and warfare

I want to explore more fully what anthropologist Eduardo Viveiros de Castro (1996) termed a 'symbolic economy of alterity'. In describing many Amerindian groups of the American neotropics, he emphasized a system of thought and practice by which predation on outside others, human and nonhuman, serves as the basis for social relations, social reproduction and the construction of self. This is also often called 'ontological predation' (Viveiros de Castro 2004: 480).

Hunting and warfare are two crucial domains for predation among lowland Amerindian groups of South America.[3] Not only do they share similar practices, but, quite frequently, they find a commonality in the logic of their doing (e.g., Conklin 2001; Descola 2001; Fausto 2000, 2007; Viveiros de Castro 1992). They are also often linked through common linguistic terms, shared imaginations in art, and through similar embodied practices (Leroi-Gourhan 1964); others have linked hunting and warfare through psychology, whether it is fear of predation (Ehrenreich 1997) or the burning desire for prestige or to outdo the last achievement (Clastres 2010). Notably, the pattern may appear in more centralized political systems, where hunting and killing game animals are essentially likened to those practiced on human prey (see also Clendinnen 1991: 115–16; Donnan 1997).

A common thread is the physical activity. Not only does hunting and combat require great physical exertion, both are technical systems that depend on and discipline the body in similar ways. Successful outcomes in either favor those with appropriate responses over a long sequence or series of operations that are informed by previous knowledge, practical action and corporeal wherewithal. Sight, smell, hearing, touch and their coordination with the hands and legs are paramount, as are training and regimen. Experience, past deeds and instinct are just as important as athletic prowess. And revised strategies emerge through the extended process of doing: stealth, quickness, brute strength, improvisation, retreat, etc. Both, crucially, are also domains for individual and team effort.

Both hunting and combat place great emphasis on intensive human engagements with an external community on the 'outside'. Whether that community is a regional ethnic group or a rival trading village, it stands as foreign and ambiguous, with its desires unknown. Moreover, relations are risky because their whereabouts and capacities of prey are unpredictable. They cast people into a network of perpetual, ambivalent interactions with external others (Descola 2005; Viveiros de Castro 1998). These matters of *unknowing* fashion the subjectivity of enemies as alters and also condition suitable responses by ego and the respective group.

Like hunting, warfare seeks to transform the quality of the social relation between the main actors (whether human, animal or spirit). Unlike many other forms of alterity, a predatorial disposition might be seen as somewhat unique in seeking to recognize the relation, and then radically transform it by eliminating or subordinating the quality of the other. In some ways, it is similar to another great problem in anthropology, the gift. Like gift exchange, warfare features diacritical moments, special players and a strong emphasis on transforming persons. Above all, it is a strategy for sociality that has competitive dimensions, often having to do with debt and expectations (Graeber 2001; Mauss 1967 [1925]; Strathern 1988; Walens 1981; Weiner 1992). But, of course, the outcomes of the engagements are distinct: they transform differently by elevating and subordinating persons differently. In gift exchange, it is to subordinate by tethering others through generosity, what ethnographer Annette Weiner (1992) theorized as 'keeping while giving'. In warfare, the relations of exchange are, by obligation, to sever and disrupt with ferocity – recognizing self and other while taking. Rather than gifting to the outside, it is taking for the inside.

Of course, in both prestige economies associated with gifting and warfare, there is often the potential, indeed expectation, to do more of it, once it has started. Clastres

(2010) generalized that a warrior's role as a warrior never ends until his death; and from the time a person kills (thereby initiating entry into warrior status) to the time he/she dies, the warrior is compelled to go to war and do something better. A similar inflation in the promise of enhancement of self (by distancing ego from others) inheres in gift exchange, a particularly conspicuous case being the chiefly potlatches of late nineteenth-century northwest coast groups (Codere 1950).

Hunting and war find another commonality in its general objective: something is captured from a dangerous outside, and brought under control by means of force. The exogenous resource is then somehow integrated into the new (captor) group. This can be through its killing and consumption (Carneiro da Cunha and Vivieros de Castro 1987; Viveiros de Castro 1992), sometimes through taking of its parts (e.g., Arnold and Hastorf 2008; Métraux 1949), and sometimes through 'adoption' or through affinal practices (Descola 2001). The physical and symbolic incorporation of enemies into the captor group has been called 'familiarization' or 'familiarizing predation' (Fausto 2000).

The motivations for engaging enemies are certainly legion (Redmond 1994). But for some groups, exhortations by men to recruit for raids make it surprisingly simple: to acquire vengeance, resources and fertility: 'Let's kill the enemy, let's do to him what he's done to our kin! Let's make war, let's get fat! Let's make war, let's fatten our women!' (Vilaça 2010: 75). Even if there are additional motivations, what essentially spurs Wari' people to war is, plainly, acts of predatory appropriation that, like hunting, ensure corporeal well-being.

Warfare and making persons

Armed conflict differentiates people. Through warfare, people ascend and descend in status. Some people are destroyed. People come to know others via actions, reputation and stereotype out of the procedures of warfare. Winners are privileged while losers may be lamented and derided. People make their names and gain renown.

At the same time, enemies are very often quintessential others, the foreigner and agent of the outside brimming with resources and vigor. Through physical and symbolic work, enemies can enrich the inside, what the anthropologist Maurice Bloch (1992: 5) referred to as a 'conquered vitality obtained from *outside* beings'.

Warfare pivots on the acquisition of resources, the gaining of tangible or symbolic capital. In Amazonian contexts, valuables are alienated and acquired, although the process has been interpreted in very different ways. The enrichment process might be seen through the lens of reciprocal exchange (Lizot 1994: 859), territoriality (Clastres 2010), transforming gendered capacities (Conklin 2001), productive consumption (Fausto 2000, 2001) or biological imperative (Chagnon 1988; Gross 1975). Different kinds of resources are gained through predation: e.g., autonomy, booty, trophies, protein capture, renown, the stealing of wives, taking of captives (Arnold and Hastorf 2008; Métraux 1949). What is significant in the first instance is how an individual is enhanced, or, perhaps more specifically, how a person's standing as a warrior is affected (Clastres 2010: Ch. 9). Elsewhere, I have termed the disposition toward such personal statuses as a 'warriorhood', particularly for the Early Intermediate Period context, when it became especially important to various cultures, and most vigorously in Recuay, Moche, Gallinazo and Nasca.

Through warfare practices, the victor acquires a new resource, prestige, payback or new subjectivity. All these move the person in a new direction, very often to produce respected adult members of their communities. Most Amerindian warfare complexes, from the Aztecs to the Iroquois, are essential for socialization and embodied practices which produce certain kinds of human beings (e.g., Viveiros de Castro 1992: 279).[4,5] The act of homicide transforms the person, because it alters how familiar others perceive him. The action confers a different status (Harrison 1993: 83). Some societies anathematize homicide. Some actively embrace it.

Anthropologist Pierre Clastres (1977: 175–78) pointed out that 'technical competence' in hunting and war is one of the few outlets for garnering prestige in Amerindian non-state societies. But any social distinction is fleeting and rarely translates into political power; rather, the 'thirst' (p. 176) for social capital and to be different via acquisition, the essence for a predatorial disposition, can only be sated by further successes in the hunt and in war. Simply, there are some people who are better at war and in the hunt, and they get rewarded, and also isolated, in a system that perpetuates itself.

Performance in war is crucial because prestige and renown are often motives of conflict. One's reputation was augmented by demonstrated achievements in combat, especially in captives and trophies taken (Clastres 2010; Clendinnen 1991; Redmond 1994; also Richter 1992). In highland Colombia, an illustrious Cauca warrior offered himself up to be eaten by his comrades, so that his strength and competencies as a fighter could be distributed (Redmond 1994: 31). It is noteworthy therefore that individual warriorhood or self-interest is often downplayed in archaeological accounts of warfare, which opt more for group-oriented, adaptive explanations, such as socio-religious integration, adaptation (survival or expansion), or as a materialization of ideology.

A study by ethnographer Denise Arnold and archaeologist Christine Hastorf considers the role of trophy-taking, warfare and political systems in the Andes (Arnold and Hastorf 2008). Drawing from lowland South American ethnography (esp. Fausto 2001 and Viveiros de Castro 1992), they make the argument that, for many Andean societies, heads acquired from ancestors and enemies were vitalizing forces. They were critical elements of political ideologies centered on their power for regeneration and growth (see especially for Nasca, Browne et al. 1993; Proulx 1989, 2001; Townsend 1985; Verano 1995). Two social types are associated with trophy head use and ideology, those with centripetal versus those with centrifugal tendencies. The former describes collectivities that are more outward looking, bellicose and characterized by interethnic strife (re: expansive, militaristic polities, capture of enemy heads) and those that are more pacific, focused on ancestors and ancestor heads, and interested in social reproduction (re: non-state, kin-based) (Arnold and Hastorf 2008: 26, 36). The interpretation emphasizes the cosmological basis and integration enabled by group ritual and fertility symbolism based on trophy head practices.

I will make no direct association of 'enemy' and 'ancestor' kinds of heads with 'expanding, centrifugal' and 'kin-based, centripetal' kinds of political systems. The record is remarkably equivocal for the origins of enemies and decapitated victims: expansive societies such as the Moche sacrifice and decapitate their own, while many less centralized societies delight in the torture and head-taking of others. We will also see that ancestors and enemies are not mutually exclusive categories: enemies can be prey just as well as predators, and ancestors can be perceived as enemies as well as conquerors. Their alterities are imagined and equally entangled, cognitively as well as physically.

The shared technologies of hunting and warfare are crucial because the ideas behind them affect other domains for social relations and cultural production. This fact resuscitates Claude Lévi-Strauss' belief that warfare formed part of the same system, but occupying a different pole, having to do with building political alliances through affinal relations and generalized exchange (Lévi-Strauss 1969).

But warfare also serves to do more, because it transforms people and acts as a scheme of action that redefines personhood, for both women and men. Beer-making, group aesthetics, corporate ritual, tool making, personal adornment, food preparation and socialization are all, for instance, intimately entangled with the practices of warfare and hunting (e.g., Arnold and Hastorf 2008; Conklin 2001; Fausto 2001; Harrison 1993). It might be noted that warriorhood, itself, was not limited to men, as the recent find of a Moche female burial (Lady of Cao) revealed. Her skin featured complex tattoos of serpents and spiders (predators) and her interment was accompanied by war clubs, spear throwers and human sacrifices (Franco Jordán 2010). In short, warfare is a sociality oriented toward acknowledging and engaging the subjectivities of other peoples.

Warfare, by its standard definition, presumes the confrontation between two or more political communities: ego in one and an enemy in the other. It is not surprising that the ideologies of most, if not all, complex societies characterize the enemy alter in formulaic ways: e.g., 'Philistines' (the barbaric other), 'Trojans' (the valiant other), 'rogue states' (dangerous and lawless nations), 'Persians' (the overwhelming horde), etc. Ideologies and the arts stylize others into outsiders, demonized aggressors, captives, tragic heroes, feuding partners, age-old rivals, etc. In these alterities, there are individuals especially notable for their signal embodiment of the enemy – e.g., Goliath, Hector, Darius, dictators. Although configured very differently, they comprise the others within their respective groups who are simply better at embodying the rival alterity.

Likewise, Precolumbian groups very commonly used parts to denote the whole. The capture of heads, of course, was common (e.g., Arnold and Hastorf 2008) and sacred relics, bundles or idols often stood in as deceased powerful ones (e.g., Houston et al. 2006). A shorthand for the destruction of communities was the capture of that community's tutelary god, or the razing/burning of its temple (e.g., Boone 2000). The metonymic relations worked because people saw warfare as confrontations between diverse elements (numina, things, animals, places, etc.) that stood for the antagonism. Just as important, the images served to inscribe and remember the outcomes and the resulting order of confrontation. We see this in the landscape of conflict between ethnic groups of Huarochirí (Salomon and Urioste 1991), which maps out their struggles, migrations and conquests as past places of confrontation between ancestral divinities. The Inca destroyed or captured cult objects, *huacas*, of enemy groups and brought them back to Cuzco, the imperial capital. This highly charged symbolic move subordinated the cult's objects and followers to the state religion (MacCormack 1991: 60–62; Rowe 1982: 109).

In sum, alterity is basic to predation, because predation demands two perspectives: ego and enemy, insider and outsider. Hunting and warfare are deeply entangled because, in practice and cosmology, they serve to elide the qualities of others as prey beings. For many Precolumbian groups in the Andes, defeat of the enemy through warfare was a form of social relations which stressed engagements and incorporation of dangerous, vital others.

Changing predator–prey subjectivities

The Amazonian literature makes clear that some enemies are more than merely game animals to be killed or destroyed for food. Occupying an outsider subjectivity with another (host) community can be significant in other ways.

Captive taking is one of the main objectives of Amerindian warfare. How a group handles its captive enemies is paramount for understanding their alterity. Not all captives are immediately killed or sacrificed (Fausto 2007: 508–9; Viveiros de Castro 1992: 285–86; Santos-Granero 2009c). In the process of acculturation to a new society, they are seen to become something different, yet tolerable by the new community. They can intermarry in their new communities, and be fed by the capturer. They become workers and sometimes slaves. Sometimes they are simply slaughtered as objects (food). For a short while, they may be perceived as (and named) pets, children, brothers and even affines of the capturer.[6] Prisoners are fed by the hosts, given the food of insiders. They are made a kind of special, temporary insider through a process that some have called 'familiarizing predation' (Fausto 2000; also Viveiros de Castro 1992: 279–82).

Many ancient American societies stressed the malleability of captive subjectivities. Mesoamerican societies, such as the Maya and Aztecs, reworked captive statuses, as part of their courtly life, visual discourse and especially in ritual performance (Carrasco 1999; Fitzsimmons 2011; Houston et al. 2006; Miller and Martin 2004). The shaming of and corporeal violence to enemies were vital instruments of political display and ideology. The terror was in the alterity-making, which transformed once feared enemies into various sorts of subordinate and nonhuman beings: pets, children, kin, eunuchs, slaves and effeminates (Fausto 2000; Richter 1992; Trexler 1999).

In Amazonia cultural products of the enemy (e.g., names, songs, dreams, cigar smoke, trophies and body parts) are considered dangerous. It's often the aim of pre- and post-combat ritual to neutralize their potential harm to the community. Stripping, torturing and renaming captives are part of this. Fausto (2000: 943) notes the practice of 're-enemization', where at different strategic points in time, the domesticated captive undergoes transformation *back* into an enemy. This can be a symbolic or physical act (e.g., redressing, body paint). The logic is that killing a pet, insider or fellow villager is neither appropriate nor advantageous, and adds little to the personal capacities of the warrior. Prisoners need to become the enemy other again before they are killed outright.

In sum, a symbolic economy of alterity basically turns on change and acculturation. It is predicated on the transformation of the alterity of the foreign being and one's social relation(s) with it. In the process, that other is internalized so that the other enhances the inside, first and foremost of the killer-person, but also that person's community.

On opposition and acculturation

Finally, before turning to the archaeological evidence of predation during the Early Intermediate Period, I want to detail the role of opposition in Andean thought and practice about warfare. Specifically, I will argue that opposition based on rivals and enemies is fundamental to certain Andean social relations. The important cognitive structure of dualism embeds the potential for complementarity. It also naturalizes the oppositions or inequalities that emerge through predatorial relations.

The structural notions of dualism and complementary opposition have long been noted for the Andes. The ethnographic and archaeological literature features many instances of dual opposition (e.g., Burger and Salazar-Burger 1993; Hocquenghem 1983; Isbell 1977; Moore 1995; Platt 1986; Turner 1996). Essentially, this worldview stresses material culture, practice, indeed ways of being, as composed of two opposed, but complementary forces. While paired, these forces are not equals, and while one side is often ranked over the other, both are required for balance or completion. The strong or upper element is seen to incorporate the other, and often stands for the whole. Such a scheme applies to many different expressions in the Andes: such as male/female, sun/moon and right/left. At the same time, dual organization frequently occurs with or are encompassed by other structures (Lévi-Strauss 1963a).

Dualism, and specifically the notion of complementary opposites, pervades many of the best-known warfare complexes in the native Americas. The Aztec Templo Mayor was dedicated to two gods, one of rain and another of fire and the sun; the same elements which when brought together (water-burning) paired as a symbol of military conquest (Boone 2000: 33, 35). The bisected stairway at Cerro Sechín, dated to ca. 1200 BC, is consonant with the imagery of converging processions of victors and the vanquished (Burger 1992a). A number of Amazonian groups refer to enemies as 'counterparts' and 'opposites' (Fausto 2001: 267; Viveiros de Castro 1992: 239).

In the Andes, the notion of dual opposition is expressed most succinctly in the Quechua terms *tinku* or *tinkuy*. Tinku refers to a pairing (of two like things, such as hands) or meeting of two elements, such as the convergence of paths or rivers (González Holguín 1989: 342–43). Both words have had an indelible impact on the scholarship on Andean warfare because tinku is used to describe ceremonial fights between moiety groups, known in historical times. But, in fact, tinku was not the common term to use for fighting or warfare. Rather, colonial Quechua and Aymara made use of words incorporating the term *auca* (enemy, warrior) and its cognates *aucca* and *awka* (see Bertonio 1879; Domingo de Santo Tomás 1951; González Holguin 1989; Guaman Poma de Ayala 1980; Murúa 2004; Salomon and Urioste 1991). Thus, making war, battles and combat with enemies were glossed as *auccay, aucanacuy, Aucani, gui, auccanacuni* and *aucasitha*.

It is notable that Bertonio (1879) uses *Aucanacuspa attini,gui*, glossed as 'To capture, or defeat another', but crucially in 'attini,gui', what seems to be a reference to tinkuy, or encounter. Guaman Poma (1980: 311) offers the construction *awqawan t'inkuq* (he who confronts the enemy), which appears to distinguish between the meeting, rooted in tinkuy, and with whom one was meeting, rooted in auca. What these seem to suggest is that war-related interaction with enemies stood as a distinct kind of tinkuy expression (a meeting of paired opposites).

We can make three brief generalizations about the lexical fields associated with auca. First, there is strong emphasis on the public nature of auca-type activities. Many auca words, for example, treat the sounds, musical instruments and shouts of war. Second, auca is especially prominent in the names and titles of people in warlike activities; these usually distinguish specific ranks of warriors and enemy warriors. The basis of social address or function obliges an intrinsic conceptual link to auca persons and confrontation. Finally, there seems to some purposeful intermingling between warrior and enemy identities, for there is no clear distinction between their usages.

That auca connotes both an enemy and warrior (from one's own side) has implications for the study of Andean alterity. This ambivalence, which alternates the subjectivities, may be related to other Amerindian warfare complexes which highlight special and changing personal statuses, and the *incorporation* of enemies (e.g., Carrasco 1999: 146; Conklin 2001: 143; Fausto 2000; Houston et al. 2006: 204–5; Viveiros de Castro 1992: 240, 286). This may refer to warriors who are partly outside their own community, because they are killers and have privileges that others do not (Clastres 2010). It may also relate to the familiarization of enemies – captives who are internalized by captor and the host group, physically or symbolically. Overall, many Quechua and Aymara words associated with warfare – centered on the term 'auca' – express a fundamental agonistic relation to the concept of an opposing other. The words may characterize the encounters as profoundly social and transformative contexts that are crucial for the personhood of the captive and captor(s).

The processes of incorporating social others serve to elucidate otherwise enigmatic native communities of sixteenth- to seventeenth-century central highland Peru (Arriaga 1999; Duviols 1973; Polia 1999). Communities were made up of agriculturalists (*huari*) and herders (*llacuaz*) who lived and worked together, but whose existence was framed through structural opposition with each other. Huari were seen as the natives, who as cultivators, were associated with arable lands and irrigation systems. The llacuaz were newly arriving conquerors; they acknowledged a homeland whereas the aboriginals did not. Associated with herding and high (puna) grazing lands, they formed an 'upper' division in the community. The llacuaz worshipped Lliviac, a god of lightning and camelids; the huari, meanwhile, venerated an underworld divinity responsible

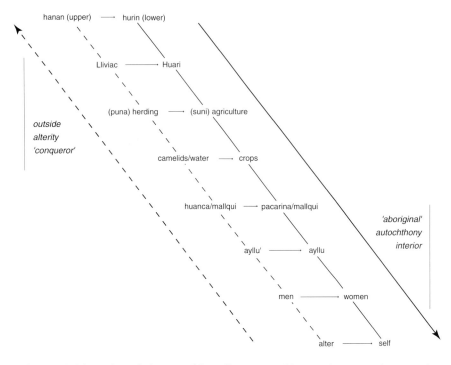

FIGURE 4.1 Schematic enchainment of *huari/llacuaz* oppositions, and processes incorporating foreign, outside elements. 'Interior, autochthonous' elements draw from 'outside' elements to define themselves, for the pattern to sustain itself (see also Viveiros de Castro 2001: Fig. 2.1).

for agriculture. The opposition was also gendered: llacuaz groups with male forces, the huari with female. The relation was founded, in large part, on the acknowledged physical conquest and incorporation of the other (Fig 4.1). Community identity and complementarity were predicated on the recognition of each other's alterity.

The huari–llacuaz phenomenon seems to have been an example of a recurring process in the Andes. There existed a persistent pattern of locals internalizing, physically and cosmologically, conquering outsiders (Gose 2008). The processes see predation and opposition as a mutual movement toward community, in which conquerors absorb and are absorbed by their subjects. Group conquest is followed by incorporation, and then locally understood as a complementary social arrangement.

But crucially, conquered Andeans, during Inca and Spanish expansions, perceived the new arrivals as ancestors, as the group's original forefathers (Gose 2008). Ancestral histories of the conquerors and conquered would be joined to shape a mutual complementary system of organization and worldview that naturalized the new political reality (Fig 4.2). This maintained many of the forms known as dual social organization, such as upper and lower divisions or moieties. The invaders' gods and sacred places would also be fitted, and placed in hierarchical terms, to match the new arrangement.

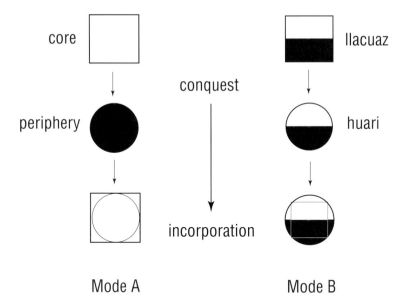

FIGURE 4.2 Comparison of conquest and incorporation schema, comparing Mode A, typical of territorial expansions (e.g., world systems), and Mode B, typifying some Andean patterns which preserve dual structures.

The socio-cosmological leeway of Andean collectivities might be seen as an adaptive strategy for survival during periods of tumult. But it is notable that historical trajectories of incorporation and new dynamics of social groups were patterned in strikingly similar, almost formulaic, ways. The patterns suggest enduring dispositions toward ambivalent others were framed uniquely within Andean ways of reckoning their world. It was one of repeated upheaval, from which order and re-organization emerge through their internalization of those others.

In these examples of Andean culture contact, it is notable that full 'integration' was avoided; there existed mutual recognition of major cultural distinctions. Communities, it seems, arranged their social and political worlds literally in concert with the other. The essence of dual organization in these examples resided in the recognition of another and that entity's alterity. If such relations served to integrate opposed groups' forces, they are also fundamental expressions of the stability of difference.

The patterns that reconcile hierarchical social relations are often reflected through local oral traditions. Ritual practices, reifying myth, also articulate beings of unequal standing into ordered arrangements (see also Descola 2005; Lévi-Strauss 1983; Turner 1995).

> The idea of creation is virtually absent from indigenous [lowland S. America] communities. Things and beings normally originate as a transformation of something else … And just as nature is not the creation but of transformation, so culture is not a product of invention but of transference (and thus, transmission, tradition). In Amerindian mythology, the origin of cultural implements or institutions is canonically explained as a borrowing – a transfer (violent or

friendly, by stealing or by learning, as a trophy or a gift) of prototypes already possessed by animals, spirits or enemies. The origin and essence of culture for Amerindian groups is acculturation … Myths address what must be taken for granted, the initial conditions with which humanity must cope and against which humanity must define itself by means of its power of *convention*.

(Viveiros de Castro 2004: 477–78)

Internalizing others, through the idiom of kinship and predation, comprises one such 'convention'. What this describes for lowland South America has some interesting implications for indigenous Andean communities. Inca and late prehispanic indigenous myths stressed group legitimacy in traditions about the establishment of noble dynasties and their gods and cults (Salomon 1991; Urton 1999). By the same token, myths that concern how products are transmitted by others to others, human and nonhuman alike, resonate strongly with the content of much ancient Andean iconography (e.g., Lathrap 1973b; Tello 1923; Townsend 1985). Some of the gifts include cultigens (e.g., maize, manioc, fish), and knowledge and technologies (e.g., pottery, irrigation).

Myths were reworked during late prehispanic and colonial times to understand new socio-political conditions (Salomon 1998: 15; Urton 1999: 64–69). Local divinities and their actions of creation were subsumed into more powerful systems and ancestor divinities. Conquests and socioeconomic turmoil resulted in demographic instability during the late prehispanic and colonial era Andes (Cook 1981; Covey 2008). Migrations, forced resettlement and displacements were not uncommon. Entire communities, often of specialists, would be moved as part of Inca imperial strategy (D'Altroy 2002). And one such instance in the colonial town of Recuay included an *ayllu*, a potting community, that became resettled as a fifth ayllu in an existing community of four (Hernández Príncipe 1923).

As we have seen, predatorial relations and how Andean societies perceived others meant constant remapping of local social orders. The ritual and economic reckoning of key places of divine action (where our ancestors made this and where our ancestors did that) form the *raison d'être* of indigenous traditions, but seen fundamentally in direct relation to those ancestor divinities of others (Salomon and Urioste 1991). Canals, the opening of fields, establishment of settlements, and lithification (e.g., standing stones to mountains) all meant lasting marks on the physical environment. Local myth left trails of primordial acts of divine behavior, but history frequently reworked and sedimented them.

In sum, this section has described how Andean societies worked out ways to recognize and internalize opposing others. It first described indigenous words that identified and celebrated the practice, things and people of war, at the same time that they entangled ideas about warriors and enemies. Both warriors and enemies are special kinds of persons who exist and give meaning to the other as opposites. But they also have changing statuses, especially as captives, which form part of the 'familiarization' process of incorporating others. A link was made to the processes of incorporation seen on a large scale with Inca and Spanish conquests, and with huari–llacuaz groups, where groups co-existed on the basis on recognizing their own status by way of structurally opposed relations with others as (necessary) alters. These comprehended conquest, subordination and acculturation as dynamic processes of complementary opposition.

Discourse on trophies: collecting the other

Where we also recognize the significance of predation is in the acquisition, display and use of trophies. 'Trophy' is a term used here to describe an object that is or represents a body part of another being.[7] Andeans, like many other Amerindian societies, made trophies from human body parts as well as elements from other beings. Infused with the potency of their prototypes, they were considered sacred and vitalizing objects, and were brought out during celebrations requiring fertility. Here, distance and the mythic seem less important as properties of the other, than on the tangible and partible of the local and powerful.

The partible other appears to have been important for many Andean societies at different levels of social organization. The Inca were especially known for practices that stressed containers of forces from powerful persons and prototypes. Not only were mummy bundles of the Inca sovereigns worshipped as ancestral divinities, Inca sovereigns had physical images of themselves, known as *huauque* or brother, made out of different materials and of varying degrees of likeness (Van de Guchte 1996). These were venerated during their lifetimes. But the effigies were carefully kept and attended to as physical extensions of the rulers, even after their death. Offerings and sacrifices were made to them. They were brought out in public display during celebrations and were deployed in battle to improve the morale of the Inca armies, having 'the same powers as the bodies of their owners when they were still alive' (Cobo 1990: 37–38).

The Incas also routinely captured key cult objects from other societies that they had conquered in their empire. Held under Inca control in Cuzco, the imperial center, these images were trophies only in the object sense of the term. At one level, they symbolized rather bluntly the extension and incorporation of distinct provinces and peoples. In this way, the collecting was not unlike that of many colonial projects in world history which filled the treasuries, museums and zoos of expanding nations (Gosden and Knowles 2001; O'Hanlon and Welsch 2000; Thomas 1991).

But Inca practice, at another level, actively transformed regional cosmologies that articulated obligations through origins: huaca capture subsumed powerful regional (ancestral) deities into the imperial pantheon and put them at the behest of the Inca (Guaman Poma de Ayala 1980).[8] It is also true that provincial divinities and oracles did not remain powerless, nor did they necessarily comply with what the Incas wanted done or to be heard (e.g., Arriaga 1999: 32–33). In Andean reckoning, mythical beings and supposedly inert things frequently revolted against masters (Allen 1998; Quilter 1990; Salomon and Urioste 1991).

The idea of huaca capture, a kind of collecting, need not describe only objects. For the *capacocha* ('royal obligation') rituals, the young, unblemished children of provincial families were sent to Cuzco, feted and conditioned for suitability, and then returned to the imperial provinces for their eventual sacrifice (Hernández Príncipe 1923;

McEwan and van de Guchte 1992; Reinhard 2005). *Capacochas* were quintessential sacrifices and trophies of a sort: freshly embodied objects taken of their biological lives so as to refashion new relations (between provincial lords and the Inca).

Their subjectivization, like trophy heads and captives, entails a triple process that transforms the person's alterity: obtaining an element from the outside, making that person into an insider (e.g., Inca), and reversing back to make the person an outsider (but wedded structurally affinally). They were acts of appropriating non-local persons and things, and incorporating them by subordinating them into the Inca universe.

Native and Spanish testimonies from Huarochirí discuss the making of sacred face masks from the skins and bones of both ancestral heroes and enemies (Arguedas and Duviols 1966: 141–43, 247; Salomon and Urioste 1991: 120–21; Taylor 1987: 371–75).

> Saying,[9] 'He [the ancestral figure Ñan sapa] is our origin; it was he who first came to this village and took charge of it', people flayed his face and made it dance as if his own persona. If they captured a man in warfare, they would first flay his face, and then make it dance, saying 'This is our valor!' And when a man was taken prisoner in war, that man himself would say, 'Brother, soon you'll kill me. I was a really powerful man, and now you're about to make a *huayo* out of me. So before I go out onto the plaza,[10] you should feed me well and serve me drinks first.' Obeying this, they'd offer food and drinks to the other *huayos*, saying, 'This day you shall dance with me on the plaza.' They actually used to bring out the *huayos* and carry them in a litter for two days. On the following day, they'd hang them up together with their maize, potatoes and all the other offerings. About the hanging of the huayos, people remarked, 'The huayos will return to the place where they were born, the place called Uma Pacha, carrying these things along with them.'

This passage elicits a number of interesting implications and ambiguities which relate directly to enemy–prey alterity and the problematic of conqueror-ancestors. First, these masks were themselves ritual objects and the foci of veneration. They were more than simply items of display or status symbols of their holders. They needed to be danced, have offerings made to, presided over public events, and were also carried as agentive objects of the defeated's personhood. Salomon and Urioste (1991: note 620) explain: ' … when a captive faced sacrifice, he asked that, immediately before his death and ever afterward when transformed into a face-mask, he always be duly fêted before entering into his conquerors' ceremonies.' All the actions given to them remind one of the activities associated with huaca and ancestor veneration.

Another notable point concerns the address given by the captive to his captor or eventual killer; the captive says to him 'brother, soon you'll kill me'. Now, this is fascinating because it employs the same term, *huauqui* or *wawki*, as we saw earlier with the Inca effigies (huauque). It is not clear whether the use of huauqui has this specific connotation here, but it is also noteworthy that none of the major translations of the Huarochirí manuscript agree on the translation of this 'almost incomprehensible passage' (Taylor 1987: 371). Arguedas and Duviols' translation (1966: 141) lacks any reference to 'brother' but refers more to the perspective of the captive.[11] Meanwhile, Taylor's version (1987: 371–73) differs on the perspective: rather than in the singular, many captives are involved and doing the saying.[12]

Notwithstanding, if we take 'huauqui' as an address to the captor, it has the virtue of describing the new relationship between the captor and the captive. It is no longer one of enmity and distance, but of kinship in 'brother'. As we have seen already, the predator–prey complex for many ethnographic Amerindian groups often construed enemies incorporated through kinship terms, often of affinal and filial relations. The captive enemies, in other words, become familiarized (see Fausto 2000: 938–39).

Finally, there is a direct link between the power of an individual and the power of an object/effigy made from parts of that individual. The sacred face effigy instantiates the vital potency of its previous owner (wearer), what both Taylor (1987) and Salomon and Urioste (1991) indicated as *valentía* (or valor), and what Arguedas and Duviols (1966: 141) translated more indirectly as 'proof that I am strong'. These, it might be mentioned, are abridged glosses for terms in the original Quechua, which connote acts and happenings of transmission of the vital force between especially capable beings (objects or persons) (Salomon 1998: 9; Taylor 1987: 373).[13] Most tellingly, the object and its wearer/holder are accorded respect because the prototype was perceived as powerful. Yet the 'power' resided in productive capacity rather than, it seems, in physical or in political reckoning.

The parts of others, when worn or incorporated, enhance the capacities of the new holder. Frank Salomon (1998: 12) has observed how in the Huarochirí manuscript, donning the skin or mask appropriated from others enables communication with beings of a supernatural kind. It is unclear, however, whether Andean skins meant also to allow the wearer to 'see' as a new kind of predator, to facilitate a new viewpoint and capacity. Ethnohistorical documents and ethnography of the Central Andes present various cases of masking with the skins and headdresses of foxes and mountain cats (Salomon 1998; Zuidema 1985). These were worn during festivals aimed to guard the fields from birds and other pests, jobs that are performed by those same animals. Wearing the skins of such animals emerged out of the desire to protect valuable fields, but, one would surmise, also to be more effective in its execution (Benson 1997: 40).

Head-taking has also been documented among highland ethnic groups in the Bolivian Andes (Arnold and Hastorf 2008; Arnold and Yapita 2006). Taken by men from men of other communities, trophy heads then become integrated into domestic production, and especially women's activities. Wrapped like seeds and babies, the heads from outsider men are seen to be sources of vitality, literally 'offspring', for the household (Arnold and Hastorf 2008: 48–49). Here they may allude to instances of gender symbolism where women transform, through blood and beer, the predatorial and incorporative activities of their husbands into fertility for themselves (Conklin 2001). It seems only fitting that infants can be perceived as enemies and affinal (Platt 2002; Viveiros de Castro 2001: 34). The labor and risk of parturition, likened to a kind of warfare among the Aztecs, also mark the ambiguity of the infant and fashion the warriorhood of women who die in childbirth (López Austin 1988). It is food and socialization that transition the infant into a sociable insider.

The foregoing sections have described why predatory relations were important for many Amerindian societies. On one level, they acted on the desire for gain – spoils, land, a slave, an affine. This rationalization must have been important at many levels of combat practice. On another level, they transformed the person doing the taking, because they effected a change in how others perceive him – as a predator, a proper adult, etc. The parts of former enemies (e.g., body parts, images/narratives, effigies) were important because they were instantiations of their vitality and acted to enhance oneself and one's community. Enemies therefore enrich: they are full of a vitality which, like most things which are finite, is high in demand but in short supply.

In the ancient Andean cases that follow, I will present evidence to show that the record of warfare and predation also features a 'symbolic economy of alterity'. First, there was a proliferation of representations of warrior-leaders during the Early Intermediate Period, especially in northern Peru but also elsewhere. The otherness of this kind of power has already been introduced in the previous chapter, but I will revisit warrior-leaders because the types of things and activities associated with them often concern predation, construed broadly.

There are three general strands of evidence for my argument. First, imagery often shows people wearing parts of humans and animals taken through some activity which makes prey out of other beings. On occasion, there are also physical examples of these trophies. Second, and in related fashion, we will see that the imagery of warfare valorized the capturing and taking of enemy others, through warfare, in the depiction in art, and in native theory about society and conquest. Finally, we will explore how settlement systems and other material culture embed notions of opposition, confrontation and the desire to recognize the enemy other.

Imagery of predation

Probably the most overt form of expression about predatorial relations during the Early Intermediate Period in northern Peru (and for many parts of the Central Andes) concerned objects that feature imagery of the enemy. I want to describe the general imagery first and then connect, where possible, ancillary lines of evidence.

Previous studies of the period's warfare imagery have employed the data for certain ends. First, some argue that the imagery shows the conquest designs of militaristic polities, and emerges out of the ideology of expanding political systems. So, for example, the elaborate pottery depictions of warriors and combat act to 'materialize' the ideology of leaders among the Moche (Billman 1997; DeMarrais et al. 1996; Wilson 1987). To a certain extent, this is also probably true for Nasca and Recuay, although scholars debate the extent to which certain 'warrior-chiefs' were religious practitioners and the political arrangements for both cultures (Lau 2011: Ch. 7; Makowski and Rucabado Yong 2000: 207–12; Silverman and Proulx 2002: 230). Second, the warfare imagery is used to relate to a group's shared ethos or set of enduring dispositions based on violent intergroup conflict, but is most apparent in elite prerogatives and media. There is no expectation for a level of social complexity or that military 'expansion' need be involved to explain the character of the imagery

(Lau 2004a, 2010b; Makowski 2004; Quilter 2002, 2008; Verano 2001). The third mode emphasizes that the imagery depicts ritual combat (Hocquenghem 1987; Topic and Topic 1997a, b) and that it is of a ceremonial essence (Donnan 1997, 2004). So, for example, the same Moche imagery of combat does not show 'real warfare'; in lieu, it represents scenes of ceremonial character, perhaps of staged contests, that are interested mainly in the capture of enemies. Scenes follow a narrative that show the enemies being defeated, stripped and humiliated, and then processed toward a Moche dignitary, to whom the prisoner will be sacrificed.

The polarized interpretations hinge on two main axes. The first concerns the degree to which the imagery depicts real-life events and things (e.g., battles, weapons, captains) or are mythic in nature (e.g., symbol, metaphor, allegory). The second axis regards the degree to which the imagery is seen to be more secular or more ritual in character. It is unnecessary to dwell on the debates here, since there has been extended coverage elsewhere that considers the issues and archaeological contexts of specific cultures (Arkush and Stanish 2005; Bourget 2001; Lau 2004a, 2010b; Quilter 2002, 2008, 2010; Sutter and Cortez 2005; Sutter and Verano 2007; Verano 2001).

More important to my argument now is the degree to which the imagery describes relations of predation. A virtue of the focus on predation is that it informs some of the categorical dichotomies that characterize current archaeological thinking on Andean warfare: between real life versus idealized, mythical depictions, secular versus ritual combat, and physical versus symbolic. In fact, I would argue that it subsumes them.[14] These issues form part of an ancient system of cultural representation and practice that study of the imagery has the virtue of illuminating, but not entirely reconstructing.

Acts of predation: hunting, combat and internalization

Like most complex societies with regional boundaries, many groups during the Early Intermediate Period – such as Moche, Recuay and Nasca – made opposing enemies and neighbors into a kind of 'other'. We can only surmise that alterities developed through certain face-to-face practices – for example, of actual combat, war preparations, enslavement, torture and ritual fights. Oral traditions and songs which concerned victories over the enemy other, such as of the huayo masks of Huarochirí, were also probably important. But it is mainly through tangible artifacts and their imagery of warfare, what archaeologist Jeffrey Quilter (2008) called 'martial arts', that we see the alterity of enemies most regularly.

Some imagery actively centered on the notion that the other could be preyed upon. The main kinds of action that constituted predation consisted of hunting, killing, internalizing (taking, capturing or eating) and wearing the parts of others. The arts of Moche, Nasca and Recuay all evidence these practices, to varying degrees.

The cultures that developed very prominent martial imageries developed them roughly contemporaneously. But they certainly had very different cultural backgrounds and antecedents (see Fig 2.1). The Moche, for example, emerged out of the Early Horizon cultures of the north coast, namely Cupisnique and Salinar, and neither of these styles valorized armed conflict to the extent of their successors. It also emerged side by side with and then superseded the Gallinazo style (Donnan 1992; Millaire 2009). Recuay emerged directly out of the Huarás style, and its characteristic white-on-red pottery featured little of the martial imagery seen later in Recuay (Lau 2011). The Nasca cultural tradition developed out of the preceding Paracas style. Although trophy head imagery is known from Paracas, depictions of fighting, especially between humans, are relatively rare (Menzel et al. 1964; Silverman and Proulx 2002).

The degree to which any of the antecedent cultures engaged in violent conflict can be debated. Settlement systems in Moche and Recuay show fortifications. There is also evidence for weapons, especially maceheads, in all of the Early Horizon cultures. At least with the imagery, however, there is confidence that Moche, Nasca and Recuay intensified the graphic emphasis on predation. This holds for both species-specific and inter-species encounters.

To be sure, there were connections between Moche and Recuay cultures. As we have seen, these were established in cultural interactions during the early centuries AD between various related north central Andean groups (e.g., early Gallinazo, early Recuay, early Moche and Vicús). However, groups of the south coast (associated with late Paracas, early Nasca and Topará styles) seem to have had little intensive interaction with these northern cultures groups, not least because of the distance (cf. Grieder 1978: 183). Interestingly, what evidence there is of Moche–Nasca interaction often regards the stylization of combat figures and their activities in war (see below).

What are some of the features of predation in all three cultures? First and foremost, all three cultures portrayed enemy combatants; human figures fight other human figures. Representing warfare is essential to the pattern of predation; it can enhance and multiply the original activity of predation. Broadly speaking, even though people might fight with enemies or consider others as prey, they need not visualize them, much less represent them in artworks. In giving them shape and space, all three cultures actively sought to acknowledge their engagements with enemy others. This recalls the notion that to represent something is to somehow want to gain something from it (Taussig 1993). That an enemy is portrayed at all through representational imagery is a testament to the appeal and demands of predating on the other.

The imagery was not only documentary. It did not only describe that combat occurred. It also represented the figures in certain stylized ways. In particular, it sub-jectivized those depicted into certain fundamental categories. These relate to those who triumph and those who do not, and those who are hunters and those who are prey. They also all show a desire to depict some act of *appropriation from* the other. The captor is shown taking a prisoner, his weapons bundle, his head, etc. A carrion bird picks at the flesh of a dead corpse. A feline assails a human by pouncing on his back. A group of warriors defeats the other group of enemies. A mythical being defeats another mythical being.

Of the three cultures, Moche combat imagery is formally more diverse, and its study has drawn more comprehensive scrutiny (e.g., Donnan and McClelland 1999; Hocquenghem 1987; Quilter 2008). At least with Moche, there was a regional precedent in the imagery of predation: Cupisnique (Larco Hoyle 1941; Salazar and Burger 2000). Cupisnique-style art of the first millennium BC rarely portrayed warriors and combat. More frequently, it depicted animal predators (raptors, felines, spiders) and the violent taking of heads. 'Spider Decapitator' representations likely represented one of the principal divinities in the Cupisnique pantheon (Cordy-Collins 2001a; Salazar-Burger and Burger 1982; Salazar and Burger 2000: 37). In later Moche art, spider figures continued as important predators and trophy-takers in portable and monumental art (Alva Meneses 2008). But the imagery also diversified to include a wide range of killer-figures dressed as human warriors and lords. These seem to anthropomorphize and secularize the act of predation, which almost certainly derived from the intensification of militarism and warfare culture later in the Early Intermediate Period.

Through compilation and study of thousands of Moche vessels and associated materials, archaeologist Christopher Donnan and colleagues have isolated a series of images that comprise the 'Warrior Narrative', discussed earlier. These treat the defeat and capture of enemies, and subsequent parading of captives and their eventual sacrifice in front of specially-bedecked lords (Donnan 1997; 2004: Ch. 7; Donnan and McClelland 1999: 69–72, 130–35).

The types of combat that the Moche depicted were almost always between people who, stylistically, appear Moche in cultural affiliation. Very commonly, warriors are elaborately attired. Characteristic elements include distinctive types of favored attire (especially conical helmet, ear ornaments), weaponry (biconical clubs, hand shield) and accoutrements (e.g., backflaps) (Donnan 1997, 2004; Quilter 2008). Very occasionally, Moche warriors are shown fighting and usually defeating people who feature different weapons, headdresses and apparel (Fig 4.3; Plate 5). This different material style might refer to other cultural traditions, perhaps of foreign ethnic groups associated with Gallinazo or Recuay styles (Kutscher 1950; Lau 2004a: Fig. 22; Makowski and Rucabado Yong 2000; Woloszyn 2008: 182–86); others favor the

FIGURE 4.3 Rollout drawing of combat scene, middle Moche stirrup spout vessel (adapted from Lau 2004a: Fig. 3; after Kutscher 1950). Moche warriors, all wearing Moche helmets and using war clubs, have the upper hand over a motley group of others, some captured, dripping blood and stripped.

notion that the others were special members *within* Moche (Donnan 2004: 117–23; Reichert 1989; Schuler-Schömig 1979, 1981).

There are some Moche scenes which show warriors dispersed across a field of battle. But many images of warfare set two combatants to face each other. There may be many pairs in any one depiction (e.g., Donnan 1997: 52; Kutscher 1983: Abb. 107–08). Moche painters most often show the fighting using hand-to-hand weapons, such as shields and clubs. The use of long-distance weapons such as spearthrowers, darts, slings and what appear to be throwing stones is less common.

Action in Moche, and indeed for most Andean images of combat, focuses on the key moment of fighting: the initial sizing up, the disabling or killing stroke, and indicative hand and face gestures. Some combatants have the upper hand, either having defeated or being in the process of dealing the decisive blow. This is usually to disable the opponent, typically a club to the face or torso, which produces blood dripping from the trauma. Very often, the victor is shown grasping the head or hair of the enemy, with the implication that a major (head) strike or capture is imminent (Fig 4.4). In modern industrialized warfare, long-distance weapons such as machine guns, artillery and predator drones marginalize the bodily skill and interpersonal activity of combat. Based on face-to-face encounters, predating on the other in ancient Peru was about the clash of persons and the dynamism produced through physical opposition between alters. It was often a shorthand for the clash of collectives.

Art also emphasized the ignominy of losing. The contrasting status often concerns the altered, denigrated condition of the losing combatants. In Moche, a number of conventionalized features express this new status: blood dripping from the face, a sprawled or upside-down position, disheveled appearance, and smaller bodies. Most important, the losing combatants are stripped of their attire, weapons and gear (Fig. 4.3). Having been shorn of the materiality of warriorhood, the enemies are bound as

FIGURE 4.4 Fineline scene of Moche warriors and defeated enemies (adapted from Kutscher 1983: Abb. 102). A captive is shown stripped, and bound with ropes, while the captor carries his gear in a bundle.

captives, tied together with ropes, and processed *en masse* – presumably back to the major Moche towns for their eventual sacrifice in the ceremonial complexes, after having been presented before Moche dignitaries (Bourget 2001; Donnan 2004). As prisoners, vulnerable body positions, placement with carnivorous animals, and the stripping of weapons and attire indicate their diminished, humiliated transformation from their original status as dangerous killers (Bourget 2006; Donnan and McClelland 1999; Hill 2000).

In all three cultures, the weapons shown being used for human-to-human combat are very often the same weapons used to hunt nonhumans. The Moche favored spearthrowers, darts and clubs (Quilter 2008). For the Recuay, clubs and maces were preferred, while the Nasca chose knives, spearthrowers, darts and feathered staffs. Shields, commonly shown among the Moche during combat scenes, apparently were unnecessary during hunting. With the exception of shields, the attire of hunters and warriors is fairly similar in all three styles.

It is interesting to note that there may have been some Moche influence on Nasca art. There were common vessel forms (face necks and long handled spouts) as well as instances of shared imagery. In particular, Nasca artists depicted running hunters and warriors, 'floating' filler and landscape elements, and feathered staffs show interest in a newfound complex centered on warfare, perhaps deriving from Moche itself (Proulx 1994; 2006: 11–12, 99–100, 117, Pl. 16; Silverman and Proulx 2002: 34). These new developments emerged largely during late Nasca times, by about AD 500.

A few Nasca and Recuay vessels show scenes of combat. But rarely are there more than a few dueling pairs in any one depiction. Hand-to-hand combat was also high-lighted in Nasca imagery, but Nasca warriors sometimes can also be armed with spearthrowers when in direct conflict with enemies. Also, as far as can be discerned, there is no recognizable extended plot of action as seen in the Moche 'Warrior Narrative'.

While warrior depictions are not uncommon in Nasca art, combat scenes are much rarer. Nasca shares some general characteristics of warfare complexes that we have seen already in Early Intermediate Period art. First, the action typically occurred face to face, and opponents directly engaged each other. At least one Nasca scene portrays figures clutching enemies with knives as if to decapitate them, apparently showing the intent to kill rather than capture the enemy (Silverman and Proulx 2002: Fig. 9.2). Second, very occasionally, the Nasca appear fighting with enemy groups, or outsiders, in their combat scenes (Silverman and Proulx 2002: 231–32). Nasca artists illustrated the alterity of enemies by their nakedness and having differently colored flesh tones. The hair and bodies of enemies are shown in disarray, and their bodies are arranged in subordinated, otherwise compromised positions. Some are seen punctured by darts and some are decapitated. As prisoners, they are also being picked at by carrion birds (de Lavalle 1986: 147, 166, 174, 176; Kroeber et al. 1998: 205, Pl. 24; Silverman and Proulx 2002: Fig. 9.2).

The severe disruptions of corporeal normality mark another major commonality of Early Intermediate Period warfare imageries. Rather than simply documenting violence or people fighting, they all typically aver victory over the human enemy. Artists stylized human predation by physically 'taking' the enemy, by his killing or capture.

For all three, as in many preindustrial societies, the key moment of triumph in hand-to-hand combat, whether the objective is to kill or capture the enemy, is expressed by the grabbing of another's head, usually by the hair. In Moche and Nasca representations, some figures have a distinctive section of hair or headgear just above the forehead, sometimes called a forelock or topknot (Donnan 2004: 89, 117; Proulx 2006: 123). In Moche, the forelock occurs on warrior figures who are defeated and captured.[15] Moche supernaturals as well as anthropomorphized predators (hybrid beings of weapons, helmets and animal) also defeat their opponents by firmly grabbing their heads.

That human enemies were likened to prey animals is embodied by conventionalized actions of striking, hurting and taking other hunted animals. Deer are captured by grasping their heads in the stylized manner of taking (Donnan 1997; Donnan and McClelland 1999: 49–51). Both deer and sea lions are the recipients of club blows to the hind quarters and head. Animal beings are also taken by their tails (foxes), by grasping their necks (waterbirds) and by fishing line (Donnan and McClelland 1999: 64, 67–68). Other circum-corporeal markers of being predated upon include: bleeding, certain expressions (open mouths, the look away from the captor) and the condition of having necks or hands bound with rope. Not being steady on their feet, sprawled on the ground or in mid-air, is another indicator of having been defeated; these are all indicative of having lost bodily control.

Much imagery was keyed to clothing and headgear of triumphant warriors and lords. This practice is crucial in the process of acknowledging warriors and successful hunters (Redmond 1994: 30–31; Verano 2008b). These same accoutrements suggest that their wearers were successful warriors to begin with. Predation on others, human and nonhuman, is reinforced by the fact that many of the combatants hold and don attire fitted with trophy ornaments. All three cultures employed key elements of animals and humans: hands and paws, tails, feathers, pets and antlers. These were incorporated into the elaborate headdresses, usually worn by high-status male persons.

By far the most common body part consisted of heads (Arnold and Hastorf 2008; Proulx 1989, 2006; Verano 1995). These may be trophy or severed, human or non-human. In the case of human trophies, heads were also grasped in hands, worn around the neck (Fig 4.5), slung over the back and appended to bags. Many related

FIGURE 4.5 Sculpture 15, with central figure scene, Chinchawas. The central male figure wears a trophy head pectoral, flanked by profile male felines. The eroded headdress very likely shows head appendages.

practices were also shown through the imagery: displaying trophies and body parts as aspects of high status, standing or talent in the process of predation, no matter whether the prey was human or animal. Thus the appropriated item serves as a sign of enhancement or success.

In Moche art, certain gear, weapons and clothing of the defeated enemy would be collected together and carefully assembled into bundles. These contained hand shields, clubs, slings and other related gear, such as spearthrowers, bags and darts. Bundles were significant because they were often shown being paraded around and carried away after the defeat by the victor or his assistants. As the gear of fallen enemies, bundles were the spoils of war.

Bundles and biconical Moche war clubs were frequently depicted in Moche art. They appear to have been trophies and symbolic of high status persons (Fig 4.6) (Benson 2008; Hocquenghem 1987); these were especially popular during the later phase developments of the Moche style (Donnan and McClelland 1999: 60, 93, 113–14, 177).[16] Anthropomorphized weapons and spoils bundles also fight human warrior opponents.

It seems that the weapons and gear of enemy alters were agentive, valuable and, above all, worth alienating and keeping. If ethnographic and ethnohistorical comparisons are instructive, the materials are important because they retain something of

FIGURE 4.6 Moche stirrup-spout vessel in the form of a war club and painted with a spoils bundle (adapted from Golte 2009: Fig. 14.5).

the enduring spirit of the enemy or embody a transformative, vitalizing essence for the victor. Both are common notions throughout the native Americas.

Enemies and outsiders

Alterity in warfare is frequently pegged to the notion of strangers and outsiders. It is not always the case, as in family feuds, but alterity often concerns people who are perceived as exogenous and different to one's community. Often, we perceive alterity through look and actions: people may wear different clothes, have a different skin color, speak a different language, worship different gods, eat different foods and have unusual customs. In short, they have different ways of doing similar things, in material as well as embodied styles.

Enemy representation in the Central Andes is inherently ambiguous. At one level, this simply recognizes that our general current understanding of ancient Andean combat imagery requires additional data. But also, I refer to the quality of intentional ambiguity that artists embedded in representations of strangers/enemies. Sometimes they trade; sometimes they raid. At the same time that they are dangerous, they are also sources of goods, materials, affines and other things crucial for enhanced living. The practices of war bring strangers closer in physical contact, but their defeat and death make their corporeal, living bodies more distant, nullifying certain types of further social relation and communication. Are they good, or are they bad? There are myriad plays of this kind. It is precisely the dangerous attraction of stranger-enemies which makes for good stories, and, incidentally, why the representation and narrative of warfare have been so compelling throughout human history.

Moche imagery, especially, illustrates how warfare and complementary opposition were materialized. In a previous study, I discussed scenes where Moche warriors rout a troop of warriors (Lau 2004a). Each Moche warrior is paired up with a foreign-looking opponent (see Fig 4.3). All the losing men feature gear and are attired like warriors and elites shown in Recuay culture (see also Kutscher 1950; Lau 2004a; Reichert 1989; Schuler-Schömig 1979; Smith 1978). The visual argument suggests that the losing side may be of Recuay culture or closely related groups associated with the Pacific foothills adjacent to coastal areas dominated by the Moche. Body decoration, including moustaches, ear ornaments and forelocks, emphasize their distinction from typical Moche warriors; some of these features also 'marked' them for death. The scene in Fig. 4.3 perhaps depicted an event (or series of events) which mythologized the defeat of enemy others, rendered in a similar way to how Attic pots show Achilles defeating Hector, the Narmer Palette shows a unified Egypt by subjugating others, or the Tizoc stone shows multiple triumphs over various rival towns (see also Arnold and Hastorf 2008; Verano 2001). Overall, what is clear in this composition – which stresses complementary opposition both in vessel form and imagery – is outright Moche triumph over formidable foes.

Considerable debate surrounds the nature of Moche warfare and the cultural origins of the combatants. Stylistic arguments for cultural affiliations through costume remain uncertain. Much new analysis focuses on the skeletal remains of the victims, thought to be captives taken through war, and burials of Moche people from cemetery sites across the Moche heartland. The research evaluates the morphological characteristics of certain skeletal elements (e.g., cranial or dental traits) or on bone chemistry (e.g., mitochondrial DNA; carbon, oxygen and strontium isotopes) to determine the degree of similarity between sample groups, taken from different populations.

Excavations at Huaca de la Luna – a large ceremonial complex in one of the largest, most powerful Moche settlements – have been especially important (Bourget 2001; Uceda 2001; Uceda and Tufinio 2003; Verano 2008a). In several walled enclosures (Plaza 3A and 3C) in the interior of the complex, archaeologists found scores of skeletons of sacrificial victims. These were all young to older adult males with injuries, both healed and perimortem, consistent with highly violent, combat-related careers. They were probably warriors, many of whom had been maimed, then killed and left to decompose in the complex, not unlike what is depicted in the sacrificial practices shown in Moche art (Bourget 2001; Verano 2001). Cut marks, puncture wounds, fracture patterns and the location of skeletal elements also stress particularly grisly practices of homicide (e.g., major blows to head, slitting of throats) and perimortem trauma (e.g., flaying, dismemberment, binding of limbs). The victims, it seems, were blood sacrifices for fertility purposes, and the build-up of skeletons derived from a long-lived pattern of human sacrifices practiced over many centuries.

The mtDNA work done thus far is not inconsistent with a model of segmented political systems headed by elite lineages. At least one sample (of burials at Sipán) suggests an endogamous elite collective related maternally (Shimada et al. 2008: 186). Samples from elite burials and from Moche sacrificial victims from Huaca de la Luna showed a great degree of genetic homogeneity. This would suggest the two groups were, first, probably from the same valley and not ethnic highlanders, and, secondly, were probably from the same or similar breeding population (Shimada et al. 2008; Shimada et al. 2005; Shinoda et al. 2002). In effect, the sacrificers and the sacrificial victims were genetically very similar, probably from the same community and/or from groups who exchanged marriage partners, especially wives. In general, groups across the Moche, Chicama and even Santa valleys had very similar mtDNA signatures: one biological population apparently shared by Moche and Gallinazo communities with different material styles (Shimada et al. 2008: 188).

Somewhat different, if complementary, findings resulted from the study of dental traits, also including a sample from the Moche sacrificial victims from Huaca de la Luna. The analyses indicate that the victims were of non-local origin, probably war captives taken during military incursions with competing polities from nearby areas as well as more distant coastal valleys (Sutter and Cortez 2005; Sutter and Verano 2007). A similar finding resulted for a sample of bound male victims at Pacatnamú (Verano and DeNiro 1993).[17]

A complex picture therefore emerges that has Moche regularly practicing human sacrifice over a long period of time in key civic-ceremonial buildings. Also, the victims were probably male warriors; and there is reason to believe that the victims may have been drawn from both local and foreign populations. The pool of local captives also included people of high status, not so far removed from those who were buried in the main ceremonial complexes.

New patterns are also emerging to more fully discern the kinds of predation for the different cultures of the first millennium AD. The geographic origins of trophy heads, for example, are being investigated through bone chemistry. Basically, the technique is premised on the fact that people from different regions have different bone chemistries. Nasca trophy heads were likely acquired from the same local populations, with no strong morphological evidence or material associations to believe they had different cultural identities or geographic origins (Knudson et al. 2009: 253). It remains unclear whether all these were the victims of internecine warfare or heads taken more generally from local people. It also shows the general insularity of Nasca groups.

Meanwhile, Wari trophy heads, found at the site of Conchopata, show greater variability than people buried at the site. The pattern indicates that trophy heads were acquired from groups with many different geographic origins, while mainly locals were found buried at the site (Tung and Knudson 2008).

That both insiders and outsiders may have been victims of ritual violence need not be surprising in the public spectacles of highly militarized societies, Precolumbian or contemporary. The Aztecs and Teotihuacanos also drew their sacrificial victims from both local and provincial populations, from those who participated in wars of aggression, violent engagements for captive exchange, and from people who had lived locally for a good portion of their lives (Carrasco 1999; Hassig 1988; White et al. 2007; White, et al. 2002). Various societies, of course, discipline their own others in highly ritualized settings, whether we take the circumstance as state-sponsored punishment or community level mob justice. Since the late nineteenth century, the more spectacular forms of discipline have taken a back seat to less public forms of incarceration and capital punishment (Foucault 1977; Masur 1989).

By the same token, the rationale and symbolism of Amerindian sacrifice turn on the notion of enemy alters being acquired from the outside, and being brought in and internalized. Thus enemies, as well as game animals and affines, occupy liminal, ambiguous terrain. Sacrificial victims may have been from or lived in the same community, but it is likely they were somehow deemed outsiders when they were dispatched.

Animal representations, relations and meanings

The value of animals in Early Intermediate Period art, often entangled with the practice and cosmology of predation, cannot be understated. Lévi-Strauss's much cited observation about animals deserves to be revisited:

> [T]heir perceptible reality permits the embodiment of ideas and relations conceived by speculative thought on the basis of empirical observations. We can understand, too, that natural species are chosen not because they are 'good to eat' but because they are 'good to think'.
>
> *Claude Lévi-Strauss,* Totemism *(1963b: 89)*

Animals are 'good to think' because humans often find parallels in their behavior and ascribe to them certain kinds of practice and human-like intentionalities that make sense to us. They organize into communities, do things together, communicate through sounds and gestures, eat and reproduce, and like to be independent but also return to their homes to raise their young. In this way, animals are significant inspirations; they provide the stuff, physical and cognitive, for reckoning and embodying *differences* in human cultures (e.g., names, myths, clans, costumes, etc.). In providing the homologies of social life that humans sympathize with, animals are seen to feature similar ways of seeing and making their worlds (Descola 2006; Lévi-Strauss 1966: 204; Viveiros de Castro 1998).

The scholar Elizabeth Benson (1997: 21) wrote generally about the significance of animals in the ancient Americas: 'Knowing how people perceive and relate to animals is a way of understanding people, especially about the beliefs and customs of people, who for the most part, lacked writing. Much of the symbolism depends on the animal's behavior.' I want to focus on one of the ways that animals are understood in the world, and specifically their roles in relations of predation – in a few words, of killing and being killed. That animals are often game for human hunting has already been mentioned, but it is also true that animals are themselves hunters. They have many skills that are of special use when hunting, or when preying on others: seeing in the dark, flight, stealth, speed and hearing. The skills are at once remarkable and superhuman, in the sense of being beyond the ken and general capacities of humans.

Animals sometimes reverse the roles of being predators and prey animals. Like humans, they prey on others but, importantly, are also preyed upon by others. And in this way, they are similar to humans: their actions and behaviors are prototypes and comparisons for humans.

I will focus especially on outward appearances, especially on what their corporeal exterior looks like and what it physically does. Of course, there are beings that appear more mythical than others and it is never certain whether more naturalistic depictions are of a 'natural' world or of a mythical world. There are also many cases where mythical hybrid beings are shown. For the moment, that is not so important to me as what certain forms do with other beings in predatorial contexts. What is crucial, I suggest, is actually a fairly predictable set of physical actions, or relations, with other beings.

I will provide a broad-brush breakdown of the general types of predatorial actions that beings of certain forms have with other beings of certain forms. My categories basically describe how certain beings predate on other beings: they hunt, take and eat them. Humans are involved. Different animals (basically taken to mean beings with zoomorphic forms) are sometimes involved. But, crucially, many animals which we know were or might be seen as potentially edible, stalkable or otherwise desirable for acquisition (e.g., viscachas, rabbits, rodents, bears, parrots, etc.) are not represented or show up surprisingly little.

It is worth noting that not all creatures in the animal world hold the status of predator or prey. Only some do (see Peters 1991: 258–59; see also Viveiros de Castro 2004: 470). For all three cultures, some animals are represented in the art, and of this sample, only a very small percentage of the potential bestiary regularly features. Only some enter into predatorial relations with humans. Some never do, but interact with other predators. Some feature always as prey. Meanwhile, humans occupy all manner of perspectives, from being predators to being prey.

What is predictable is that the animals which are given emphasis might be said to occupy multiple perspectives or points of view. Crucially, they are points of view that humans sometimes also occupy or actively covet. Only some beings feature the capacity, usually great predators and the principal species of prey for humans. First, the animals usually are those able to 'occupy a point of view', and, second, sometimes have the capacity to take the point of view of another. I take this as a meaningful step in a new ordering of social relations between humans, nonhumans and spirits that moves beyond nature/culture or secular/religious dichotomies. What I want to look at more carefully is how the forms of these beings relate to their capacities to interact with other social beings (see Table 4.1).

In addition to the triumph of certain humans over other humans, the representation of predation in art imagery features three other overt modes: humans predating on animals, animals predating on humans and animals predating on other animals.

Recuay is appropriate to begin this section, in large part because its artisans depicted these three modes in perhaps the most straightforward fashion of the three cultures under discussion. Nasca and Moche have greater diversity in the creatures represented, but they also represented animals more human-like, and some humans more animal-like.

Recuay art also emphasized a range of animals and humans engaged in predatorial relations. But it is configured very differently, compared to Nasca or Moche. Also, in

TABLE 4.1 Local animals in Recuay

	As predator (eats)	As predator (takes)	As game animal (is eaten)	As game animal (is taken)	As game animal (trophy is worn)
Deer	Never	No	No	Yes	Yes (antler)
Feline (pumas, mountain cats)	Yes (humans)	Yes (humans)	No	Yes (by humans)	Yes (paws, head, skin)
Serpent	Yes (eats humans, felines)	No	No	No	Yes (body)
Condor	Yes (humans)	Yes	No	No	Yes, on headdresses
Owl	No	No	No	No	Yes, on headdresses
Human	Never shown eating others	Yes (other humans)	Yes (by felines, birds)	Yes (by felines)	Yes, trophy heads and hands
Camelids	No	No	Maybe (seen associated with sacrifice)	Never seen hunted	No

Recuay art, consumption and taking are the primary modes or acts of predation, rather than killing or disabling.

Its imagery emphasized certain predators: felines (pumas and mountain cats), raptors and serpents (Hohmann 2010; Makowski 2000; Makowski and Rucabado Yong 2000). The main birds are condors, owls and perhaps hawks. There are also animal predators that cannot be identified specifically, but appear to be carnivorous mammals, probably felines or canines. Deer, in Recuay art, are game animals, and other common creatures include dogs, camelids, ducks and certain types of birds. This latter group might be best described as 'domesticated', familiar animals. Birds, for whatever reason, are rarely shown hunted, killed or eaten, but they are often seen on the tops of houses and as parts of headdresses. Other animals which do not appear to occupy prey statuses include amphibian figures.

Humans rarely fight one another. There are only a few images of decapitation (e.g., Makowski and Rucabado Yong 2000: 198). But certain persons, usually warriors and leaders, often wear anthropomorphic trophy heads. These adorn headdresses and pectorals or are clutched in the hands. They also feature on or in bags slung over the back or on the side. Headdresses often feature trophy hands or representations of hands.

Acts of human predation on animals, on the other hand, are much more common. These include an unusual stone sculpture of depiction of humans in the act of capturing or clubbing felines (Fig 4.7). More commonly, stone sculptures depict what has been referred to as the 'central figure' theme (Lau 2002, 2006b). The design centers on a male figure, shown frontally. The male figure often features accoutrements of a successful warrior or chief: weapons, trophies and an elaborate headdress.

He is flanked by a pair of creatures. Most often these are rampant felines on a stone sculpture (Plate 15A, B, C). The paired figures are never identical and occupy flip sides, as in split representation. Like many other parts of the world where such designs existed, the central male is seen as commanding or mediating between them, what art historian Terence Grieder (1992) said marked an 'ideology of authority'. This is especially apt, because the intervention of the central figure seems to call attention to the obeisance of the figures, but also sometimes their physical transformation (Lau 2011: 237–38).

FIGURE 4.7 Recuay horizontal slab sculpture, showing in profile male felines and humans with clubs, perhaps a hunting scene. The humans hold clubs with both hands. Originally found in the Huaraz area, the sculpture is now lost (photo courtesy of Donald Proulx).

Peruvian scholar Rebeca Carrión Cachot (1959) noted that the central figure theme is also very common in post-Formative cultures of northern and central Peru. In Recuay ceramics, the central male figure often takes the form of the vessel: his body doubles as the vessel body. Notably, ceramic representations frequently substitute out the feline creatures in favor of other beings, including serpents, serpent-felines, birds and women. The women often hold out objects for the main figure. No matter the physical form of the flanking figures, the overall figural arrangement emphasizes the centrality of the main figure and foregrounds his power to mediate others.

But this order, referring to cross-species interaction, is also seen reversed. Recuay ceramics and stonecarvings depict creatures who 'take' or predate on anthropomorphic figures (Plate 16). They hold the heads and bodies of humans, as if trophies and play-things (Fig 4.8). Most commonly, these are recognizably felines, foxes or scavenging mammals. Others show carrion birds, some with distinct head elements of vultures or condors (Plate 17). These animals pick on human heads and the innards of dead human bodies (Grieder 1978: 138, 148).

The meanings of these images are unclear. These may be related to notions of defleshing and to local Quechua oral traditions about the role of predatorial animals in transitioning the deceased into the afterlife (Walter 1997, 2002). The representations may also pertain to general notions about death, regardless of whether the cause was natural or anthropogenic, as being the result of homicide, whose agents can be human and

FIGURE 4.8 Recuay handled bowl. On the flanged edge are avians picking at human bodies. The moribund figure, perhaps a captive, features closed eyes, turned head and the suggestion of genitals, while the bird firmly grasps the flanged edge with the talons. Caraz collection.

nonhuman (Taylor 1996: 202). Thus the animals who 'take' the corpse, are the person's symbolic killers – agents of the process of death.

But they might also relate to themes of human sacrifice and treatment of captives during the Early Intermediate Period. The Recuay shared two unusual themes with Moche ceramic artists in this regard. First, both styles portrayed birds picking at the bodies of fallen humans. And, at least with Moche, actual remains of carrion birds have been found associated with mutilated victims, all young males who were probably war captives or criminals (Rea 1986; Verano 1986). The other theme concerns a bird drinking from a ring-based vessel, a bowl or goblet (Wegner 2011). For Moche, at least, the subject of the 'bird with a bowl' emerged during Moche phase IV and continued into phase V, and symbolizes the drinking of 'captive's blood' (Donnan and McClelland 1999: 136). The Moche avian figures appear to be raptors with long tail plumes; they are often speckled, crested across the head, and have two stripes below the eye (e.g., Donnan and McClelland 1999: 77, 136, 140), that feature similar elements found on ospreys or falcons (Koepcke 1983: 39, 42; Peters 1991: 267–68; Yacovleff 1932: 62–66). This design occurs only rarely in Recuay (Hohmann 2010: Appendix p. 22); in general, the bird and vessel are much less elaborated and distinctive.[18] Notwithstanding, while the representation of carrion birds might be perhaps seen as coincidental, there is less possibility of thematic convergence with a bird drinking from a ring-based bowl. Both Recuay and Moche share two fairly specific themes of what appear to be the post-mortem treatments of people defined by their alterity.

Recuay art features very little of the diversity of interspecies combinations seen among its contemporaries. The most common is the feline–serpent (e.g., Lau 2011: Fig. 56), which resembles the long lived concept/figure of *amaru* in the Central Andes (Urton 1996). There are also occasions, perhaps, of birds with feline maws, but Recuay art lacks the range of mythical animal–human hybrids seen in Moche, Nasca and Paracas art. Along the same lines, humans very rarely wear masks or show corporeal features (outside of headdresses) that transform them morphologically into distinct beings. This only holds for pottery figures, for effigies on stone sculptures have facial features resembling funerary masks (Lau 2008). And Recuay art does not seem to overtly stress 'ritual impersonators'. The entire complex of shamanic transformation, so popular in antecedent Chavín art, seems to have been muted in Recuay (Lau 2011: 237).

Interestingly, camelids are never shown hunted in Recuay culture. This would contrast with Nasca, for example, which shows humans actively stalking camelids, probably the wild varieties, guanaco and vicuña (Proulx 2006: 144). This is probably because the Recuay did not see camelids, especially ones already domesticated, necessarily as prey animals to be hunted.

Camelids are shown, however, as forms of gifts and sacrifices. One of the most distinctive genres of Recuay ceramic sculpture consists of ornately sculpted vessels that show a handsomely attired figure, typically a male, leading a camelid by a rope (Plate 13). The rope leads one to believe that the camelid comes from one of the domesticated varieties, llama or alpaca, that are bred and kept, rather than hunted. The images do not show physical violence to the animal, but the moment of presentation *with* the male figure. The sacrifice of camelids was one of the most important offerings in the ceremony of highland groups: offering camelids was obligatory in festivals, burial rites, house buildings and dedications, etc. It was the host's duty to provide and kill the camelid, and circulate the meat as festive generosity. Meat from herding complemented chicha from cultivation. In depicting the presentation of camelids in Recuay art, the theme concerns transactions between familiarized animals, or domestic camelids. Rather than being prey taken from the outside, camelids are animals already on the inside.

Predators in Nasca

Nasca artisans depicted a much greater range of animals than Recuay (Allen 1981a; Proulx 2006; Townsend 1985; Yacovleff 1932). Animal imagery featured especially on pottery and textiles. As symbolic expressions, these media provide a 'window' on Nasca society (Silverman and Proulx 2002). Whereas textiles were certainly important, drawing especially from antecedent styles such as Paracas, pottery became the hallmark medium for expression of predation in the Nasca tradition (Proulx 2006: 143; Silverman and Proulx 2002). Many of the creatures resemble those from earlier representational styles of the south coast, namely those associated with the Paracas style (Paul 1992; Peters 1991). The most important land predators included felines and foxes; those of the sea included killer whales and sharks; and the domain of the sky was lorded over by hawks and vultures.

Early south coast textiles also emphasize nonhuman predators. Ann Peters (1991: 249–51) has stressed that weavers highlighted predator animals at the top of their respective food chains and habitats: killer whales, sharks, fur seals and sea lions dominate the waters of the Pacific Ocean, while the condors, the pampas cats and foxes characterize the inland valley flanks that rise up into the highlands (Fig 4.9). One can find that apical predators have other animal substitutes, or 'succedanea', in the art, but which are frequently habitat-specific. A killer whale figure can be replaced by a shark, just as a condor can replace a falcon figure. Thus, in the pattern of 'substitution of animals with ecologically similar roles', she argues there are key positions that denote predator of the land, of the sea and of the air. The substitutability of like beings in formally similar positions resembles the interchangeability of flanking beings in the central figure theme in Recuay art.

Another important aspect of Nasca tradition imagery is the compositeness of some of the figural representations, where some figures bear human and nonhuman animal characteristics (Peters 1991; Proulx 2006; Roark 1965). This is a very common feature of Nasca imagery and its cosmology, but seems less marked in Moche and much less so in Recuay. Debate swirls over whether these represent ritual practitioners (i.e., shamans), supernaturals, masked-impersonators or embodiments of telluric and supernatural forces (Silverman and Proulx 2002: 137–40). At this time, it is premature to say that any one alternative is mutually exclusive; as we have seen with Recuay and Moche art, important figures seen as mythical have real-world presences. The reverse is also true: individuals (or their descendants) frequently strive to engage the supernatural, by taking on aspects of that divinity.

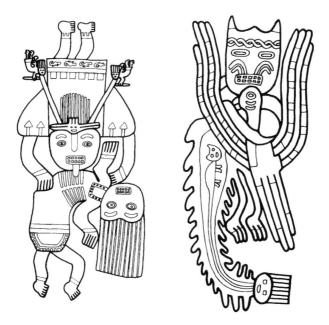

FIGURE 4.9 Designs on Paracas/Early Nasca textiles. The left image shows a winged anthropomorph grasping and 'tasting' another, while the right image shows a feline
creature holding a large avian (adapted from Peters 1991: 7.23, 7.84). Both physical
actions connote a predatorial disposition.

The compositeness of figures almost certainly relates to the funerary function of
much of early Nasca weavings as well as other objects that adorned mummy bundles –
the function being to celebrate the transformation of the deceased into divinities.
Besides the embroideries of composite beings, Peters (1991: 250) has noted that gold
masks (fashioned as whiskers) and diadems (depicting birds' heads and wings) 'transformed their wearers into images of the most powerful predators of the natural world
around them'.

Birds occasionally are shown with fish as well as small mammals in their mouths.
Various raptors, including falcons and ospreys, may have been favored as capable
predators, as mid-air bird killers and fishers, respectively, but curiously excluding owls
(Peters 1991: 267–70). Condors are also seen as predators, holding smaller animals
(usually small mammals – rodents, foxes and camelids), but are also depicted with
their beaks around naked human figures and trophy heads (Peters 1991: 271–72).
Felines frequently are shown 'embracing' birds, what can be seen to be their 'taking'
(see Peters 1991: Figs 7.22 and 7.23; Fig 4.9 this volume).

Nasca art depicted mythical beings with a core form with various traits identifying
an animal species or main figure, on which were then affixed features that differ-
entiate each as a variation of the being (or theme) (Proulx 2006; Silverman and
Proulx 2002). Among the most important are the 'Anthropomorphic Mythical
Being', 'Horrible Bird', 'Mythical Killer Whale' and 'Mythical Spotted Cat'.
Common additions, called 'signifiers' (Roark 1965), might include a mask, trophy

FIGURE 4.10 Nasca carved design on bottle gourd, showing masked and winged anthropomorph who holds a trophy head and weapons (adapted from Silverman 1993:
Fig. 19.22).

head, weapons and other diagnostic anatomical features of other creatures, which otherwise modify the figure's body. It might be surmised that these mythical beings, based
already on predator bodies, are thus given extras which express their alterity, but especially
their capacity to perceive and act purposefully as killers, like humans (Fig 4.10).

By comparison, domesticated creatures were less commonly represented. And
rarely are they subject to 'signifiers' that might concern their predatorial capacities.
This follows the artistic choices of other Andean cultures that favored non-local,
exotic animals associated with faraway lands (Miller and Burger 1995), socioeconomic
wealth (Lau 2011) or myth (Bourget 1994; Lavallée 1970). For example, crabs, sea
urchins, mollusks and guinea pigs form important parts of diet but only figure occasionally in Early Intermediate Period south coast art:

> The conspicuous scarcity of animals, plants and activities associated with human
> subsistence in Paracas Necropolis block color textile imagery is combined with
> an overwhelming emphasis on relations of predation in the natural world …
> Predators at the apex of the alimentary pyramids of the south central Andean
> coast are most frequently depicted.
>
> *(Peters 1991: 310)*

The artistic emphasis on animal predation in Nasca occurred alongside warfare-related
imagery, especially during the later phases of Nasca, by mid-millennium. There are
representations of warriors (Fig 4.11), representations of combat (discussed earlier), as well
as standalone male figures, probably warrior-chiefs, without explicit allusion to mythical
animality (Roark 1965; Silverman and Proulx 2002: 135, 149). As in Recuay and Moche,

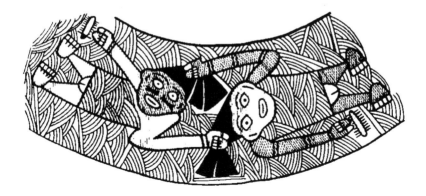

FIGURE 4.11 Nasca image of fighting warriors, showing their dual predicament of capture and suspension in a spider web (adapted from Proulx 2006: Fig. 5.119).

the use of predation imagery in Nasca was part of a growing social emphasis on militarism more generally, and especially ideologies based on successful warrior leaders.

'Taster figures' are also frequently represented. With their tongues, tasters orally engage something else important as a form of predation. Peters (1991: 305–7) has observed how the figures at the end of appendages emanate from primary figures: they form a hierarchical arrangement, linked to the vitality of exuviae and action originating in the primary figure.

In Nasca and Paracas, the pampas cat and the fox seem to have been important for the kinds of orientations and comportments they share with humans. In particular, all are primarily land predators and eaters of other animals. It is notable that certain anthropomorphic figures wear the skins of felines and objects of other predators (Paul 1990: 43; Proulx 2006: 122). Deer were not nearly as important as hunted prey for the Nasca (Proulx 2006: 147). The parts of these other beings – through impersonation or simply association – were important for transferring desirable capacities of the creatures:

> The animals shown … could be considered their competitors or their collaborators in killing pests … A parallel seems to be drawn between human beings and the predators of the natural world. Those predators are given the dress, the tools, and the status symbols of human beings, and human figures dress in the wings or whiskers of the local lords of the animal world. A strong analogy is made between the senior men buried with numerous and elaborate textiles and those predators who are able to move among the realms of land, sea and air.
>
> *(Peters 1991: 310)*

Deer are occasionally depicted on Nasca textiles (Peters 1991: 278), but their skins were important as wrapping material for the bundle. Finally, human beings also feature as prey beings. Parts of them appear as trophy heads, and sometimes they occur as the prey/objects taken by larger figures (Fig 4.12).

FIGURE 4.12 Nasca predator imagery, showing killer whale with severed head (top) and large avian (below) with a severed leg, probably a condor (adapted from Proulx 2006: Figs 5.46, 5.116).

In short, south coast predation imagery of the Early Intermediate Period stresses the taking from other beings. By carefully observing human and nonhuman beings, they focused with great acuity on the behavioral and formal characteristics of creatures and represented them in art. Elements from other beings were especially important for constructing and re-presenting other composite beings, including persons manifesting as bundles and hybrid anthropomorphic images.

Ambivalent animals in Moche and other styles

I wish to turn now to Moche art, which, like Nasca shows a tremendous diversity of animal types. I will emphasize those species most commonly depicted as prey (e.g., deer, sea lions, foxes, raptors) and then I will explore the ambivalent imagery of felines.

There are certain depictions of human–animal and animal–animal actions that are rarely shown in either Nasca or Recuay. For example, seldom do animals hunt or fight others in Nasca or Recuay art. In Moche styles, however, artists often anthropomorphized animals and transformed them into warriors with weapons and warrior attire (Donnan and McClelland 1999: Fig. 4.66). These figures might be in the physical action of running or fighting. The best known forms consisted of fox and deer warriors, but other species find representation as well: sea lions, monkeys, marine and riverine invertebrates, and birds.

In Moche art, humans hunt a limited array of game species: deer, sea lions and birds (apparently, raptors). Deer were especially popular as game animals (Donnan and McClelland 1999: 121). They were hunted with the help of dogs, and were either bludgeoned with clubs, shot with spears and darts, and/or trapped via nets and then dispatched. Foxes were perhaps trapped using nets as well (Kutscher 1983: Abb. 68). The Moche are also shown collecting land snails and fishing with lines and nets. Curiously, some who are shown with warrior capacities, such as foxes, monkeys and (Muscovy) ducks, are not portrayed as being hunted.

Compared to Recuay, Moche artists gave much more emphasis to the predation imagery of octopi and spiders. Both are skilled predators who use their limbs to snare, bind and then overcome their victims. They are solitary hunters of great speed, who make a decisive kill for subsequent consumption. They are also predators who eat other predators and harmful animals. For example, most octopi prey on other marine invertebrates (crabs, lobsters and other shellfish); but certain species can also catch fish, even sharks. Spiders, meanwhile, consume insects, many of which are pests to crops and humans. The emphasis on spiders in Moche art drew from earlier Cupisnique precedents (Cordy-Collins 1992; Salazar-Burger and Burger 1982). This antecedent imagery featured on stone bowls and ceramics, where spider decapitator figures are seen with knives and holding severed heads.

Spiders are quintessential predators with a rich symbolism of behavior that the Moche found useful for their religious ideology (Alva Meneses 2008). These may be related to the morphological and behavioral characteristics of certain spider species on the north coast.[19] The animal provided unique models for authority and social relations. Spiders are predators who catch victims through a web, in which they are central and isolated; not only do they protect against insect pests, they also have associations with divination, rains and agricultural fertility (see Salazar-Burger and Burger 1982). Donald Proulx (2006: 114–15) has suggested the depiction of humans ensnared on webs, sometimes suspended or in the act of fighting, may allude to the capture of humans through predation for sacrifice.

It is not coincidental that references to animal/predatory others are fundamental to the Moche 'Sacrifice Ceremony' (Donnan and McClelland 1999). In the depiction, whose practices are embodied in real life by Moche dignitaries, the major officiants have animal associations, which characteristically have reptilian, feline and raptor features (Fig 4.13). These part-human, part-animal attendants cut the throats of captives, then catch and bring their blood to the fanged Warrior-Priest. In other words, these fierce predators feed the top predator, the high Moche lord.

Certain animals in Moche art were ambivalent creatures. Some species are depicted as prey, but they are also depicted as warriors and predators. In particular, felines, certain birds and deer occupy multiple positions in the predator–prey relationship. Sometimes they are seen fighting and/or hunting; sometimes they themselves are being hunted, in subordinated positions (Donnan and McClelland 1999: 122–23). Prey species are also sometimes depicted as anthropomorphic warriors and killers (holding knives) (Donnan and McClelland 1999: 135).[20]

FIGURE 4.13 Moche rollout drawing of 'Sacrifice Ceremony' (adapted from Kutscher 1983: Abb. 304). The main protagonists of the image (except the neutralized captive) have predatorial animal features, and help bring blood nourishment to the main lord, carrying a head effigy club.

FIGURE 4.14 Moche fineline image of deer hunting, with nets and spearthrown darts (adapted from Kutscher 1983: Abb. 81).

In Moche art, the notion of changing statuses applies especially to depictions of deer and humans. As we have seen already, deer were a favorite topic of hunting imagery, and deer are the most common sort of animal hunted in Moche imagery (Donnan 1982, 1997) (Figs. 2.4, 4.14). The Moche had very conventionalized ways of depicting hunted deer. Both females and male deer were hunted. Deer very frequently are shown with antlers as well as their sexual organs. They also often feature spots and other distinctive markings across their bodies. They have mouths wide open with tongues dangling from their jaws, as if exhausted or dying (Donnan 1997: 54). When downed or killed, deer are shown with open mouths, rope ties, the exposure of sexual organs and face and body painting with spots. All these appear to make equivalencies between deer and enemies as game animals (Donnan 1982, 1997).

It is notable that deer warriors are also represented as captives, suggesting that captured enemies were associated with deer. This would suggest that deer and enemies were seen as prey animals, and that combat was like hunting (Donnan 1997). One telling commonality concerns the physical action. The Moche depicted deer being gathered and trapped in nets, and then downed by spearthrown darts and bludgeoned with clubs.[21] Enemies are, likewise, usually disabled by clubs, and scenes of combat and processions occasionally feature nets. At the same time that combat and deer hunting were seen as group activities (working in packs, cooperatively), a pair of enemies squaring off essentially replicates the behavior of rutting bucks – competition for superiority.

Sometimes deer are seen fighting with anthropomorphized beans, and shown as warriors, apparently indicating a contrast between kinds of resources: meat and cultigen. It also stands as a complementary opposition between the subsistence economies: one element produced through agriculture, the other element the hard-won objective of hunting. Deer, of course, are also detested pests for ravaging the fields of farmers. Yet it is curious to find the qualities of deer compared to those of warriors. Deer are not known for their ferocity, usually run away from confrontation, and do not fight back, nor are they known for their smarts. It is true that hunting deer is an elite, often royal, activity, seen as privileged sport or having ritual significance around the world (e.g., in Europe, India, Australia, Andes). But they are not common models for warriorhood in the native Americas.

One distinctive quality of deer is that they can be taken, tamed and habituated to live with people. By transforming into 'pets', they relinquish their own agency and become reliant on their captor-owners. This rapport stresses their violent subordination, for captive deer warriors were often depicted the same way as captive warriors: bound by the wrists behind the back, stripped with genitals bared, and sitting cross-legged. In short, like human captives, deer are seen to be familiarized, taking on a new 'insider' perspective, if only temporarily.[22]

Monkeys were perhaps conceived as cognate sorts of beings (pets, warriors and victims) in the Nasca culture. Monkeys were certainly important in Nasca pottery but also as stand-alones in other media, such as geoglyphs. They are depicted as naturalistic creatures but also as mythical figures, part human and part monkey (Proulx 2006: 98–101, 142–43). Monkeys were primarily pets in Nasca culture, and coastal Peru more generally, and probably imported from lowland regions (Proulx 2006: 143). Notably, some monkey representations are portrayed with weapons and in battle with more human warriors; monkeys are also sometimes shown decapitated.

The rich imagination of captives as subjects was not limited to Moche imagery. It informs directly on the practices of human sacrifice and mimetic representations at

Huaca de la Luna discussed earlier. In particular, clay effigies of captives were intentionally destroyed in deposits that also contained sacrificial victims (Bourget 2001: 96ff.; Donnan 2004: 137–39; Verano 2008a: 202–3). It has been suggested that the effigies represent the victims in some way. If so, the images may have been to document the transformative statuses of prisoners (alternating between enemies and domestic captives), which are somehow useful to the captors during their captivity. They apparently lost their use and were destroyed at the same time that the captives were killed.

It should be mentioned that skeletal analysis indicates that Moche sacrificial victims were not always killed outright; many seem to have survived injuries and must have resided in the captor region for some time before they were sacrificed (also Verano 1986: 132–33, 2001: 120). This extended period of 'familiarizing' encounter seems to have been the main difference between Moche predation, and those of the Nasca and Recuay. The Moche extended the timing and process of predation, making expressions of predations at once more prolific, public and monumental. This would explain the multiple images of captives as well as the great emphasis in their mimesis across various media. Making recurring acts of predation on their enemies allowed time and opportunity for various audiences to witness the emergent alterities of captors and captives, which allows the 'multiplication of the acts of predation' (Fausto 2000: 947). In optimizing every last opportunity with the captives, the Moche reinforced the kinds of group enmities and boundaries that sustained the warfare practice and public ideologies of theocratic elites in urban contexts (Carrasco 1999; Swenson 2003).

Notably, in Moche art, the presentation of foodstuffs or tribute to the lord resembles the presentation of prisoners in the sacrifice ceremony scene, where a lord is presented with a goblet of blood taken from prisoners who have their throats cut. Some containers of foodstuffs include paired gourd halves and jars have legs and walk toward the seated lord. While the gourd halves have food inside and are tied together with a cord, some jars are tied around the neck, just like captives, and pour out their contents into bowls, literally giving of themselves (Donnan and McClelland 1999: 113). These are sacrifices of a different kind, but both make the explicit argument that lordly figures are gifted the vitality/sustenance of subordinate things (prey). When embodied containers are emptied, they are also deliberately broken or killed, and abandoned.

The Recuay also depicted, with great interest, the ambivalent qualities of certain animals. Felines had especially rich roles in ancient imagery. To be sure, they were markers of high status, and often the symbols of rank and leadership position. In the central figure scene, two profile figures stand on either side of a central male anthropomorph, a figure I take to be a generalized reference to local chiefly leaders taken as ancestors. The skins and body parts of felines were also actively appropriated for use on clothing, as well as general representation on Recuay imagery. Feral cats (e.g., pumas, tigers, jaguars) also occasionally 'tolerate' new masters, at least for a while – but they do not seem to have been favored for sacrifice representations, for whatever reason. Notably, both Moche and Recuay artisans sometimes showed felines as pets (Donnan 1978: Fig. 140), where they luxuriate as companions of human lords (Plate 18, Fig 4.15). These artworks stressed the importance of feline meanings as symbolic assets (taken from the felines) that enhanced the human person.

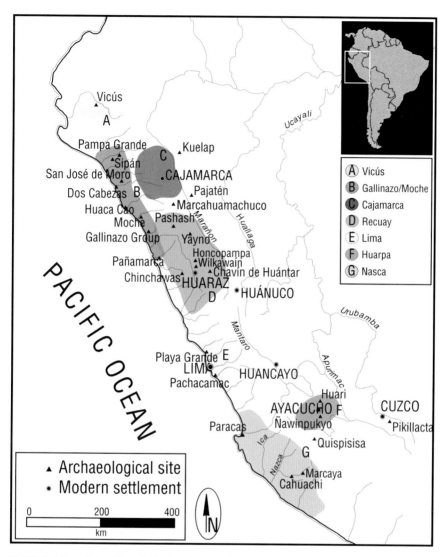

PLATE 1 Map of the Central Andes, showing location of major Early Intermediate Period cultures dating to the first millennium AD.

PLATE 2 Photo of Peru's lower valley, Nepeña (coast). Coastal groups farmed fields in the floodplains using irrigation canals for waters descending from the Andes mountains.

PLATE 3 Photo of Nevado Huantsán and the Quebrada Rajucolta, in the Cordillera Blanca. Wide glacier-cut valleys are prime areas for pasturing herds. The meltwater from the snowcaps flows down toward the Pacific Ocean. Andean peoples considered some nevados as ancestral instantiations.

PLATE 4 Fortified settlement, Yanamayo drainage, Ancash. By the beginning of the Early Intermediate Period, many settlements across northern Peru began to emphasize fortifications and hard-to-access locations, suggesting a strong concern for protection and defense. A massive semi-circular enclosure measuring ca. 50 meters across and tall terraces protect the hilltop and create a layer cake effect; all other sides are flanked naturally by cliffs.

PLATE 5 Moche effigy vessel, representation of a warrior. The hair forelock, face painting and ear tubes are characteristic of enemy captives in Moche art. He chews a cud of coca in his right cheek. UK collection.

PLATE 6 Middle Horizon style vessel from the Callejón de Huaylas, excavated in the chullpa sector of Ichik Wilkawaín. The seated position, mace in the right hand and left-handed shield are typical of the earlier Recuay practice of depicting ancestors, as are the headdress with upturned trophy hand objects and wad of coca in his right cheek. But the red slip, eye modeling and the polychrome bands are Wari stylistic influences. Photo courtesy of Juan Paredes.

PLATE 7 Deep Recuay bowl with short tube spout, with interior designs. Each of the designs is reminiscent of the frontal face motif in Recuay art: having a central round element, out of which emerge appendages. Frontal faces are also important in Cajamarca pottery and sculpture. Pomabamba collection.

PLATE 8 A, B Front and side views of Recuay vessel, showing Janus-figure woman, holding infant and bowl. The female head is covered by a shawl, fastened with nail-headed pins, and is complemented by a male (?) head, facing the spout. The figure wears a garment covered with red geometric designs, including triangular feline-serpent heads. Parental feeding and nurturing of children are fundamental to a 'moral economy of intimacy'. Chacas collection.

PLATE 9 Recuay double-chambered vessel, showing two seated anthropomorphic figures, eating or perhaps chewing coca. Pomabamba collection.

PLATE 10 Recuay ceramic vessel, showing ceremonial activity, likely a form of ancestor veneration, in front of a (funerary?) building. Three women in shawls present cups to a male personage, also holding a vessel. The designs on the building resemble those of stone sculptures found in the Recuay heartland. Lima collection.

PLATE 11 Recuay ceramic vessel, showing a circle of embracing women dancing around a male personage, who holds a cup in his right hand and mace on the left. The vessel was part of the burial furniture revealed in a funerary platform located directly across the Mosna river (La Banda zone) from the Chavín de Huántar temples (Museo Arqueológico de Ancash, Huarez collection).

PLATE 12 Recuay ceramic jar, showing a female effigy carrying a vessel strapped around her head. Recuay art strongly emphasized that the brewing and distribution of chicha maize beer were important activities of women. Camelid rearing and sacrifice were common responsibilities of men. Scale units = 1cm. Jancu collection, Huaraz.

PLATE 13 Recuay ceramic vessel, showing a man with a camelid, holding a club and shield. Camelids were important sources of wealth and prestige for Recuay groups during the Early Intermediate Period. Chacas collection.

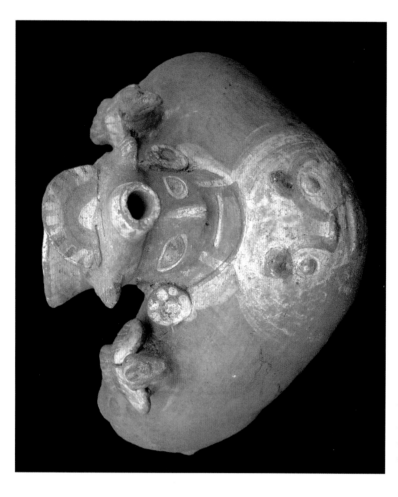

PLATE 14 Recuay ceramic vessel, chiefly effigy. Note the spout issuing from the main figure's head and two flanking condors. The figure wears a pectoral ornament in the feline form around his neck. Similar forms show the body as a severed leg, on which the carrion birds feed and out of which grows the chiefly (ancestral) head. Pamparomas collection (photo courtesy of Kevin Lane).

PLATE 15 A, B, C Carved horizontal slab sculptures at Chinchawas, ca. AD 600. All three sculptures would have adorned important buildings. Each shows a variation of the central figure theme, in which a frontal figure, usually explicitly male, is flanked by two male feline figures.

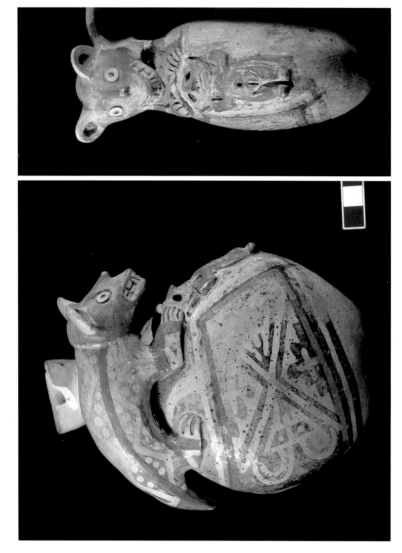

PLATE 16 Recuay double chambered bottle, showing a feline or canine creature grasping the dying body of a woman. Scale units = 1cm. Jancu collection, Huaraz.

PLATE 17 Recuay stone slab sculpture, showing three birds, probably condors, picking at a bodiless human head, from the site of Pashash. Cabana collection.

PLATE 18 During the Early Intermediate Period, certain persons become both like predators and masters of animal predators. Vessel representing a seated ruler with pampas cat, Moche North coast, Peru, AD 250–550, ceramic and pigment, 19.4 × 19.1 cm, Kate S. Buckingham Endowment, 1955.2281, the Art Institute of Chicago.

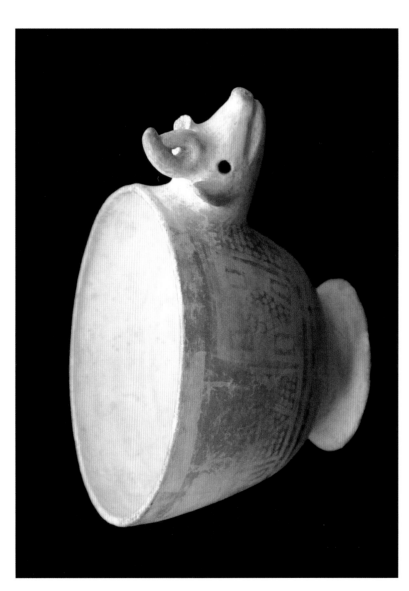

PLATE 19 Recuay open bowl, with a modeled deer head adorno. Two-tined antlers are typical of huemul deer (*Hippocamelus antisensis*), a variety common to the mountainous regions of highland Ancash. Pomabamba collection.

PLATE 20 Large settlements with monumental structures were built throughout the Recuay world, on defensible high areas with good strategic vantages. The impressive tombs and high-status buildings of Pashash occupy a prominent spur of ridgetop (midground, right), near the modern town of Cabana (foreground).

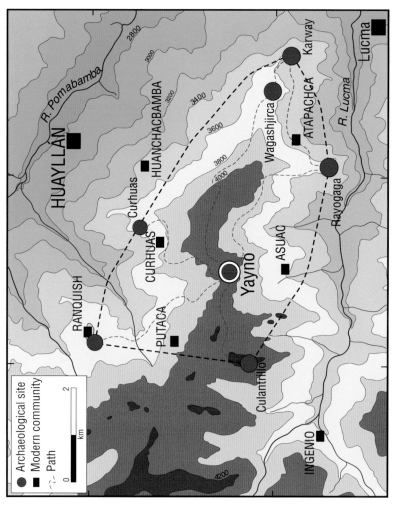

PLATE 21 Site cluster centered around Yayno, Ancash. Defensive villages, all on high ridgetops, ring the large monumental center.

PLATE 22 View from the top of Yayno site, 4,150 masl, overlooking high-walled residential compounds, quadrangular (left: c41 and c40) and circular (right: c50). In the background is the Cordillera Blanca, including the dual peaks of Huascarán (left), the tallest mountain in Peru (6,768 masl).

PLATE 23 Masonry stonework of c41, Yayno. The masonry uses thin uprights and carefully arranged chinking stones to make a veneer facing on either side of a mud/rock fill. The uprights employ dark limestones with white quartz streaks and granitic rocks, variably textured and colored through weathering. The patina includes red, orange and yellow.

PLATE 24 Maceheads from highland Ancash: left (cast copper metal, fluted cylinder); center and right (ground stone). Most Recuay weaponry was hand held and meant to bludgeon opponents. Private collection, Chacas and Caraz.

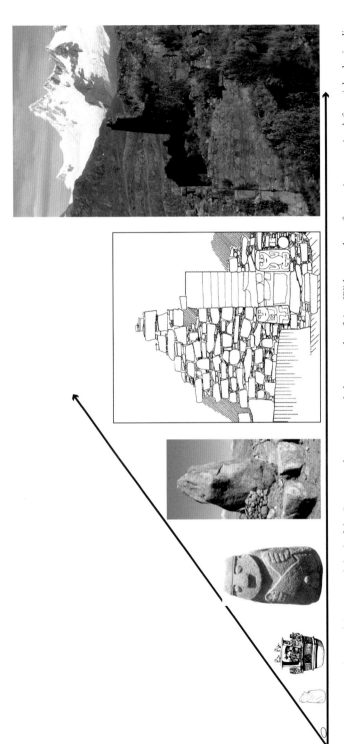

PLATE 25 Myriad forms of the ancestral dead of the Recuay culture, arranged along a scale of size. With a number of exceptions, moving left to right also implies greater genealogical distance, time from biological expiration and size of ritual community.

PLATE 26 Recuay polychrome ceramic vessel, from Jancu tomb, depicting avian. The eye stripes suggest a hawk-like raptor, rather than a condor. Jancu collection, Huaraz.

PLATE 27 Recuay ceramic heads, broken from effigy jars found at Pashash. Jars depicting similar chiefly personages were buried with the nobles of many Recuay groups throughout the north highlands. The location of the spouts connotes that the liquids issued from the chiefly figure, and more specifically, his head and body. Cabana collection.

PLATE 28 Ceramic effigy vessel, showing a portly figure with Wari-style four-cornered hat with hands tied behind the back. Wari people, apparently, were occasionally perceived as enemies, worthy of capture. Recovered from a chullpa tomb at Yarcok, Pierina mine area, near Huaraz. Scale units = 1cm. Photograph courtesy of Victor M. Ponte.

PLATE 29 Middle Horizon-style open bowl, with three modeled figures in the interior, excavated in the chullpa sector of Ichik Wilkawaín. Two are arranging a headdress for a seated figure, probably a mummy bundle or stone sculptural effigy of a bundle. The action was likely seen as a key moment in the installation or celebration of the ancestor. Photograph courtesy of Juan Paredes.

PLATE 30 Recuay sculpture of a mummy bundle. Besides the anthropomorphic imagery, many such sculptures are found in and around tombs and cemeteries. These stone uprights/monuments (huancas) were considered ancestors by historic Ancash groups. The flexed position and prominent genitals likely pertain to the bundle's association with (inchoate) renewal and fertility; it is also quite possible that such sculptures, carved in the round, may have been wrapped in fine cloth offerings. Museo Arqueológico de Ancash, Huaraz collection.

PLATE 31 Recuay architecture often incorporated burial spaces into settlement architecture. The image shows a defensive perimeter wall built directly atop a cave entrance, where bundles were kept, Yanamayo drainage. Ancestors may have been seen as foundational for the community, marking the place for living and being a source of protection.

PLATE 32 Recuay stone sculpture, cross-legged mummy effigy with warrior gear, including hand shield and club. His elaborate headdress features trophy hands (or representations), and on his left arm is a coca bag, with three fringes. Huaraz collection.

FIGURE 4.15 Recuay vessel, showing prone chiefly figure, flanked by profile felines, perhaps mountain cats (adapted from Carrión Cachot 1955: Lám. XVIIa). Note how the spouts issue from his body.

But the opposite is also true. Sometimes, birds, but especially felines, predate on humans; it is an appropriation or transaction from humans. Thus, felines hold them like pieces of meat and eat at their internal organs while the human bodies lie prone (Plate 16, Fig 3.6B–C). Notably, the stylized actions also feature in Moche art, where felines attack and bite at humans (Benson 1974). Even in the Recuay central figure scenes, feline–serpent heads emerge as appendages out of the headdress worn by the central male and appear to reference the act of consumption (Lau 2006b: 244–46) (Plate 15A, B, C, Fig 3.5). Of all the kinds of nonhuman beings, felines, most overtly, have this multivalent capacity to occupy multiple perspectives. They can be prey and pets, just as they can be predators and killers. But, for whatever reason, they are never shown as food.

★ ★ ★

In sum, Moche, Nasca and Recuay artisans valued the depiction of animals in their vibrant imagery. Many animals were favored because of their role in patterns of predation. Humans, as the ultimate predators (and also the ones telling the story), frequently engaged with animals as hunted prey and as pet subordinates. On the one hand, apical, nonhuman predators, such as felines, hawks and killer whales, were significant models for human warriors and groups of warriors (e.g., orders). They were celebrated perhaps because their killing behavior and talent in predation were enviable and to be patterned after; and their talents in predation might be seen as superhuman. Meanwhile, enemies and opponents were closely associated with game animals, and were hunted and captured using the same weapons and similar techniques. Some kinds of animals hold ambivalent statuses, often alternating between enemies and tamed beings; these resonate with the idea that outside beings are internalized by predating groups.

Good to eat (animals as predators and prey)

When Lévi-Strauss queried why animals were chosen for embodying important cognitive categories, his famous adage that animals were 'good to think' opposed the notion that animals were 'good to eat'. But, in fact, some animals are good to eat, just as some animals are good to think because they eat (others). Another way to get at the heart of Amerindian predatorial relations is through the mouth and stomach.

The analysis of faunal remains from archaeological sites provides important evidence to see how humans interacted with animals in the past. Faunal assemblages inform especially about the types of animals that people engaged with on an everyday basis, typically as food items. Other special contexts for human–animal contact can be discerned, such as the role of animals in postmortem corpse handling, offerings, as well as in burials (e.g., Donnan 1995; Rea 1986; Verano 1986).

It is common, however, to find that the faunal records are rarely consistent with the art imagery (Fig 4.16). What was good to represent rarely meshes completely

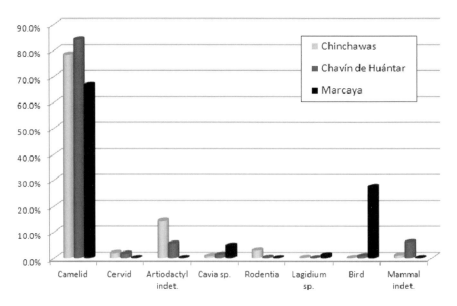

FIGURE 4.16 Summary of faunal assemblages from Chavín de Huántar, Chinchawas and Marcaya. Animals commonly represented in art imagery (predators, animals from far away and special sacrifices) rarely appear in the residential refuse of ancient communities. Most meat protein seems to have come from domestic camelids.

with what was good to eat or, more accurately, what was eaten. And even animals seen as prey, such as deer in Moche art, do not automatically equate to finding their remains in food refuse (M. Shimada, in Donnan 1997: Note 5).[23] In fact, we can say that, in the art styles of the Central Andes, food species, more often than not, had less priority than certain types of predatory carnivores that featured more heavily or were more elaborately theorized in artworks. When an Andean group portrayed an animal a lot, they did not usually see them as edible.

Like their contemporaries in Nasca and Moche, Recuay groups represented animals in their art imagery, and shared a number of cosmological views about their otherness. As we have seen, the principal animals in Recuay imagery consisted of pumas, mountain cats, condors, hawks, owls, snakes and other humans. These preferences resonated especially with chiefly male symbolism and certain nonhuman, ontological types associated with predation, virility and violence. It is notable that most of these are all recognizably highland creatures, beings that local peoples were probably familiar with and had seen directly. But these animals rarely show up in faunal assemblages and, to be sure, did not form part of the regular diet (Lau 2007).

There were a few species that were portrayed and consumed. In Recuay, we find that camelids, deer and guinea pigs made up the bulk of the animal meat contributions. Camelids show up regularly in the art, as do deer, but much less commonly (for abundance of representations, see Hohmann 2010: 7–8 (Vol. 2)). In terms of faunal assemblages, the few reports available show overwhelming representation by camelids. Most camelids were almost certainly domesticated llamas or alpacas, and reared for their meat and other products. And guinea pigs were probably raised locally at the household level.

So far as is known, neither camelids nor guinea pigs were much valorized for their body parts to be worn or displayed as trophies. They are not prey in the sense of being stalked, hunted and killed. Deer, however, were probably hunted in high grasslands or verdant intermontane valleys (Lau 2007). The Recuay hunted both white-tailed and huemul (or *taruka*) varieties (Plate 19); the dual tined antlers of the latter occasionally featured as headdress trophy adornments in pottery imagery and had ritual significance in later times. In terms of number, however, by far the most customary animal depicted in Recuay art was the feline. Serpents and raptors are ancillary. There is very little physical evidence, however, that humans interacted much with any of these species in quotidian life, and certainly not in food refuse assemblages.

We might compare the different ranges of animals seen in the art and in the faunal assemblages of the Chavín culture, the main culture in Ancash before the onset of the Recuay style (see Miller and Burger 1995). Chavín arts celebrated the distant exoticism and protean imagery of lowland animals and their symbolism. Harpy eagles, caymans and jaguars were paramount in Chavín imagery (Burger 1992a; Conklin and Quilter 2008; Lathrap 1974; Tello 1923). In general, the transition to Recuay culture, which developed in the same region following Chavín, featured similar emphasis on predation in artistic representation, but on the capture of local animals.

Much the same can be said of Moche and Nasca art, even despite the greater diversity of species represented. These cultures favored depicting animals that were native to their local environmental settings: the northern and southern Peruvian coasts and coastal valleys, respectively. Animals in the art are typically those indigenous to the Peruvian coast: deer, felines of different types, foxes and birds of the interior areas. Meanwhile, creatures of and by the sea include various forms of seabirds, fish and marine mammals (whales, sea lions, etc.) and invertebrates (octopus, shellfish, etc.). Even jaguars and monkeys probably found homes along the coast. Meanwhile, the general earlier emphasis on anacondas, harpy eagles and caymans – species found in Amazonia – was largely abandoned.

One of the last major essays by the influential archaeologist Donald Lathrap concerned the cosmological importance of jaws (Lathrap 1985). Focused on the emergence of political authority and 'Formative' societies, he argued that many of the early ceremonial complexes of ancient America were essentially conceived as great portals to a supernatural domain. They were seen as the giant maws of apical aquatic predators (e.g., caymans, killer whales, anacondas) who are also mythical providers (Lathrap 1985: 246). In this model, leaders acted as key mediators between places and people, for articulating with the supernatural. The anthropologist Mary Helms (1998: 52) has also suggested that the symbolic value of game animals and predators diverged with the intensification of food production and sedentism.

But one aspect that deserves further mention, in any discussion about jaws, is teeth. Not all jaws need be ferocious, nor can all jaws chew on and consume others without teeth. Mouths are important for feeding and eating, but what makes them important, to reach others, is their voice and bite.

For many ancient Andean cultures, including those of the Early Intermediate Period, teeth are important indicators of a killing, dangerous, ambiguous or predatory quality. Felines and foxes almost always show teeth. Sharks and killer whales are known for their teeth. Even fish, serpents, spiders and birds are sometimes represented with teeth. In northern Peruvian art styles, we understand the anthropomorphic figure to have a general predatorial disposition when that figure has interlocking teeth. Curiously, the Recuay rarely portrayed human figures with bared, snarling teeth. When they did, they feature on figures who are decapitators. Other teeth-baring figures in Early Intermediate Period art drink from sacrificial cups, who carry weapons, fight (others) or are associated with shamanistic transformations and other ritual activities, which are often deemed by Amerindian groups as a kind of predation (Fausto 2000). Teeth, it would seem, mark special beings who were seen as predators, who kill and consume other living beings.

Although predation imagery was emphasized long before, it takes a decidedly distinct tenor during the Early Intermediate Period. Animals in Chavín were exotic, heavily speculative creatures employed to reach out to those who were within and outside its heartland. By moving beyond the lived animal world, Chavín fashioned a naturalizing mythology to proselytize outsiders with an ideology based on predatory animals. Moche, Nasca and Recuay, meanwhile, all represented largely familiar creatures, feral as well as domestic, based on or native to their worlds. Of course, many of the creatures featured supernatural elements, but even those elements were grounded in local prototypes. Mythologizing the native and familiar had the effect of associating people to these creatures, thereby differentiating people internal to the society. Chavín colonized foreign animal worlds to internalize outsiders, while Early Intermediate Period groups embraced local animal models to naturalize hierarchical social relations.

In sum, the principal animal types that feature heavily in Early Intermediate Period cultures were rarely ever primary food animals, or those that were domesticated. The symbolic realms of Moche, Recuay and Nasca highlighted predators – animals and human alike who had status, in part, because they preyed on others. Only rarely in the cultures, do we see animals that are good to eat become particularly good to think. This is because the animals that were good to think – that is voracious predators – were precisely the ones that eat (others). The alimentary allusion thus emerges in alterity process – but unlike the forms of nourishment associated with domestic insiders, predatorial relations occasioned forms of consumption with the outside.

Conflict and predation in the archaeological record

Beyond imagery and contexts informed through imagery, the archaeological record for predation and interacting with enemy others is much less plentiful and rich. In this section, I want to review several kinds of evidence that can be related positively to how Andean groups during the Early Intermediate Period oriented interaction with ambiguous others. The first concerns settlement patterns and community arrangements centered on defense. The other concerns weaponry. Both of these sources of evidence are well-established in the literature, but rarely do they figure as forms which recognize alterity.

What I aim to show is twofold. First, the kinds of evidence resulting from purposeful ways that ancient groups interacted with social others. Second, it will be shown that remnant settlements and arms do not only demonstrate a physical concern with social others, but that they also recognize and seek to engage, at a cognitive level, their alterity. The interpretations here are not meant to be comprehensive as much as they are meant to serve as lines for further research on the topic.

Settlement patterns

Fortified sites and buildings are among the most basic and pervasive physical expressions of a regard of dangerous others. They address the common concern of safeguarding oneself, group and belongings from another. At their most basic, fortifications are to protect things and people within, while keeping unwanted agents out. They were to exclude enemies, but we should not rule out their potential utility for managing other sorts of beings. Animals and supernaturals can be guarded as well as kept at bay. Regardless, fortifications are *for* others: they seek to engage others in certain prescribed sorts of ways.

In the northern Peruvian Andes, fortified settlements have been a fairly common, indeed even predominant, settlement type since the late Early Horizon, or what is the last half of the first millennium AD. They never seemed to have been prominent in the south coast until after the Early Intermediate Period, so I will focus my discussion in the northern area.

In the Moche world, most settlements were established close to the rivercourses and/or areas where irrigation canals could extend (Kosok 1965). However, settlements were also on foothills and clustered in zones where the valley constricts, which were useful for controlling exchange routes, irrigation intakes and coast–highland traffic. These types of sites have been argued to protect lower valley areas from highland (ca. over 1500 meters above sea level) groups. Buffer zones and gateway communities mediated ambivalent relations between coastal and highland groups (Billman 1997; Daggett 1985; Dillehay 2001; Millaire 2008; Proulx 1982; Topic and Topic 1982, 1983; Wilson 1987).

Late in the Moche sequence, between AD 600 and 800, there was greater intensification of defensive projects, including large walls, protective enclosures and other buildings which suggest greater amounts of conflict with enemy groups. The waning of earlier demographic centers coincided with the development of extensive, nucleated settlements such as Galindo and Pampa Grande. With perimeter walls and a 'bottleneck' position, Galindo's architects certainly had an interest in protection against unruly neighbors. Both sites, however, show innovations in town planning, which sought to separate groups internal to the overall community, especially those common spaces versus more elite, restricted spaces (Bawden 1982; Lockard 2005; Shimada 1994). Thus the settlements emerged as the outcomes of at least two specific kinds of alterity. One concerned the fear of raiding enemies, presumably from upvalley locations. The other concerned the alterity of elites, leaders and other high-status members of society, who became increasingly distanced from commoners during the late Moche period.

Although Nasca frequently shows warrior imagery, Nasca groups do not seem to have emphasized defensive architecture or settlement patterns. There is little to suggest that Nasca warfare included large-scale engagements with the enemy, nor does it seem to have been for control of territories or political domination. Warfare may have intensified in later Nasca phases, when political groups competed for scarce agricultural land and water resources, as well as providing a source of victims for ritual decapitation, especially in later phases of the Nasca sequence. Settlement surveys in the Nasca region do not find much evidence for defensive sites or for fortifications (Proulx 2007; Schreiber and Lancho Rojas 1995; Silverman 2002a; Silverman and Proulx 2002: 235–36); this lack is especially marked for later developments given the intensification of warfare-related themes in late Nasca imagery (Proulx 2006; Roark 1965).

In contrast, the wide majority of Recuay occupation sites can be considered fortified hilltop settlements (Plate 20). This holds for villages, large regional centers and ceremonial sites, and this seems to have been the predominant pattern over time.[24]

The defensive features typifying Recuay and Moche sites were fairly similar, including trench/ditch systems, high perimeter walls, parapeted walls and high location with limited access (Arkush and Stanish 2005; Topic and Topic 1987). Buildings and walls were agglutinated to ring around areas and settlements, and innovative arrangements of buildings provided lines of defense against vulnerable areas (Lau 2010b). Recuay fortifications were not for securing borders or large regions; rather they seem to have safeguarded largely independent communities and, at most, special groups, of settlements.

Some Recuay sites formed clusters of hilltop villages which, in concert, protected a paramount settlement (see Lau 2010b; Redmond 1994: 29, 36, 55). For example, a series of four or five smaller villages afforded a ring of defense around the major center of Yayno (Plate 21). All are found lower down in elevation, within a few hours hike (down) from Yayno, and directly adjacent to pockets of arable lands. Today, footpaths converge at Yayno and it seems likely this may have followed prehispanic practice. The smaller villages themselves were defended by elevated, strategic ridgetop positions. Each village features multiple defensive features, including perimeter walls, walling in vulnerable spots (usually blocking gullies), restricted access, trenches and tightly packed residential compounds.

All this made for a highly defensible system with a paramount center at the top-most, central point. The Recuay groups, centered at Yayno, were therefore eco-nomically and ritually linked, but also likely cooperated against neighboring others during times of need. Moche defensive settlement patterns suggest that one major strategy concerned large basin-centric territories against ambivalent others. For the Recuay, their main concern was against other neighboring villages.

Recuay's most famous buildings are large structures bearing monumental façades and very elaborate stonemasory (Lau 2011). At Yayno, the best built buildings are walled residential compounds that alternate circular (max. diameter about 26 m) and quad-rangular layouts (max. 35 meters on a side); the largest compounds are multi-storey, having rooms built atop each on their outer wall (well over 10 meters tall) which faced into an open central courtyard area. Because of their domestic refuse and restricted access, it is surmised that these were residential complexes for many coexisting family and kin groups. It is notable that there is great variability in both forms: some are larger and much better made than others of the same class (Fig 4.17). Basically, there are a few monumental versions in each class – which are interpreted as the complexes of local elites. The reason for cohabitation and the fortifications was probably to protect from outsiders (that is, other villages and communities), while the high walls of every compound also served to create some buffer from people and factions internal to the settlement (Plate 22).

At other sites, such as Pashash, the monumental area features a series of large structures whose main example, the Caserón (or 'big house'), shows a formidable, unbroken wall façade, measuring over 15 meters in height and 30 meters across (Grieder 1978: 14). The corners feature especially large blocks, alternating the long and short sides. Tinyash, a Recuay-related site, features a large building, whose tall monumental façade is adorned with a row of light colored stone that rings around the enclosure like a halo.

Throughout the Recuay world the elaborate, cyclopean walls of monumental buildings must have impressed outsiders. This stands as another source of engagement with the perspective of others, to dazzle and inspire awe through monuments. All of

FIGURE 4.17 Reconstruction drawing of entrance and west façade of compound c24, Yayno (adapted from Tello 1929: Fig. 3).

the major buildings at Yayno are found within the zone delimited by the trenches, further reinforcing the impression of a formidable citadel atop a mountain. The finest stonework on all the major buildings at Yayno alternates large upright boulders (up to 2 meters tall/wide) of light colored granites and dark, white streaked limestones, all aligned to rows of descending size moving up the wall (Plate 23). Weathering on the granites gives them oxidized red and orange patinas and heightens the aesthetic effect.

Besides their defensive functions, some settlement arrangements and buildings are made to effect a gut response on the part of the visitor or enemy. Here the builders sought to effect awe, respect or trepidation in others. By the Middle Horizon and Late Intermediate Period, building extensive defensive architecture was still very common, but the connection with fine stonework (and its aesthetic of noble surfaces) seems to have been lost.

Weaponry

Weapons constituted another mode for engaging the other, both physically and cognitively. Early Intermediate Period groups had rather simple kinds of warfare technology when compared to coeval societies of Europe and Asia. There were no analogues to gunpowder, seige engines and elaborate armor; bladed weapons were never popular. Animals were not directly involved in combat, although camelids may have been used for carting equipment and supplies. At the same time that these were unnecessary, they were also likely ineffective in many parts of the Andes.

Despite very elaborate metal technologies, including strong alloys and casting, warrior equipment by and large employed weapons of stone and wood. The favorite kinds of weapons, and those that were apparently quite successful throughout Andean prehistory, were arms that did not weigh much, that were not contraptions that needed much preparation time, and that very likely could be used for other sorts of tasks (e.g., hunting, cutting, pounding, etc.). Weapons were handheld, eminently portable, and were *quick* to use. They slashed, punctured, broke and bludgeoned others. They often disabled enemies to be killed and predated upon later.

Heavy equipment and plunder, live and inert, are always burdensome in warfare. Transport for even small raiding parties might need to consider deserts, rocky ravines and steep gradients. A little of this emphasis might be implied in the art imagery of the Moche, where the *principal* activity of warriors was running and parading, not fighting.

In general, the weapons of Early Intermediate Period cultures indicate an emphasis on short-range, hand-to-hand combat. Clubs and maces were privileged in scenes of combat as well as being more frequent in the archaeological record. Both Moche and Recuay groups emphasized clubs and maces (Larco Hoyle 2001: 207–11; Quilter 2008). Recuay clubs are of two main types, those hafting a perforated stone (often biconical, star- or donut- and cloverleaf-shaped), and those which attach a copper-metal club head, cast into fluted cylinders (Plate 24). Unlike the war clubs of Moche (with conical ends used for jabbing strokes to stun and induce nosebleeds, and basal spikes for piercing), the Recuay ones seem to stress bludgeoning potential of the heavy end when swung, probably with one hand.[25] Shields were used. At least from the imagery, these seem to be single hand-held shields, rather than full-length body shields.

Projectile weapons are also known. Slingstones are common at many residential sites (Lau 2010b), and piles of slingstones characterize fortified settlements in Moche midvalley areas (Topic and Topic 1987). In Recuay hilltop sites, these are river-rolled stones (ca. 3–6 cm wide) and are distinct from typical, rough stones found on rocky hilltops. They were likely collected and brought up to hilltop sites for different purposes, one of which was certainly as projectiles delivered via a sling or thrown from the hand. Of course, most hilltops in the Andes have plentiful rocks to push over the slopes that can be just as dangerous to attackers downhill.

The Moche and Nasca also used knives and blowpipes (Donnan 1990; Proulx 2006). Nets, thrusting spears and atlatl darts (perhaps tipped with poison) are also depicted, often with long barbed points, and appear to be associated with hunting, especially of deer (Bourget 2001: 94; Donnan 1997: 57–58). These are rare for Recuay, although long weapons are sometimes shown in the imagery (Grieder 1978) and atlatl hooks have been found in highland Ancash (Lau 2010a: Fig. 136H).

Early Intermediate Period cultures therefore privileged face-to-face contests and direct physical triumph in their weaponry. Clubs and shields were preferred over long-distance weaponry and fighting methods. Most weapons were meant for direct, one-on-one encounters bent on hand-to-hand combat, rather than in group forma-tions or formal lines. They were intended to emphasize the disabling/capture of others, rather than outright killing and distance attacks. It is notable that there never seemed to be an 'arms race' in the Early Intermediate Period, where opposing communities continually innovated more efficient weapons. The lack of interest in a technical edge for annihilating enemies may have been because the procedures of post-combat predation were just as important for some groups as the combat itself.

Early Intermediate Period weaponry could be highly elaborate, made with technical skill, and highly unique objects. They were objects that mediated social relations with others, whether as weapon or grave good. In some ways, it was part of the warrior, but we have also seen that this can be alienated from the original owner. One might say their effectiveness was in relation to the person wielding the weapon, rather than based on the technical military efficiency of the weapon in and of itself. The weapon also related its holder to the insider community. Just as importantly, the weapon was for enemies. In this way, weapons were made for others to see, contemplate and admire. They were certainly to gain advantage, both physically and cognitively, over others.

Summary

In this chapter, I have focused on how peoples of Peru's first millennium AD recognized social others who had 'predatorial' dispositions. Sometimes the alterity corresponded to enemies and foreigners; other times they are associated with affines, conquerors and captives. This chapter stressed how predation and being predated upon counted as forms of social relation.

Outside beings, broadly conceived, embodied vital resources that were incorporated through transformative, often violent, engagements. The archaeological record of ancient Peru demonstrated various material outcomes of enemy confrontation through mind and practice. Predatorial relations occurred in the ancient Andes at varying scales and in various domains.

Much art imagery during the Early Intermediate Period concerned predation. I focused especially on Moche, Nasca and Recuay. We saw predatory creatures, predatory acts and their aftermath. We encountered zoomorphs and anthropomorphs in conflict, often with one another, or put into opposing and subordinating positions. Humans took on aspects of animal predators, or vice versa. Killing and consumption of a symbolic economy of alterity contrast with the nurture and feeding found in the domestic milieu. Some subordinated humans (enemies, captives) were compared to animals (deer, tamed being, pets).

Representations of predators (enemies, captives, nonhuman predators) are part of that impulse to acknowledge their alterity. Early Intermediate Period cultures represented the human enemy through certain conventions: defeat and capture; attire; body position and ornament; and, sometimes, size. These were understandings of the comportment and corporeal statuses of the defeated other. Interlocking teeth and associated instruments for killing and consuming (broadly conceived) almost always index predatorial beings in Early Intermediate Period art.

To judge by comparison to the ethnographic literature, there were resonances with the notion that one of the main aims of warfare is precisely to win something from the other. Enemies were subdued and incorporated through violent capture, display of trophies and the spectacle of sacrifice. Crucially, the external perspective and subjectivity are not obliterated, but rather recognized and often reworked. Such triumphs certainly enhanced the fame and authority of the victors, lords and warriors. Many groups, it was argued, also managed the subjectivities of enemies – from feared others to captives to pets to enemies again – before they were killed, as part of an extended predation process. Thus warfare, conflict and predatorial relations, in general, involved not only a subordination of others, but an enhancement of oneself through the contributions from others.

It is interesting to note how Central Andean cultures seemed to have placed so little emphasis on war divinities. Huitzilopochtli was the patron god of the Mexica (Aztecs), but was their god of war. War gods are also important to various First Nations groups in North America. One explanation would be that many ancestors were conceived as heroic warriors. In this way, Huitzilopochtli's war cult, aggrandized by the success of Mexica expansion, is simply a heightened example of a broader pattern. In having war gods legion, predatorial relations enter therefore into the domain of ancestral divinities. It is to Andean ancestors that our attention now turns.

5

THE DEAD AND THE LIVING

And you, señores malquis [ancestor bundles], señoras guacas [sacred object/place], give us life and health, let there be no sickness in the town, may the Indians multiply and have good fields, may they have possessions, let there be no frost, nor worms in the fields, and let them not be harmed by the Spaniards.

Plea to ancestors by idolater (in Doyle 1988: 183)

I start by reviewing potential traits of the ancestral dead in the Central Andes. They are considered old beings, often with physical characteristics typical of the old. They are hard, wrinkled. They do not move too fast and frequently need help. They like cool, dark places and like to be with others of the same kind. They are irascible and fickle. They are needy, and require tending and respect. They like food and drink, and songs and stories; they like to be the center of attention. They have long histories, extraordinary faculties (often of 'sight') and enviable knowledge. They are at once stingy and generous. They don't smell quite right. They have valuable things and frequently impart them as gifts. They can bestow bad fortune and barrenness, just as well as wealth, wisdom, resources, good wishes and kindness.

This quick summary about the alterity of the ancestral dead may sound like someone's characterization of the elderly. But, in fact, I would argue that the countenancing of consanguineal elders and the formal properties of old persons is precisely the relation basic to the otherness of the ancestral dead in the ancient Andes, especially of the Recuay culture, the focus of this chapter.[1] The main difference, of course, is that we rarely keep our esteemed dead at hand for regular visits and festivities. But we might have an heirloom or a photograph by which we remember them from time to time with a drink. It may not be surprising, then, that highland Andeans often use local terms meaning 'grandparents' to describe past peoples, ancestors and antecedents in general, including many of those outside generational memory (e.g., Allen 1988: 56; Salomon 1995: 337–38; Walter 2006: 178).

In this chapter, I consider the dead as a special type of social being, who is both the source and agent in a 'social economy of ancestrality'. By this, I mean social relations that reproduce society, based on patterns that give considerable cultural weight to interactions with the ancestral dead. It is based on the belief system that sees life as a cyclical process in which the dead reciprocate the living for their veneration. It is also based on the notion that genealogy is the basis for personhood and certain forms of social differentiation. Although deceased, the sociability of ancestors remained via their images. To flourish or fail was owed to relations with them. Let us explore how the potency of the ancestral dead resided in their alterity.

Death practices and cosmology in the Andes

As with many societies around the world, death for native Andeans formed part of the cultural practices and cosmology that sought to manage the well-being of the living. Death and burial feature as an extended series of practices that address the instabilities that arise when reacting to biological death, the need to dispose of a corpse, and to reorganize the collectivity coping with the loss – or, rather, bodily trans-formation – of a former member. And how a society resolves these questions, many of an ontological nature, tells much about the forms of social relations in that society (Bloch and Parry 1982; Descola 2005; Huntington and Metcalf 1979).

Here I am interested in the dead, especially the ancestralized or 'enshrined' dead (Salomon 1995), as a kind of social other. Much of our knowledge about ancient northern Peruvian religious practices derives from colonial era descriptions. These include work by writers knowledgeable about the different regions of the former Inca realm (e.g., Cobo 1990; Guaman Poma de Ayala 1980). Notable insights regarding the cosmology and treatment of the dead occur in documents emerging out of colonial persecution of pagan and 'idolatrous' religious beliefs (Arriaga 1999; Doyle 1988; Duviols 2003; Mills 1997; Polia 1999; Salomon and Urioste 1991). Ethnographic studies are also significant for understanding beliefs and practices about death in more recent times, especially as they relate to the advent of Andean Christianity (Allen 1988; Bastien 1978; Gose 1994; Harris 1982; Salomon 1995; Spalding 1984).

In many regions of the prehispanic highlands, the esteemed dead were key com-ponents of ancestor cults. I will be describing ancestors as specific named deceased deemed to have influence over the affairs of the living. My reference to the ancestral dead follows Doyle's argument (1988: 241) that, once placed in their collective burial repositories (discussed later), they became ancestors because they joined a world of beings who 'shared the quality of sacredness' imbued in places of group origin. We do not know whether ancient Andean groups, least of all of the Recuay culture, also recognized a 'general dead' as opposed to those who were considered ancestors.

The cults were religious practices centered on ancestors, whose veneration attended to the notion that the ancestors continued to look after descendants – in the form of favor in crops, herds, health, wisdom, reproductive fertility, etc. Ancestors were therefore agents of well-being, with whom the living entered into a contract of reciprocity.

Each collective, or ayllu, had its own ancestors, and they were often ranked, according to a sacred kinship system (Doyle 1988: 90; Zuidema 1973). The system concerned group origins, and tracked primordial actions (and kin relations) of those people who settled the landscape and gave rise to specific ayllu collectives. At the highest position of a given group's genealogy was the founding progenitor(s), who, in bundled form, was called a *mallqui*. So, for example, all the bundles in one burial repository would be ancestral persons, but presumably descendants of the founding mallqui. Some progenitors also had the capacity to lithify as monuments and features of the landscape.

There were therefore many kinds of ancestral divinities who could readily be fitted into greater (and lesser) levels of ritual organization. For example, there were smaller objects, associated with lesser ancestors and household fertility, that were more associated with the cult practices of the family and individuals. These were heirlooms and passed down from the parents to the children, but did not feature heavily in cults of founding ancestors (Arriaga 1999: 35–36). On the other hand, when the Incas conquered its provinces, the empire helped to integrate its provinces by incorporating, cosmologically, the regional divinities to whom people in the provinces were still beholden. The regional divinities took their place below the supreme gods of the Incas.

Just as important, ancestral divinities took touchable, material forms (Plate 25). Ancestors manifested at many different scales and sizes: mummy bundles, body parts, built spaces and various other forms of non-mimetic simulacra (e.g., mountains, caves, rocks, pebbles). They need not feature corporeal continuity nor consubstantiality. Having images of the dead was essential because the various cults centered on tangible embodiments of ancestors, and veneration often involved regular interactions with the images. Physical proximity and sensory engagements (in particular: sight, smell, touch, eating) were paramount; these promoted an intersubjectivity of shared action and being (with them). The most important activities with the ancestors included receiving libations and songs, providing consultations, and their resplendent display in public circumstances. In other words, the images act and do stuff in the proximity of living beings (Lau 2008). The cults demanded collective representations about the agency of objects and ancestrality over many generations.

Colonial exigencies: resettlement and inquisition

It is axiomatic to say that the sixteenth and seventeenth centuries count amongst the most tumultuous times in humanity's short occupation of the Americas. The settling of the Europeans in the new territories changed the shape of world history, by unleashing new economic, technological and social transformations that ensued in each side of the encounter (Diamond 1997; Gade 1999; Wallerstein 1974–80). Its cultural dynamism and social differentiation provide numerous insights into the process of alterity and engagements with the other in earlier times.

In the late sixteenth century, Viceroy Francisco de Toledo sanctioned a program of Indian resettlement in new Spanish-style towns across Peru. Referred to as *reducciones*, the towns developed so that native Andeans could be more easily governed, taxed and Christianized. In the highlands, the reforms displaced communities and emptied homesteads dispersed across the landscape, and especially those people living at high altitude and hard-to-reach areas.

In one fell swoop, the policy struck irrevocably at the heart of traditional Andean society and culture. Concentrating people in the new towns, usually in more temperate valley bottoms, disrupted patterns of economic production and social organization based on customary vertical orientations. But it also created tremendous distance between natives and their places of cult, usually located at high places, caves, outcrops and cemetery sectors near the abandoned settlements. This was equally pernicious as it was effective, for it took people far away from their esteemed dead, the cult objects (persons) with whom they drew descent and with whom they had duties. The reducciones resettled people some 0.5 to 2 leagues away from their necropoli (Doyle 1988: 112). Religious officials rationalized that distancing native Andeans from the cult centers would bring their idolatry to halt: out of sight, out of mind (Toledo, in Gose 2008: 123; Arriaga 1999: 80).

As it happened, Andeans, not least of highland Ancash, did not shed social relations with the dead so easily (Duviols 2003; Hernández Príncipe 1923). The necessity for regular interaction with the dead, even if banned, would continue long after the Toledoan reforms. This was because native Andeans could hardly imagine social life without the dead. The alterity of the esteemed deceased, long bound up with regeneration, descent and reciprocity, remained a powerful organizing principle for Andean communities; the living regularly engaged the dead at all levels of community life.

Spanish surveillance of indigenous religion was especially fervent in the body of writings known today as the extirpation of idolatries documents. These were descriptions made by Spanish clerics to chronicle their campaigns against native practices in rural parts of Peru (late sixteenth to early eighteenth centuries). When it became increasingly recognized that Christianity had failed to take in major areas of the Viceroyalty of Peru, the Spanish launched a series of brutal campaigns to root out or 'extirpate' pagan practices, what Pierre Duviols (1971) called 'the war against autochthonous religions'.

What they found was not a unified religion *per se* – one that shared god(s), doctrines or centralized priesthoods. Rather, they encountered an innumerable series of cults, both small and covering large regions, centered around ancestral divinities that were, especially at the local level, linked to death practices. This was what made their job at once terrible and challenging, for they could not simply extirpate one cult and pretend to be done. Death, not surprisingly, was everywhere. Equally important, death in the Andes was deeply embedded, indeed embodied, in social life as well as in people.

There is already a rich published literature on the idolatries, many of which are compendia of the eyewitness testimonies provided by both Spanish officials and the Indians themselves (Arriaga 1999; Doyle 1988; Duviols 2003; Gose 2008; Griffiths 1996; Mills 1997; Polia 1999). It is from a general reading of these that I will make comparisons to the ancient cases.

The idolatries documents are of particular relevance in informing prehispanic practices. First, many of the documents concern the rural areas of what is present-day

Ancash, and especially its highlands and areas just to its south. The regions had certainly been affected by the conquest and had integrated into the overall colonial system of reducciones. But surviving pockets of non-Christian religious beliefs and material cultures were the target. For many regions, the testimonies describe 're-visits' to areas where pagan practices were particularly stubborn and sprouted up again. Also, some descriptions concern geneaologies and historical memory of ancestor cult practices before and during the Inca reign (ca. 1450–1532), attesting to its core nature (Zuidema 1978). Finally, there are clear, usable links between the archaeological evidence and the types of objects and contexts described in colonial-era ancestor cults (DeLeonardis and Lau 2004; Isbell 1997; Kaulicke 2001; Korpisaari 2006; Lau 2008; Tello 1929).

Alterity in the idolatries

> They were also careful to preserve the pieces of the broken and half-burned huacas. … the respect, love and fear which the Devil inspires in them is astonishing to see … [T]he old men say … that we ought to go and remove the huacas from their hiding places. But when we go, taking them for guides, they proceed unwillingly … trembling, perspiring, and biting their tongue so that they can hardly talk or move their hands and feet … I think the Devil reminds them of the tender love they have felt for their huacas, the care with which they have guarded them, and the grief they will feel if they are deprived of them.
>
> *Lic. Rodrigo Hernández Príncipe, letter to Arriaga (1968: 85)*

There is something profoundly moving about the testimonies emerging out of the Spanish persecution of native religions. Their essential basis distinguishes two highly stylized categories of people in a clash of cultures, communication and will (e.g., Gruzinski 1993; Todorov 1984). In simple terms, the idolatries documents reiterate what needs little saying: the Spanish saw Indians as pagans, and Indians saw the Spanish as oppressors.

But the same documents record each group struggling to recognize and come to grips with the other through the means they had at their disposal. On one side are the priests, rationalizing, in remarkably bureaucratic fashion, the laborious project of religious repression and the sometimes extraordinary tasks to which they were assigned. They too were conscious of monitoring by their superiors. Yet the documents do not merely chronicle the work of God. They are about the imperfections of others, and stand as moral meditations on how to improve them, to make their souls worthy of salvation. In this way, native Andean alterity provided both the evidence of error and the site for corrective change, for assimilation by learning the ways of Christianity. The idolatries documents are also checklists chronicling the various detective exploits (and failures) to make them better, purging them of pagan habits and sowing faith in the one true God.

On the other side, the Indians clamored to resist the alterity of the Spanish and the Christians. Various testimonies by Indians during their interrogations conveyed certain Spanish lifeways that, for whatever reason, were either unpleasant or downright unacceptable. Food was one source of grievance, for it was said that the Spanish ate dirty, contaminated food, especially the meat of Old World animals, such as mutton, pork and chicken (Doyle 1988: 149).

It was priests who most commonly wrote about the clashes of faith during the early seventeenth century. Awkward confrontations between the clerics and natives were inevitable because of drastically different materialities of religion and person: where to keep corpses; what constituted priesthood and sacrifices; what were signs of divinity; where did the soul go; what was proper ritual. The accounts are especially impressive because they show the dogged determination of both the Spanish church officials and the natives. The former were tireless in their persecution of pagans; the natives desperately tried to reconcile a new social world while clinging to old, suddenly outlawed and dangerous, habits of worship.

A social economy of ancestrality: the dead as benefactors

The ancestors were worshipped because descendants saw their existence as due to the work of these progenitors. Ancestors created the various kin collectives (ayllu) and owned the fields which provided sustenance (Doyle 1988: 177). Ancestors were, in short, responsible for ensuring continued fertility and well-being among the group.

What did the ancestors provide in return? The chapter's opening epigraph, a supplication made by a descendant to his ancestors, provides a quick summation about the domains of influence held by ancestors. They had a hand in life and health, wealth and fertility of people and land.

Ancestors featured powers in specific domains. The first consisted in imparting to the living special types of knowledge, expressed through rituals of divination (e.g., of weather, propitious moments for activities) and ritual specialists. Also important were their public presence and acknowledgment of important life events, such as naming ceremonies, marriages and house raisings. They were also sources of key resources: entitlements to land as well as rights to water. Probably the most significant capacity was to bestow divine favor, such as increased fertility (e.g., herds, crops or humans), protection against enemies and poor yields, and guidance in certain tasks (such as being a leader). They were directly responsible for the livelihood of their descendants, both individual and at corporate levels. Misfortunes in any one field might be attributed to unhappy ancestors.

The power of an ancestor was most pertinent to his/her respective descent group. Social relations parallelled each other. Benefits and effects were directed at individuals as well as at collectivity, just as ancestors were venerated individually as well as in the collective (usually centered at the beginning and end of the agricultural cycle) (Doyle 1988: 147).

For many Andean groups, the ancestors and other special divinities could communicate directly to their followers (Curatola and Ziółkowski 2008; Doyle 1988: 151–52, 178, 208). They had powers to speak, give visions or communicate through an intermediary religious specialist. The dispositions of the dead and ancestor bundles were also divined through examining the innards of sacrificed guinea pigs and llamas (e.g., Arriaga 1999: 51; Doyle 1988: 208). Likewise, the knowledge concerned major issues of well-being: propitious times (e.g., sowing, harvests), consultations (e.g., names, marriage partners) and predictions (e.g., weather, results of warfare).[2]

We are now in a position to see what death practices were like in the ancient past, with special respect to reconstituting alterities of the dead. While recognizing the limitations of both the archaeological and ethnohistorical record, a social economy of ancestrality provides a framework for a more nuanced understanding of prehistoric materials.

Prehispanic death practices

Diachronic patterns in the treatment of the dead provide important insights into changing alterities of the dead through time. Major patterns during the Early Inter-mediate Period are of particular relevance. These have to do with the form, location, popularity and character of ancestor cult activities.

Burial practices in the north highlands before the Early Intermediate Period are not well known. Burials in cists and expedient tombs under large rocks and boulders are the most common during the centuries immediately preceding the Early Intermediate Period (Bennett 1944; Lumbreras 1974a: 50–51; Matsumoto 2006; Ponte 2001, 2009). In neighboring areas, there is evidence of stone-lined tombs as well as richer offerings associated with monumental ceremonial centers (Kato 1993; Onuki 1997).

In general, the pre-Early Intermediate Period patterns include relatively modest subterranean graves, under-rock burials, reuse of older constructions and location near residential settlements. These were characteristic funerary treatments in Ancash and continued well into the colonial period.

With the advent of the Recuay style, funerary constructions showed a greater array of form, size and quality of work (Lau 2011). The variability indicates greater social differentiation and greater regional cultural diversity. Compared to earlier times, Recuay groups evince much more elaboration of burial spaces and their attendant ritual practices. Intentional re-use and episodic visitation of burial sites also appear to have intensified (DeLeonardis and Lau 2004; Gamboa 2010).

Most Recuay tombs appear to have been subterranean or at least partly under-ground. Typical subterranean tombs had a single main chamber with a small entry space (e.g., Bennett 1944: 21ff.; Lau 2010a: 118–20; Orsini 2007: 88; Ponte 2001: 228–29; Tello 1930: 271). In general, the larger, more elaborate tombs are char-acterized by multiple burial chambers and more features, such as niches, orderly stonemasonry, large stone jambs/lintels and large roof slabs (Fig 5.1). The tombs often had passageways that linked to rooms with small compartments, presumably for interments and offerings. Larger than cist tombs, they had the capacity to accom-modate more than one interment, or bundle. Long galleries, some 3 to 20 meters in length, also served as burial spaces as well as passageways to burial chambers. Some sites feature dense complexes of multi-chamber tombs. Areas reserved only for the dead, perhaps for extended families or kin groups over many generations, were

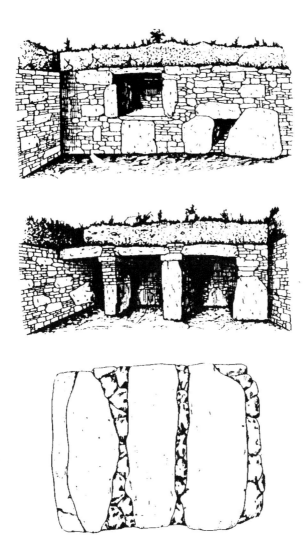

FIGURE 5.1 Recuay subterranean chamber tombs, Katak (adapted from Tello 1930: Fig. 6). Compartments and main spaces were used for interments as well as to place grave furnishings. Over 150 distinct funerary chambers were tallied by Julio C. Tello.

certainly part of a growing tradition about recognizing and making separate communities of the dead (Bennett 1944: 64; Gamboa 2010; see also Mejía Xesspe 1948; Tello 1929: 40).

By about AD 400, Recuay funerary practices began to more emphatically stress certain individuals as important members of society. Directly opposite the main plaza of Chavín de Huántar, investigations on the eastern side of the Río Mosna found Recuay-period tombs built into Early Horizon deposits (Gamboa 2010). A burial platform contained a series of burial compartments: pits and cists, some of which were lined with stone. Some interments, accompanied by Recuay ceramics and evidence of previous manipulation of the corpses, were mostly poorly preserved. The most elaborate tomb was dedicated to an adult male and female, buried together and accompanied by eighteen ceramic vessels; one shows a multi-figure scene showing embracing women around a central male lord (Plate 11). Comparison with the other nearby interments, which are simpler and contained more modest offerings, suggests the male and female pair may have been progenitors of the group housed in the funerary complex.

The tomb of Jancu is another important Recuay burial context (Wegner 1988). Builders situated the tomb directly underneath a large boulder, and carefully partitioned the interior space by propping flat stones against each other. The chamber was accessed through a carefully made gallery and entered through a series of thresholds. The grave furniture included a set of at least fifteen vessels (Plates 12, 16, 26), many with figurative modeling of human and predatory animal figures (Wegner 1988). There was at least one interment, flexed and seated, who was found wearing a gold foil frontlet. Overall, the Jancu tomb appears to have constructed a distinctly artificial world, based on stylized social relations, for interactions with the dead and various effigy forms.

At Pashash, near Cabana, the site of the richest Recuay burial ever documented, abundant luxury offerings were made at different times to the tomb of a high-status individual. They included metal adornments, fine ceramics, beadwork and carved stone objects. The fine ceramics stress the importance of male chiefly dignitaries (Plate 27). Metal garment pins, decomposed textiles and spindle whorls suggested that the main interment was of an older woman. Overall, people repeatedly honored the person with distinct caches of very lavish offerings, apparently one of many nobles to be honored this way in the funerary complex (Grieder 1978: 48, 55).

Major transformations in mortuary behavior therefore characterized groups of the Recuay culture. They show substantially greater variability in scale of burials, distribution of Recuay-style materials, and in elaboration. Burials offerings and ritual equipment become much more frequent as well as much more finely made. Also notable was the increasing use of large burial constructions with multiple interment spaces, probably for collective interments of high-status lineages. Certain esteemed deceased, it seems, attracted offerings, caches and general attention over a period of time. Elsewhere, I have likened these individuals to cynosural bodies who command attention by others who follow their movements in and across their respective universes (Lau 2010d).

The seventh century AD, near the end of the Early Intermediate Period, began to see major transformations in the material culture of funerary practices. Most important, a distinctive new burial form became increasingly popular: the *chullpa*.[3] The chullpa was a mortuary building, usually located above ground, meant for housing, display and veneration of the dead. As part of ancestor cults, chullpas, and use of collective tombs more generally, continued well into historical times.

There were both large and small chullpas. The largest in the region measures over 15 meters long and nearly 10 meters high, with as many as twenty-six funerary chambers and compartments (Bennett 1944; Buse 1965; Isbell 1991; Tschauner 2003). The largest

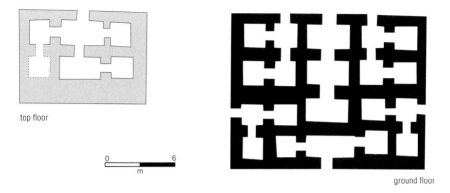

top floor

0   6
m

ground floor

FIGURE 5.2 Layout of chullpa MCS-1, ground and top floors, Honcopampa (adapted from Tschauner 2003: 201). The many chambers provide some structured flexibility for organizing ancestral bundles, offerings and associated ritual practices.

were also often the best constructed, with built-in features such as niches, massive roof slabs, ventilation shafts, drainage canals and decorative stonemasonry (Fig 5.2). Many also probably featured stone sculpture and were set atop low platforms.

The clustering of funerary buildings became more prominent during the Middle Horizon. Whereas some necropoli existed during Recuay times, by the end of the Early Intermediate Period and during the Middle Horizon, many small and large communities began to feature sizeable sectors dedicated to chullpas and related mortuary buildings.

Some general observations can be made at this point about alterity. First, chullpas proliferated across highland Ancash dramatically during the Middle Horizon. This was part of a much wider proliferation of the form in the north highlands, including Cajamarca and La Libertad (Isbell 1997). In addition to its increasing popularity and wide dissemination, it appears that funerary practices based on above-ground tombs became increasingly important to display interactions with the dead. The physical appearance of chullpas and the performance of public ritual also likely helped to mark social boundaries (Lau 2000).

It is also clear that the chullpas show great variability in appearance and quality of building. Chullpas in the north highlands are characterized by different sizes and shapes: they were built with different materials and had different plans, number of rooms, door orientations and unique artifact assemblages. In other words, there was no rigid or prescriptive template for their making or use. The form and its attendant practices could characterize collectivities of varying socio-political arrangements. They were certainly not restricted to high-status groups or nobles.

A related point is that the new chullpa ceremonial patterns often intervened into antecedent forms and practices. There was a constant interplay of new and old forms. Chullpas were placed on or near existing mortuary buildings and spaces, surmounting previous constructions, such as subterranean galleries and chambers. Carved monoliths, a holdover from Recuay times, also were re-purposed (Lau 2006b). The monoliths, many depicting ancestors and associated supernaturals, adorned the thresholds to chullpas and also stood nearby as freestanding statues. The capacity to incorporate local cultural traditions suggests that many groups did not reject or surrender former practices, beliefs and objects. Rather, older customs found a new context for expression by being co-opted and reworked.

What this implies is that people began to see older ancestors somewhat differently. Their alterity, if you will, changed. For one thing, there were many more of the ancestral dead about; inclusion in chullpas, it seems, was much more inclusive by the time that chullpas proliferated. Also, overt wealth disparities between the esteemed dead and common dead do not seem to have been as great. To date, there have been no extremely high-status burials in chullpas that come near to the wealth accumulation found in tombs such as Jancu or Pashash. Finally, if the great proliferation of chullpas suggests a proliferation of ancestors, we would expect, by extension, that there was wider engagement of their alterity.

Wari: foreigners and purveyors of the modern

Wari culture, beginning during the seventh century, certainly played a role in the new ceremonial patterns. Wari-style material is frequently attributed to the rise of a powerful expansionist state, associated with a cultural style based in Huari (Ayacucho). While Wari does not seem to have invented the above-ground *chullpa* tomb, it seems to have played a role in its increasing frequency and popularity. There are several ways that Wari could have effected this pattern.

One was that the chullpa interment style was an intrinsic part of its political expansion, a policy or an institution that piggybacked on territorial or hegemonic rule. So, for example, Christian church architecture did not originate in sixteenth-century Spain, but it was certainly an essential element in its religious ideology and colonial policy in the New World. The other possibility was presented by archaeologist Bill Isbell (1997). He argued that chullpas arose and intensified in use during the Middle Horizon as a *reaction* to the state, and most notably against Wari imperialism. A form of local resistance, it reinforced conservative traditions and kin-based (ayllu) social organization: ancestor cults and the use of the chullpas 'represent creative responses by supporters of kin community interests, in a struggle to protect local control and resist the demands of an increasingly influential and privileged class of elites' (Isbell 1997: 297).

While these hypotheses remain debated, it is clear that Wari presence and chullpas are frequently linked. This is because Wari-related materials, usually decorative pottery of either imported or emulated styles, are often found inside or near chullpa complexes and in residential settlements associated with chullpa complexes (Bennett 1944; Lau 2005; Paredes 2005; Paredes et al. 2001). They occurred as parts of cosmopolitan assemblages, where people appear to have been interested in collecting objects from various prestige styles and regions (Burger et al. 2006; Lau 2005, 2006a). Exactly for what purpose is not clear, but this new disposition for cultural heterogeneity, especially in funerary assemblages, was shared by other cultural groups of northern Peru (Castillo 1993; Castillo et al. 2008; Topic and Topic 1984). It remains to determine more fully whether the materials and cosmopolitan practice resulted from relations of domination, resistance or some other form of interaction.

There is no doubt that Wari constituted another alterity for people in Ancash and probably for other areas of northern Peru. Wari style and materiality were largely alien to many of the northern cultures before the late Early Intermediate Period. Most Wari architectural characteristic forms, such as heavily compartmentalized orthogonal complexes and D-shaped ceremonial structures, were innovative forms, if only due to the new organizational and religious functions for which Wari put them to use. The best known occurrences of D-shaped structures in Ancash occur at Honcopampa, a large center populated by local lords, some of whom were probably allied with the Wari state. Featuring high walls, large interior niches and limited access, the structures were probably for feasting and offering practices (Cook 2001; McEwan 2005; Meddens and Cook 2001). The intermediate position of the D-shaped enclosures between chullpas and the elite palaces was probably an intentional architectural device. It showed how local leaders refashioned forms of political authority, by mediating residential and funerary spaces, via the idiom of Wari-style ceremonialism.

We can also see that north highland groups imagined Wari people in certain ways. Not many examples exist, but Wari figural representations are occasionally found in tombs in Ancash, probably made by local potters for the burials of local elites. The first category treats Wari as people with dazzling, elegant clothes and personal accoutrements. This includes colorful and technically sophisticated textiles, for which Wari were almost certainly renowned (Oakland Rodman and Fernández 2001); the polychrome character of the cloth aesthetic, of course, was also almost certainly an appeal of their ceramics, whose style began to be quickly emulated in local circumstances (Plate 6). Some Wari people were also known for their headgear: the four-cornered hat. The second component of Wari alterity is of people who were associated with festive generosity, drink and reciprocity (for labor, in celebrations, exchange, etc.). There is a vessel showing a figure wearing a four-cornered hat, for example, who holds a shield in one hand and drinking cup in another. Finally, north highland groups saw Wari people as enemies. One vessel (Plate 28) shows a figure wearing a four-cornered hat, who has his hands tied behind his back, the typical position of a war captive (Ponte 2001: Fig. 24).

Current evidence suggests that Wari's presence in Ancash, at least early in the Middle Horizon, was probably fueled by trading interests, especially for rare items and materials (e.g., *Spondylus* shell, Cajamarca ceramics and perhaps materials such as camelid fiber and metals) (Lau 2005, 2006a, 2011). The chullpa sites coincided with wider transformations associated with the early Middle Horizon. Sites with chullpas often show greater evidence of long-distance goods, especially obsidian, prestige pottery styles and other rarities. That all the largest chullpas are found in the Callejón de Huaylas (the intermontane valley of the Río Santa) is consistent with Wari's keen interest in the area, the valley's surge of economic interaction, and a growing openness to new cultural networks facilitated by Wari (Lau 2005). Much more positive data are needed to determine whether there was ever a Wari military conquest or territorial takeover of north highland Peru.

By the eighth and ninth centuries AD, Wari had greater cultural influence over highland Ancash, where local potters began to change their styles to embed stylistic dispositions more typical of Wari and other contemporary cultures, especially Cajamarca. But by AD 900 or so, Wari influence rapidly abated, both in terms of local stylistic developments as well as trade goods (e.g., ceramics, textiles or obsidian) (Burger et al. 2006; Lau 2005, 2010a). The practice of chullpa making certainly continued, and in unprecedented numbers. But their lack of elaboration, small size and limited grave offerings suggest a series of small collectivities, probably kin-based, with limited wealth differentiation. Settlement evidence and recent excavations show relatively little evidence of strong social differentiation during Ancash's late prehispanic periods (Herrera et al. 2006; Ibarra 2003a; Mantha 2009).

By the end of the first millennium, all throughout the areas where Wari had an initial foothold, there was a rapid cessation of Wari presence. Wari presence at sites such as Chinchawas, Wilkawaín and Honcopampa quickly diminished. This was part of a broader pattern, what was the next great period of pan-Andean alterity, in which various regional groups, from the south coast to the north highlands rapidly evacuated any formal Wari associations from local cultural assemblages. The cosmology or the social forms associated with the Wari state probably grew weaker. Also, local groups were probably increasingly emboldened to go their separate ways. By AD 1000, Ancash groups saw and referenced very little Wari cultural impact ever again.

Patterns through time

In sum, there were major transformations in burial practices during the Early Intermediate Period and these have important implications for local perceptions about the dead and changing alterity of the dead through time. First, very simply there was a popularization of ancestor cults. More and more communities began to adopt multi-chambered burial spaces in their ceremonial practices. There were also more burial constructions during the Middle Horizon than in the Early Intermediate Period. Second, there was a greater emphasis on the dead to congregate in bounded areas, or clusters (necropoli). Third, there was also a greater emphasis on the dead who dwelled in complementary parts of the communities. Funerary sectors near residential areas of sites were increasingly common and dedicated to mortuary activities. Fourth, the kinds of materials accompanying burials became more diverse: the dead and their cults were stylized as more cosmopolitan. Finally, developments at the end of the Early Inter-mediate Period saw less ostentatious mortuary practices than in the centuries before, a pattern that would more or less continue into historical times.

The increasingly regular engagements between the living and dead contrast with many coeval developments of neighboring areas. Although post-inhumation manipula-tion of interments did occur (Millaire 2004), groups of the Moche period, for example, employed deep underground chambers and piled adobe construction over tombs, in effect sealing them off and limiting revisitation or manipulation of the burials.

These features characterized what Isbell (1997: 291) called the 'huaca cemetery' pattern: a style distinct from the 'open sepulcher' type, associated with the advent of chullpas in the north highlands. He asserts,

> Society's most important men and women were placed in appropriately important locations within the *huaca* temple, and their bodies must have disappeared forever because access to the graves were frequently made impossible by subsequent architectural expansions. These elite could not have been venerated founders of *ayllus* who could be seen and embraced during rites of propitiation.

The huaca style was popular on the north coast for north coast elites (Pillsbury 2001; Quilter and Castillo 2010; Uceda and Mujica 2003).

The evidence from the Recuay area and the north directly bears on the generalizations, enhancing some details of the pattern recognition. Recuay subterranean tombs, long before the advent of chullpas, featured many of the behavioral patterns associated with 'open sepulchers': relatively open access, additional burials, stone upright markers, revisitation and ancestor veneration (Lau 2000, 2002). It seems likely that tombs such as funerary complexes at Jancu, La Banda and perhaps at Pashash emerge out of a cosmology that, in tenor, emphasizes esteemed progenitors or founding ancestors.

To be sure, the chullpa form certain radically reoriented practices. These tombs stressed, first and foremost, easy access to the dead. It also implies a new temporality which attended to the regularity of their veneration and the anticipation of new burials: of new members of this kin set being inserted into the new afterlife community. Situated above the ground with clear, if small, doorways, these buildings and their contents were much more open to revisitation. Many cemeteries developed in proximity to living communities. And doorways into chullpas were rarely blocked with large slabs, as was common in subterranean tombs (Grieder 1978: 45–49; Lau 2002: 291–92; Wegner 1988). Subterranean tombs could be re-entered, but people employing chullpas made access to the dead a conspicuous priority. They were also much more visible on the landscape, especially those located near residential settlements, fields and pastures.

Discussion: alterities of the dead

The foregoing has outlined the rationale and various contexts for changing religious patterns in highland Peru. It first introduced the basis of Andean ancestor cults, and then focused on the richest corpus of evidence: the idolatries descriptions. It then went back in time to cover the archaeological patterns of the first millennium AD, using the information from ethnohistorical times as the principal framework to understand the more ancient past. It is an opportune time now to provide a more extended discussion about the alterities of the dead, both during the first millennium AD and during the period associated with the idolatries documents.

Ancestral points of view

How did Andeans see their dead as different? Probably the best way to approach this question is to see how people made effigies of the ancestral dead and how they engaged with them as physical objects (Plate 29). My points here will focus on the relationships between the formal and symbolic qualities of ancestor effigies, a topic treated elsewhere, both for Recuay and for other Andean cultures more generally (Lau 2006b, 2008).

Native Andeans were apparently quite comfortable with dead bodies. Because access to ancestors was vital to social life, it was important to have them in relatively close proximity. Mummy bundles were kept in areas not too far away from the residential areas and, as we have seen, they were often the focus of physical interaction at various times of the year. There were also various forms of the dead (cadavers, bundles, statues, effigies) that duplicated their presence, for exultation as ancestors and when the decomposing body became no longer accessible.

Spanish officials who described Indian idolatries were especially aggrieved by the time and attention Andeans devoted to the bodies of the dead. The overt obsession with the dead, manifested in the stealing of bodies from Christian cemeteries, was seen as the largest encumbrance to effective conversion (Cobo 1990: 39; Doyle 1988: 5). The Spanish saw dead bodies as sources of pollution and corrupting objects that needed to be disposed of, in the ground or by being destroyed. A favorable fate for the soul, emancipated from the disposed corpse, was the purpose of Christian burial.

Native Andeans, meanwhile, understood dead bodies and their simulacra as tangible instantiations of key, powerful beings. Much effort in prehispanic mortuary practices sought the curation of the deceased's essence; in lieu of their removal, they needed ongoing care and proximity. The bodies were vessel-images who were at once creator-progenitors (for a given group) as well as direct conduits for that group's vitality (Lau 2008; Salomon 1991, 2004). Hence, they were the source and inspiration for the cults, and it was vital to keep them in good stead.

In many ways, the dead shared many of the characteristics of the living. Just as there were houses and communities for the living, there were houses and communities of the esteemed dead. Indeed, for many archaeologists, it has been difficult to distinguish domestic buildings intended for living inhabitants and those above-ground buildings (chullpas) intended for storage of ancestor effigies, even when the tombs are clustered together (e.g., Bennett 1944). Tombs are customarily set apart from the rest of the village, creating small necropoli or communities of the dead.

In this scenario, the dead maintain cultures and traditions just as the living do. They have a *habitus*, a set of durable dispositions that inform action (Bourdieu 1977). They eat, live and work, just as biologically living people do. While they do all these things, they do them differently because their corporeal forms are different. That is, the main basis for differentiation resides in their bodies.

They no longer maintain human form or capacities, precisely because their bodies are not up to it. Ancestors can no longer work fields or herd camelids; they can't because they're bundled and ossified. They need to be carried, and as ontologically animated beings, they are understood to be slow and heavy. They move and act at a different pace. Rather, their work is at a more basal, originary level: to ensure the rains come, that there are fields to farm, camelids to herd and wisdom to transmit. They are most important in public ceremony and become especially vital during monumental time, that is, that temporality attributed by people about the past, usually via political ideologies and sanction (Herzfeld 1991). Their materiality of permanence (dryness, hardness, stone or likened to stone) goes hand in hand with the perceived perpetuity of their work. Their work seeks to achieve the same goals as the living: to promote the group's reproduction, and ensure survival and well-being.

Hence, the alterity of the Andean dead very much regarded their bodies and the transformation of corporeal status (live to ancestral forms). Ancestors might simply be seen as very old, special sorts of people. This follows the notion that progenitors see their descendants as children, while the descendants see ancestors as elders. The fact that they no longer live and work as humans (for their new bodies are unable) is precisely the condition and prompt for their potencies to emerge. To justify their being, they also need to be useful; they *need* to reciprocate. This is basically what Viveiros de Castro (1998) calls a different perspective, the vision of the world according to a species-specific corporeal form.

Interactive bodies

Faith in the productive capacity of progenitors was crucial in the alterity of the dead. Without help from written sources, asking how ancient Andeans perceived their dead can really only be answered by seeing what they did to and around the ancestral dead in archaeological contexts.

Let us first consider what most images of the dead were like. Ancestor images were, put simply, objects that were infused with the supernatural power of esteemed forebears (Lau 2008). Ancestor effigies could take many different forms: mummy bundle, stone sculpture and figurines. But even common pots and distinctive, but unworked, pebbles could serve as an ancestral instantiation. All these featured parts of the prototype or conveyed some essence of the original (Salomon 1991).

Even when cult objects were destroyed, however, new images could replace them (Hernández Príncipe, in Arriaga 1999: 103; Doyle 1988: 66). Bits of the surviving remains (ashes, rock, hair, fingernails, textiles, etc.) were believed to still harbor ancestral power.[4] Such remains were the materials that Spanish extirpators were especially careful to dispose of (in rivers, by burial, or burning) out of sight from the Indians, lest they were to make the cult images anew (Arriaga 1968: 25–26, 31, 131). Thus many types of ancestor effigies were possible, but I will focus on those images that are most commonly represented in the archaeological record: mummy bundles, stone sculptures and ceramic objects. These construct similar kinds of alterity.

Probably the most common form consisted of a mummy bundle. This had the quality of containing physical matter of the dead person – such as hair, fingernails, bones, dried flesh and personal effects. Essentially, these were dried human bodies who were wrapped in textiles. In the highlands, this was produced by removing the soft, putrefying tissues, while leaving the skin, flesh and bones to be dehydrated in the freezing nightly temperatures of the mountains. They were positioned in the flexed or tucked position, like a fetus, and rarely in a seated or extended position. Father Bernabé Cobo (1990: 39, 42) observed that the Incas made use of embalming techniques that preserved the skin and flesh from deteriorating in composition or smell; he marveled, 'Some of the bodies lasted this way for two hundred years' (cf. Doyle 1988: 219).

The mummification preserved the form of the deceased, a technical procedure that made it last longer. The Recuay sometimes represented mummy bundles in stone as well as in ceramics (Plates 25, 30). These too had the effect of stabilizing or materializing the originary form (a biologically living being) for posterity. Stone-carvers indelibly cut an image out of the rock, just as the firing of ceramics fixed another's perception of the ancestral other. At least with mummy bundles, new wrappings could cover or replace old, worn and deteriorating ones.

The variable forms of Recuay ancestral bodies are almost certainly related to Andean native concepts of death and dying, which theorize corporeal transformations as an extended process of dying, of which biological expiration is one, albeit highly important, moment. Specifically, anthropologists Frank Salomon (1995: 328–34; see also 1998: 9–11) and George Urioste (1981: 15–18) have detailed a 'death continuum', consisting of varying physical states and associations with the expiring body and its transformation after death: from softer and wetter, to harder and drier.

Outside of the organic matter of the cadavers, stone was probably the most important surrogate material for ancestor simulacra. No doubt it was favored because of its material properties. It is abundant across the Andes, and comes in many potential colors and textures and from sources that are of symbolic importance (Dean 2010). It can be finely worked. Moreover, that work can be enduring over many generations. It can also be moved with effort and be part of larger constructions and contexts. But it was also favored because of its generative properties, having to do with stone's animacy and potency as concentrates and repositories of ancestral pasts (for Ancash, see Howard 2006; Lau 2006b, 2008).

In highland Ancash, stone had long been favored for sculptures as well as for standing stone monuments, known as *huancas* (Bazán del Campo 2007; Bazán del Campo and Wegner 2006; Burger 1992a; Doyle 1988; Falcón 2004). The first huancas appeared by the Early Horizon and their use continued until colonial times. Stood as uprights, phallic in shape, and embedded into the soil, some have argued that huancas were the symbolic complements to mummy bundles, which are seed-like and are found in womb-like caves (Duviols 1977, 1979). There are also sexual connotations of the footplow and its movements. One of the most famous standing uprights in Ancash, the Lanzón, was established as a key cult image of the monumental complex at Chavín de Huántar early in its creation: it staked out a sacred center as a foundation and provided the focus for subsequent veneration (Burger 1992b: 270; Cummins 2008: 282).

The best known stone carvings, portraying the esteemed dead, come from the Recuay tradition (Grieder 1978; Lau 2006b; Schaedel 1948, 1952). Known examples are associated with villages or large centers with nearby cemetery sectors.

The myriad representations of ancestors share fairly common characteristics. Many are positioned upright in a seated, tucked position (Plates 25, 30). There are also views of frontal figures, flanked by other beings. The body is often completely wrapped (if a bundle). And all that might be exposed is the head and face.

The most elaborate work showing the ancestral simulacra often went toward rendering the head and face. This was important for different reasons. Probably the most important was that, for many Andean groups, the face was the locus of recognition. While the Recuay did not practice naturalistic portraiture, the identity and associations of the ancestor effigies were probably never in doubt. Ethnohistorical documents suggests that little worked sculptures, standing stones and even pebbles were easily recognized as ancestral embodiments. But effigies of the dead also frequently wore different kinds of headdresses and ear ornaments that probably helped to signal some sort of identity, affiliation and rank.

Second, the head was the primary site of the ancestor's engagement with the world. It was where an ancestor effigy was seen to interact with social others. Most of the physical interactions expected of ancestors are those that emit from or are directed toward the figure's ears (songs, prayers, queries), nose (of offerings, chicha) and mouth (predictions, food and drink).

The eyes are of great importance and, at least with Recuay, are always shown oversized and wide open. I suspect this is because, as a primary sensory organ, they demonstrate the life of the ancestor, his alertness and potential for seeing the world and the people around him. It is impossible to pass by an effigy without its recognition; at the same time that ancestor witnesses all the people and all the events for which his favor is needed. The open eyes allow for mutual acknowledgment of co-presence and action. Cobo (1990: 42) remarked that the Inca fabricated a mummy effigy so that '[its] artificial eyes were open, and this gave the impression that it was looking at those who were present'. To perform activities under the gaze of ancestors and crucial others legitimated statuses and power relations. Some data exist which lend support to this conjecture. The interactive visual quality of Recuay figural ceramics may allude to a special form of subjectivity during ritual encounters, perhaps heightened through intoxication, and shared between chiefly/ancestral figures and their followers (Lau 2008, 2010d).

The final formal quality of ancestor images, which reflects their alterity, is that they frequently occur in numbers. Ancestors, like old folk, are quite gregarious with their own. In Paracas and Early Nasca cemeteries, bundles were frequently placed together, forming their own afterlife collectivities. In Recuay, subterranean and above-ground mausolea were clearly built to preserve and curate multiple interments; caves also served this purpose. Such collectivities presume a special world, or 'house', for the ancestral dead, in which they are seen to socialize with their own, until they are engaged with again during the various rituals initiated by their living descendants.

Housing the dead: forms and formulae

> They are persuaded that the dead feel, eat, and drink, and only with great pain can they be buried and bound to earth. In their machays [burial caves] and burial places in the fields, where they are not interred, but placed in a small hollow or cave or little house, they have more rest.
>
> *On Indian burials, Pablo José de Arriaga 1968: 64*

Although the archaeological record of these patterns is imperfect, much formal variability can also be discerned. The available evidence demonstrates that many Andean groups did not abandon or break ties with their deceased, as much as they tended them, physically and symbolically, in perpetuity.

Ancient Ancash groups maintained their dead in environments that allowed their continued presence among the living. They designed most, if not all, of the burial structures to contain physical human remains inside, protected and preserved. Mortuary buildings, what Isbell (1997) called 'sepulchers', were to do away with the effects of interment in soil or in the open. The constructions mitigated against the processes of decay due to the elements, animals and other humans. The different kinds of tomb architecture were repositories for the dead and in this way resolved a fundamental human concern: the putrefying corpses of deceased ones.

Siting the housing for the dead also speaks to their alterity. Topography and the availability of building materials (e.g., stone) were certainly important factors. In general, groups favored high areas with strategic vantages and rocky prominences of land. Proximity to key land- or waterforms was also important. Special features such as caves, springs, lakes and rocky outcrops were often seen as origin places, or *pacarinas* – embodying the progenitor or a founding or milestone act by him/her in the ancestral past (Arriaga 1968: 24; Doyle 1988: 71, 241; Salomon 1995: 322). Caves, in particular, were emphasized as burial spaces, not least because they were durable and helped to preserve bodies, images and grave offerings. Some caves are also obviously very large, with interiors and hollows that could accommodate large numbers of individuals. On most occasions, perhaps because caves were unavailable, groups built environments that simulated the qualities of cave interiors.

Caves are especially important in Amerindian thought because they are quintessential places for fertility and emergence, and are seen as conduits to the underworld and supernatural realms (Bassie-Sweet 1991; Heyden 1981; Prufer and Brady 2005); they are also inextricably related to group origins from the earth (Salomon and Urioste 1991; Urton 1999). For the Andes, this held for much of the complex of death-related culture, for interment practices, the ancestor cult, the images of the dead, and their various settings frequently embedded the symbolism of growth and fertility (Bloch and Parry 1982; Duviols 1979). The language of death practices and ritual elements are also pertinent (e.g., Duviols 1979). Burial constructions and the treatment of the corpse marshaled symbolism from the life–death transformations of living forms, both plant and animal.

One expression of this concerns the physical connections between tombs and specific locales or landforms. They facilitated the living to enter and connect periodically to a specific, selected locale. The locales frequently marked or were associated with *pacarinas*. Taking root at these mytho-historical locales (e.g., instantiated by a rock, cave, lake or mountain), mausolea were established to tap into the ancestral potencies where progenitors came from and resided. It was not unusual for groups to build structures directly on top of interment places, showing both the symbolic and physical connections of ancestors as foundations (Plate 31). Importantly, tomb constructions were often renovated, adding new extensions and chambers (DeLeonardis and Lau 2004). In addition to new burials and contexts, entire new buildings were added when necessary. These physical connections between the dead evince how the living perceive networked relationships between members of the tomb collective over time.

Skeptical of Christian treatments of the dead corpse, native Andeans often returned to church cemeteries to recover their dead and put them back into the customary repositories: caves and chullpas. For them, they reasoned that the dead needed to breathe, did not like being in the ground or the extended position (e.g., not flexed, fetal or seated). The unpleasant stench of decomposing cadavers also stirred them to remove them from Christian graves (Doyle 1988: 205). Keeping the dead out in the open air, the Jesuit inquisitor Arriaga (1968: 56) observed of native sentiment, was done so that their bodies were not cramped and did not rot (also Doyle 1988: 205).

Rather than decompose in the ground, open exposure allowed the corpse to dessicate. It may not be surprising, then, that groups in the Callejón de Huaylas occasionally built ventilation ducts and shafts into their burial structures to circulate fresh air (e.g., Bennett 1944: 16). This helps to explain why *chuño* freeze-dried potatoes and bundles are both placed on top of straw (Doyle 1988: 212, 224), to provide soft, breathable bedding preferred for reducing damp, protecting against pests, and making superior products (Mamani 1981: 240, 245) (Fig 5.3).

FIGURE 5.3 Freeze-dried potatoes, or *chuño*, for sale in Huaraz market, 2004. Many different varieties of potato are dried and, when ready, are stored on top of hay to limit damp and avoid decomposition. Peel is easily removed when the interior tissue is hydrated.

There are interesting parallels between preserving human bodies and high Andean procedures for preparing chuño, meat jerky (*charki*), and other kinds of freeze-dried products. The freezing temperatures typical of the Andean highlands dry out wet tissue, making the item hard, shriveled, light and portable. Anthropologist Catherine Allen (1982: 182) writes of contemporary Quechua speakers in the Cuzco highlands, 'As potatoes turn into ch'uño, they are said to die. I was told repeatedly that ch'uño is *wañusqa* (dead).' Archaeologist Bill Sillar (1996) has also noted the similarities in the form, use and beliefs of storage structures for potatoes and chullpa mausolea for ancestor bundles.

Importantly, the process allows the items to be more reliably stored, peeled and transported for later use. Very old chuño, made of select potatoes and carefully aged between one and up to twenty years, is highly valued for consumption (Mamani 1981: 245). This is precisely the goal of many Andean treatments of the dead associated with ancestors. Like these products, the ancestral dead, once transformed, were enriched sources of renewable sustenance, a kind of future-looking risk management.

Water brings fields back to life, as the rainy season transforms the sere and dried-out vegetation into a verdant landscape again. Water and people's hard work makes them useful again. This can be of chuño or charki, which rehydrate when soaked or when added to soups. Soft wheat and barley cereals are also opened up like this. Maize kernels are soaked to make them germinate for use in chicha maize beer. In essence, the work of rehydration, what can be likened to the practices of ancestor veneration (libations, clothes, food, songs, attention, etc.), was seen to activate the latent potency of dried out things (also Allen 1982; Gose 1994). Similar technical operations and commitment (both physical and symbolic) work to saturate the items, making them soft and pliant, who then can return the favor of nourishment.

It is worth noting that the hydration process does not recover the original quality of the original product. Chuño can never be potatoes (*papas*) again, just as ancestors can never be biologically living people again. Indeed, the transformation alters, irreversibly so, its character. Chuño and charki, when rehydrated, no longer look the same as they did when in their original, fresh forms; their color and flavor change. They also smell pungently, in dried or rehydrated conditions. In this light, it is interesting that the Quechua term for ancestor bundle, *mallqui*, also describes a 'seed', 'sapling' or 'young plant' (Duviols 1979: 22; Salomon 1995: 328, 340; Sherbondy 1988; Sillar 1996: 282). The group of terms appears to emphasize a bundle's young or energetic state, rather than an old, ossified form. The form of eggs is often the originary state of mythical ancestors, for highland as well as coastal groups. Of course, the nurture of things, housed in a special, protective form, characterizes many kinds of inchoate, latent beings. Just as a baby grows in a womb, and eggs in a nest, seeds and tubers might find their nourishing space to be their chakra, or field. So the living entrusted their most precious sources of vitality to burial spaces.[5]

The entire mortuary complex can be said to contain components at sequentially smaller scales. Hence, the world contains houses; necropoli contain tombs; tombs contain bundles and other container objects; pots contained offerings; bundles contain the remains of esteemed dead; and the dead contain the basis for the group's continued prosperity. This was not so much a fractal system (Fowler 2004: 48–52; Wagner 1991), as much as it was a nested series of differently constituted social bodies. The overall burial necropolis involved a series of containers, each smaller than the previous, which enveloped the entire collective and its people through time at different scales. Crucially, they all have the purpose of distributing and concentrating the vitality issuing from death.

Proximity, ritual, aggregation

Tomb design stressed the careful arrangement and temporality of ritual for the ancestors, attending to their needs and alterity. Access into Recuay tradition tombs is often restricted at certain points: through antechambers and doorways. For the multichambered tombs, the internal spatial divisions functioned not only to segregate interments, but identified separate zones of tasks. The antechamber, for example, was often used for leaving offerings, while niches held ritual equipment, and the exteriors immediately outside tombs were places for burning. The compartmentalization also prescribed intervals in movements and distinguished engagements with the deceased.

Caves and the simulated cave spaces of tombs provide clues to the interactions with the deceased. These burial environments are very often dark spaces, and the accessways and low ceiling may restrict certain motions. Walking and standing upright are rarely possible and, very commonly, the visitor can move forward or backwards only by crawling. Besides the disorienting darkness and crowded spaces, most ruins of these buildings today reek of refuse and damp. Without good upkeep and functioning ventilation, such spaces in the past probably smelled of decomposing bodies, organic materials and food offerings. Leaving the tomb through narrow passageways can only be described as a shock to the senses; not only is there fresh air, clear vision and sunlight, there is unencumbered movement and re-orientation. I have suggested elsewhere that a possible objective of such environments was to make the visitor deferent, perhaps even supplicant like a child, to the ancestral bundles and effigies (Lau 2011). As a practice of objectifying inclusion and genealogical position of different actors, what better way to embody the descendant status of the venerating individual?

Overall, Recuay burial practices are consistent with Amerindian cosmologies and the ethnohistorical evidence that stress the regenerative capacity of death through telluric and biological metaphors (e.g., Boone 2000; Duviols 1979; Fitzsimmons 2009; Heyden 1981; Houston et al. 2006; López Austin 1988). The ancestral dead were seen as old, organic forms but, crucially, with the potential for renewal. With a proper environment and attention, they could flourish and provide for their young in perpetuity.

Keeping the dead apart in their own communities and dwellings also alludes to their otherness. It is at least partly due to the living wanting to maintain some distance from the cemeteries, all the while keeping them close. This probably results from general notions about the polluting aspects of the dead (often associated with corpses) or their potential danger to communities (both during burial as well as due to negligent disposal) (Douglas 1976; Hertz 1960; Walter 2006). But it also regards the fact that the ancestral dead can be said to have and make their own communities.

Not all residential settlements were established within walking distance of the burial grounds. But it seems that most were during prehispanic times. The priest Arriaga (1968: 24) is again insightful on this detail: 'They also venerate their *pacarinas*, or places of origin … This is one of the reasons why they resist the consolidation of their towns and like to live in such bad and difficult places … the reason they give for living there is that this is their pacarina.'

The growth of a necropolis implies continuity of use by one or more source community over time and, in related fashion, an enduring social connection between the community and cemetery's physical locale. This might give regard to the notion of territory and what land belongs to what group. An individual collective tomb (e.g., chullpa) served as the mausoleum for a given group over time (Fig 5.4). The tomb spaces and its environments also performed as the key backdrop for associated ceremonial practices and regular interaction between the living and the dead. As long as the group and cult continued, additional interments and relationships could redefine the dead community, constantly re-ordering a group's social past and genealogy (Salomon 1995: 347; Zuidema 1978: 46).

The record today is a palimpsest of a diachronic process that has been curtailed and its features merged into one, largely synchronic, context. In one cave chamber in southern Ancash, as many as eighty mummy bundles were reported (Antúnez 1923). In one large chullpa at Chinchawas, a minimum of twenty-four individuals were revealed through excavations. The positioning of the bundles was probably arranged through a practical compromise that took into account issues of space, the kinds of kin relations that the mummies embodied, and the decisions of the last ritual collectivity that reordered the burial space.

What is very common is for later structures (e.g., chambers, galleries) to be added to existing funerary structures, or, on a larger scale, for entire new buildings to be located in necropoli. Additions appear to have been to relate new burial contexts and interments to the old ones, and had the net effect of creating larger and more complex mortuary aggregations over time. All these developments are potential expressions of the changing social memory of the collective (e.g., Huntington and Metcalf 1979; Joyce 2001a; Salomon 1995; Silverman and Small 2002). Unfortunately much of this is largely lost to us due to exposure, time and tomb robbing.

From time to time, the archaeological record shows how mortuary practices may have acted as important sociopolitical expressions that addressed the alterity of the tombs and their contents. For example, some local groups in the seventh century showed their new embrace of above-ground mausolea by building chullpas directly over subterranean tombs (e.g., Ichik Wilkawaín, Chinchawas). Chambers were added to some, while others were sealed – by ritual communities who apparently re-organized ancestral orders. In similar fashion, the establishment of D-shaped structures (at Honcopampa), ritual buildings of apparently foreign style, may have sought to reimagine the dead under the new ritual-economic ideology spread by Wari. These developments were more than merely adoption of new forms of ritual

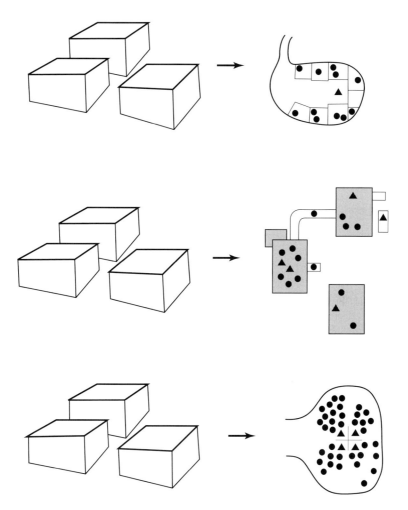

FIGURE 5.4 Hypothetical reconstructions of necropolis formation. Triangles (▲) locate apical ancestors, while circles (●) locate more common esteemed deceased. Each scheme presumes flexibility for accommodating new interments and new arrangements by the descendants. Top row: subterranean tomb with interior partitions. Middle: chullpa cluster and additions. Bottom: cave.

buildings. The developments laid claim to the necropolis space, asserting physical appropriation, exclusion and/or completion of previous arrangements.

The proliferation of chullpas occasioned a new style of ritual practice that imagined and engaged the dead differently from before. These very likely did not contradict earlier beliefs and practices. But we have also seen how chullpas were different, indeed overtly unusual, in their early appearance in Ancash. Insofar as the current radiocarbon evidence shows, this intrusion came around the early part of the seventh century AD. It became so popular that it was the predominant mortuary mode for nearly a millennium. In short, mortuary spaces and practices for ancestor burials were often malleable and contested over time. The inevitable loss in death ensured flux and new social arrangements for the living and the expired.

Nurturing ancestors: effort and embodiment

Reciprocity between the living and the dead fueled Recuay's social economy of ancestrality. A diversity of practices went into the ancestor cult, and great attention was paid to the changing statuses and dispositions of the deceased. Regular care and attention for the bodies of ancestors were vital to the ritual system. One priest warns about routine activities with ancestor bundles: 'These mummies are more harmful than the huacas, because the worship of the latter takes place once a year, whereas the dead are worshiped every day' (Lic. R. Hernández Príncipe, letter to Arriaga 1968: 86).

Nurturing ancestors featured wrapping the body in fine textiles and the accoutrements of exalted and high status. This holds for both the making and the subsequent veneration of the ancestor. Just as other living beings shed skin, leaves and peels, providing new wrappings for the ancestor was an important ritual, which symbolized renewal. Typical dress included full-length garment, a shirt and a head covering (Arriaga 1968: 27, 55; Doyle 1988: 228–29). Some people were also given feathered headdresses as well as bags filled with coca. All these offerings by others reinforced the notion of the ancestral other as living, sentient and requiring of new acts of devotion. It is noteworthy that Recuay iconography, in stone sculpture as well as ceramics, frequently portrays ancestor effigies decked out in fine attire and accoutrements (Lau 2006b, 2011). Specific resemblances include coca bags, feathered headdresses, full-length garments and shawl pins (Plate 32).

Other forms of ancestral recognition occurred through offerings. In addition to textiles, food and other offerings were made to the dead because the worshippers believed that the dead needed sustenance. Without this, the dead were unhappy, unsatisfied and unlikely to share of *their* vitality (Arriaga 1999). Famously fickle, the fear by the living is that the ancestors do not do what they are supposed to do, which is take care of them. Or worse, they also have the power to withhold health and engender misfortune or illness (Doyle 1988: 141–42).

During ethnohistorical times, the quintessential offerings included chicha maize beer, coca leaves and llama fat. There were also additional offerings: *Spondylus* shell (in whole valves, pieces, beads), different types of ground meals and powders from cultigens and minerals, pieces of metal and coins (during colonial times) and dried maize (whole cobs and kernels). The extirpators itemized many of these offerings as abuses given to the dead (Arriaga 1999: Ch. 4).

Specially prepared chicha was critical (Arriaga 1999: 39): it was sprinkled on ritual objects, poured as libations to the ancestors and other divinities, and poured directly into tombs, besides being drunk by the various participants. Some batches were made from the corn collected as contributions from different households (Doyle 1988: 150). Camelids and cuys (guinea pigs) were sacrificed, and their blood and flesh were offered, the latter sometimes sprinkled on the ground, buildings and cult objects.

At least during colonial times, there were also important prohibitions in the constitution of proper ancestral persons. For example, the 'dirty' meats of chickens, pigs and sheep rarely featured as offerings to the ancestors; indeed, these were prohibited from being eaten during burial rites. It was customary that offerings were of native animals and native products, which befitted the respected status and special food needs of the esteemed ancestors. While deer and other wild species are present in relevant faunal assemblages, they are found only in trace amounts, suggesting that camelids and guinea pigs were customary as offering animals (Lau 2007).

It is interesting that the broad complex of ancestor veneration should focus, in very great part, on materials that have been processed and transformed, in some way, from their natural state. This holds for both the ethnohistorical evidence as well as archaeological contexts of ancestor veneration. Thus the lard and blood come from a dead domesticated animal, and chicha and coca have also been processed through fermentation and drying, respectively. *Spondylus* and coca, as long-distance trade goods, were also products of considerable work. The various powders and meals have been ground down. There was therefore great emphasis on anthropogenically transformed things and their use as offerings in ancestor ceremonies.

The offerings made to the recently dead in their burial ceremony (*pacarícuc*) were somewhat different. In addition to the customary kinds of offerings made to ancestors, there seems to have been a wider range of foodstuffs offered to the recently deceased. This includes yams, potatoes, manioc, avocadoes, peanut, lucuma fruits, beans and potatoes (both fresh and freeze-dried chuño). These were all foods that the deceased, while living, enjoyed eating (Doyle 1988: 210).

We can speculate why these items may not have been appropriate offerings to ancestors. Many of them remain relatively 'natural', unchanged; they have not gone through drastic anthropogenic procedures to change their qualities or properties. No doubt where wealth was 'in people', work and symbolic effort were seen as gifts. The food also connects to their individual humanity more, rather than to their new othernesses as divinities.

There were probably equivalencies made between the kinds of offerings and the ancestors, due to their transformations; they made the offerings particularly suitable or transcended any food restrictions for the ancestors. It is notable that descriptions of offerings made to ancestors rarely include raw potatoes, or 'fresh' fruits and vegetables. These were either not seen as 'valuable' enough or had not been transformed enough. The more typical offerings (e.g., coca, chicha, blood, textiles, *Spondylus* shell, cuys and camelids) all embodied effort and the transformative contributions of others, and were therefore highly appropriate tokens to bestow on their main source of wealth, founding progenitors.

Many of the propitiation rituals occurred in open areas, just outside or near the tombs. These were called *cayan*, and were located on platforms highly visible from afar and accessible to many. Interestingly, all across different parts of highland Ancash, such spaces, often delimited by walls, have been found which performed as the settings, often associated with nearby funerary structures, for public ceremonies and intensive feasting (Gero 1992; Herrera 2008; Lau 2002; Tello 1929). Even D-shaped structures were probably for ancestor ceremonies at Honcopampa. The modest sizes of the spaces suggest relatively small ritual collectives. These may have served no more than a hundred people – much less than the thousands we might envision in coastal plazas or those of Inca administrative centres.

It was in these open areas that festive activities publicly engaged and recognized the alterity of the ancestors as sentient, divine beings (Carrión Cachot 1955; Doyle 1988; Duviols 2003; Hernández Príncipe 1923; Herrera 2008; Ibarra 2003b; Lau 2000, 2002; Mantha 2009; Millones 1979). Large quantities of food and drink were consumed, for entire communities (live and dead) convened because the major ancestor ceremonies coincided with the sowing and harvesting of crops, also cooperative ventures. Food and especially chicha lubricated the integration of various groups. A generous supply was *de rigueur* at any ancestor celebration for it was symbolic of the abundance desired and provided by ancestors.

Through ritual and chicha, well-being coursed through the collective social body, living and ancestral. Indeed, renewal through ancestral 'flows' is implicit in Recuay decorative ceramic vessels. The main function of the tomb vessels (pottery, gourds) was to contain offerings of liquids, including the blood of sacrificed animals, but especially chicha. Chicha and the dead may be linked because they are sources of vitality from things which are slightly decayed, anthropogenically transformed, and in need of tending.

Testimonies tell us that even common vessels could perform as major huacas, and the function to contain chicha was paramount in their ritual significance (e.g., Hernández Príncipe, in Arriaga 1999: 96). This purpose is enhanced, however, by the fact that many decorative vessels depict groups in celebration. Or they may depict chiefly figureheads of those groups (Lau 2010d, 2011), who figuratively give of themselves in the act of pouring. Death and the cult of ancestral persons demanded a process to produce and circulate flows of vitality provisioned by ancestors and their earthly representatives.

Summary

This chapter has explored the alterity of the ancestral dead. It relied on ethnohistorical evidence of death practices and cosmology to help understand the Early Intermediate Period and, specifically, the rise of a social economy of ancestrality for highland Andean groups.

The ancestral dead were perceived of as a special kind of social being, who had dispositions and habits very similar to those of living humans. Their alterity pivoted on their roles as esteemed progenitors and sources of renewal. Like their descendants, they live in houses with their families, and eat, drink beer and socialize. The ancestral dead were old entities, and characterized by being hard, intransigent and unyielding. Ritual work in this social economy was to make them pliant and give of their enriching vitality: food, beer and the substance of kin.

We have seen, in both ethnohistorical and prehispanic times, Andean groups regularly attending to the dead as social beings. Ancestors were honoured during public events and ceremonies. Their veneration occurred during seasonal events based on the agricultural calendar and also whenever ancestral favor or acknowledgment was required. Retrieved from their repositories (usually caves and tombs), they were celebrated in nearby open contexts with dancing, feasting and offerings. This included new textiles and copious amounts of drink, food and songs – all acts of effort and devotion. The ancestors were also carried, sometimes in litters, and danced with, as if they were alive. The festive events coincided with collective recognition of one's elders, genealogy and community.

The various physical engagements with the dead constituted vital forms of sociality. As social beings, their recognition and interaction with the biologically living continually helped shape social worlds. Through the remembrance of loved ones, connections with the dead and the living persons were publicly expressed. The cults occasioned very stylized forms of ritual practice between kinsfolk. The movements and activities of the participants, usually concerning offerings of liquids, enabled the nourishing of bodies as a formulaic operation. By feeding their prototypes, the descendants could be seen as repeating the embodied acts that engendered them. Mimetic artworks (effigies) and rites were part of prescriptive memory practices that coordinated flows, generosity and genealogy. The outcome was a series of revitalized bodies: ancestral and social.

Funerary practices sought to make more durable the bodily presence of people's ancestors. Diverse kinds of burial constructions and ritual spaces served as containers for the tangible ancestral forms, but they also helped to interact with them. Mausolea, large collective burials and necropoli – all for corporate burials – gave great emphasis to increasing access, visual prominence and overtly materializing social links to the ancestors.

The death process transformed named deceased into cult objects, who were then treated as the pivots for religious mediation. Ancestral effigies were fashioned especially as dessicated mummies and ossified, flexed interments. But many kinds of objects depicted and/or were instilled with the partible potency of ancestors because groups stressed durable and solid physical bodies, and some ancestors, especially ones from the deep past, were lithified as stone sculptures, pebbles, outcrops and mountains. The objectification process also occurred at different forms and scales, from grave items to buildings and landforms.

In part, it was probably because ancestors had the uncanny quality of embodying different forms, that ancestor cults were so enduring. This was the case even during great times of cultural change and when there was extreme prejudice to move away from traditional ritual dispositions. Even without conquests and resettlement, however, historical contingency and local politics of burial ensured constant transformation. Ancestor others were, above all, willful agents in constituting new social relations and histories.

6

CONCLUSIONS

The foregoing has been an exploration of alterity in prehistory. The 'Recognition of Others' refers to both the ancient perceptions of others and our contemporary surveillance of them. A study of this kind obliged an examination of diverse material remains and contexts of the archaeological record as well as reliance on the representational imagery of artworks – all framed within understandings informed especially by ethnography and other documentary sources. Alterity, in general, has seen very little treatment in the archaeological literature, and this work makes a step toward fuller consideration of its utility for archaeology.

Different strands of evidence were assembled to build my arguments. By obligation, I privileged some kinds of data over others – and many of the arguments drawn from the available data must be considered hypotheses for further investigation. Much argumentation relied on insights from ethnographic and ethnohistorical comparisons, encompassing many miles and centuries beyond the region (Central Andes, northern Peru) and the time period in question. Equally significant may be potential disjunctions in social complexity as well as the contingency of local histories and environmental contexts. These are significant issues, to be sure. But they are also unavoidable ones if we want to reconstruct understandings of the world that are not necessarily our own and, in the case of the deep past, cannot be our own. The archaeological record is exceedingly rich, but enigmatic and often intractable without comparison.

This book focused on several important kinds of alterity, based on the social and symbolic 'economies' with others. By this I mean the social relations vital for personhood and social reproduction. The first concerned those associated with regions, both environmental and cultural. The second concerned the alterity of familiar others, those on the 'inside' primarily associated with kinsfolk and the residential community. I then examined the alterity associated with the outside, associated with foreigners, enemies and predators. Finally, I considered the alterity of the ancestral dead and their relationships with the living.

Throughout, it was seen that these are fluid categories, with sliding scales for identification. Often there is overlap. This was to evaluate my basic proposal: that perception of and engagements with the other were fundamental to ancient Andean cultures and their associated peoples. In some cases, alterity comprises the background of difference in which identity emerges. In other cases, alterity process is a purposeful confrontation between rival perspectives. In some cases, alterity gives rise to social relations, or is the basis for sociality.

We have seen that various patterns centered on the transaction and internalizing of something crucial from the other. What helped to make persons and 'culture' of groups during the Early Intermediate Period frequently relied on the recognition and actions of others. Other beings were seen as a source of vitality and nourishment – and the great emphasis on alterity was precisely to capitalize on what could be gotten out of the engagement. The desire of alterity concerned how to live with and benefit by way of these others.

Alterities crosscut different domains and are of different scale. Each one comes with specific kinds of material expectations characterized by different intensities and distances between self and others. The ones treated in the foregoing ('the dead', 'predators', 'kinspeople', 'outsiders') seem to have relatively stable qualities, which help us see them archaeologically but is also partly due to the observation that alterities of these kinds tend to be more durable and self-sustaining. Yet, like archaeological studies of identity or ethnicity, there is no magic formula for approaching ancient alterity as a cross-cultural phenomenon. Its complexity as a process and instability in cultural expression make this all but impossible. Nevertheless, ethnography and historical records will almost certainly furnish viable comparisons to understand some forms, while helping to settle alternative viewpoints. Finally, there are certainly many other othernesses, and I have by no means exhausted the range of potential alterities.

I used a framework of alterity not only as an heuristic device for contemplating the past or archaeological method. Rather, the move committed to the idea that the alterity process, the process of making othernesses, is crucial for informing the study of ancient cultural patterns and social change. The Early Intermediate Period (ca. AD 1–700) of the Central Andes, with its unprecedented socio–political dynamism and distinctive patterning of material culture, provided a unique space for interrogating cultural difference in prehistoric contexts.

From a systemic perspective, part of the great challenge of understanding the time is reconciling the great diversity of cultures and their long history and insularity as regional traditions. Many of the most prominent – Nasca, Moche, Recuay, Lima, Cajamarca – endured for the greater part of a millennium, and each one was characterized by a very different art system. The onset of the Early Intermediate Period, I argued, was spurred on by essentially an about-face on the issue of the Chavín cult: a wholesale rejection of things Chavín. If it was the belief in the Chavín other (one itself based on esoteric otherness) that allowed for rapid expansion of the Chavín community, that cultural unity faltered just as quickly when the Chavín cultic system was called into question.

The wane of Chavín influence shattered the previous cultural integration into fragmented local and increasingly regionalized systems throughout Peru. Concomitantly, it promoted a series of new patterns almost simultaneously: new art traditions, new kinds of residential practices and leadership ideologies, reduced long-distance trade. These all privileged factional interests, and had the virtue of all being largely different to one another. The regional art traditions endured for many centuries, and became increasingly the purview of increasingly powerful nobles.

Although forms of interaction clearly existed, cosmologies, mythic traditions and funerary practices remained, in the main, very different from one another. Groups were conscious of each other, but each regional art tradition chose to keep core elements of form and imagery intact, over many centuries. Finding common alterity first in rejecting Chavín, over the next six or seven centuries, groups of the ensuing period promoted active difference to the ways of doing things of 'other' cultures. As we have seen, this was not simply a pattern of isolationism, since trade and interaction are evidenced. Rather, in the face of others, groups actively guarded local common patterns such as techniques of making (ceramics, sculpture, metalwork), as much as the belief systems and mythologies that underwrote the remarkable ritual practices of Early Intermediate Period groups. Both to us and to their contemporaries, the ancestrality of Recuay groups cannot help but seem rather alien compared to Moche's 'Warrior Narrative' or the multicolored menagerie of Nasca. It was during the Early Intermediate Period that regional identities and alterities dominated in the Central Andes.

In this great time of cultural diversity, however, it is interesting to observe that alterity processes of each culture were patterned in such strikingly similar ways. Thus the dead were seen as sources of life and regeneration. Predators were dangerous consumers – part animal, part human – who instigated corporeal transitions. Insiders nourished, outsiders were integrated. Captives and body parts were incorporated and displayed. People subjectivized objects to interact with them as if they were alive. Even in difference-making, there may have been something still profoundly Andean in the recognition of others.

Alterities in archaeology: moving forward

Besides the role of alterity for ancient Amerindian societies, I wish to follow up on several themes potentially of more general interest, and examine what present and future contributions on ancient alterity might also emphasize.

First, alterity was seen as being crucial for the rather differentiated look, the regional cultural heterogeneity, of the Early Intermediate Period. Knowledge about other groups and their cultural dispositions played a significant role in the making and representation of alterity; there were conscious choices to construct the other. This was first seen in the intentional move away from Chavín style, and then the long rather insular trajectories of regional art traditions at the crux of the Early Intermediate Period. Here, the heterogeneity consisted of many 'insides'. What constituted the 'outside' had meaningful effect. More so than other times of Andean prehistory, the key brokers of style and identity (nobles, artisans, traders) during the Early Intermediate Period focused on otherness precisely to locate and coordinate something about themselves.

Second, alterity cannot be divorced from the processes of social complexity. Many of the most crucial developments of the Early Intermediate Period were accompanied by innovative and intensified ways to perceive and represent powerful others. These increasingly centered on beliefs about how collectivities, warriors/enemies, ancestors and leaders originated and were 'made'. Some of these cultural frameworks did not exist before, were intensified from antecedent foundations, or were irrevocably transformed from antecedents.

Institutionalized leaders, by way of their material accumulation and authority, cannot help but be laden also with an alterity. This, as we have seen with the Recuay case, concerns their distinction from normal social relations based on social/genealogical position (they assumed a privileged domestic position), but also the symbolism that reinforces their specialness. Alterity helps to resolve the question of Recuay chiefship by demonstrating a mode where social actions between unequal others recognize the position of 'chief'. It is notable that many, if not all, Recuay human representations seek to collapse the distance between the past and present, the dead and the living, ancestors and chiefs. It was a mimesis that telescoped fluidly between myth and history, image and practice. In telling about the storied transgenerational careers of leaders, they show us the politically organized subjection that is at the heart of any political system. My emphasis was on Recuay, and further research should explore how alterity played a role in other kinds of socio-political arrangements. But if Recuay is indicative, much Early Intermediate Period art focused on the actions that confer authority by way of their stylized engagement with others.

Third, the emphasis on alterity helps us retool understandings of the social. Alterity comprises the perceptions of others, but there is no prescription for the kinds of others. In this book, we have examined a range of alterities taken on by beings who interact with humans: the ancestral dead, animals, enemies and prey, kin. Many of the interactions were seen to be social relations. And one could argue that these beings are more social (in having conviviality, institutions, culture, moral framework) than some humans. If the 'social' is problematized in this way, then many of the expectations for things in the lexical field of the social might also be renovated, or at least re-imagined productively. Society and social complexity are the first things that come to mind.

Ultimately, I see alterity (recognition of others) as having actively shaped social practices and change. Alterity counted as a key factor during the critical juncture of Andean prehistory, and underwrote one of most notable periods of cultural production and artistic florescence in the world.

I wonder if we take for granted how important perceiving others is to us in our everyday lives. Others, and their perceptions of us, are why we go to war, raise our young and why we work and provide care, why we self-identify a certain way. Alterity effects and motivates precisely in those domains we have examined: dwelling, authority, region, warfare, death. Put another way, there is no warfare without enemies. There is no life without the dead and no dead without the living; no humans without nonhumans. In short, there is no sociality without recognition of social others.

Coda: converging perspectives

It is striking that the language and imagery of sixteenth- and seventeenth-century church missions were so focused on Christian indoctrination as organic, vegetative processes – for these parallelled the native rationale for ancestor cults. Just as Andeans saw their ancestors as sources of growth, as seeds and 'young', the Spanish saw them as deeply rooted 'incitements' to idolatry that needed extirpation to cultivate a different kind of Indian, encultured through another faith.[1]

The endeavor of the Spanish extirpations was not simply to destroy idols and pagan faiths. It was to save souls for the one true God by teaching them the error of their former ways and revealing the mysteries of Christianity (Arriaga 1968: 67). Explaining their false conviction, writes Arriaga (1968: 90–91):

> This too is for lack of Christian teaching and preaching, which must be strengthened not only by planting the truths of the Christian religion in their hearts … But neither mission nor [extirpation] visit will be profitable, however long or permanent, if what is planted is not watered, cultivated, and nurtured, so that what has been pulled up by the roots may not spring up again.

Written for the Spanish crown and church officials, a crucial goal was to rally for support to perform repeat visits and spread, by growing, the one true religion.

'Extirpate', of course, comes from the Latin: 'to root up, destroy, or remove root and branch (a tree, plant)', according to the *Oxford English Dictionary*. Pagan religious practices were seen as a 'disease' and a 'pestilence' and Christianity was considered the 'remedy' (Arriaga 1968: 8–9, 73). But the process was laborious, because the incitements and causes of idolatries were legion and rhyzomatic, sprouting up wherever there was not a firm presence. Arriaga (1968: 21) writes:

> Great diligence was employed … in removing these objects [of idolatry] from their sight … we tried by continual sermons and catechisms to remove them from their hearts, but it is greatly to be feared that roots so ancient and so deep will not yield entirely … To make sure they are really uprooted and will not flourish again, a second and third plowing will be required.

In doing so, the church advocated creating new kinds of embodied others. Arriaga observes on Indian conversion (1968: 142): 'Our purpose is to teach them to work and to develop into the kind of men they should be. We will pluck the finest fruit when these tender plants come to bloom … '. We have already seen how indigenous burial cults partook of this language and symbolism. Ancestors, in their crypts, were tended like organic beings, so that they continued to produce for the living. The crucial difference, of course, resides in Spanish and Andean notions of the afterlife and associated practices. For the Spanish, it was the eternal salvation of souls, growing new kinds of people during their lives. For Andeans, the physicality of bodies was paramount, growing people via their death.

The rhetoric of the missionization process was certainly aimed at Spanish audiences. But one also wonders whether Indians may have found solace in these words as shared symbolic space – a recognition of perspectives. Perhaps there was some inkling that the new mandates could be reconciled with traditional ways. Regardless, for Indians as well as Europeans, faith in others changed the course of their histories.

NOTES

1 Recognizing others

1 An argument made perhaps most memorably by Taussig (1993: 236ff.).
2 In this way, it is not unlike Arjun Appadurai's 'social life of things', which sought mainly to contextualize commodities (1986).
3 See Lau (2011) for my unpacking of this term, specifically in relation to Recuay objects and architecture.
4 Taken as the notion of the self or belonging to one's community.
5 Paradoxically, I often feel less Chinese the more I try to talk in Cantonese; I identify more with my Chinese side when I speak English. Feeling abler in English, other aspects of identity, such as difference in appearance, surface and come to the fore when speaking to another English speaker, say a Caucasian.
6 What Viveiros de Castro (1998) has called Amerindian 'perspectivism'.
7 Of course, this harks back to different 'social contract' approaches for the rise of government and political authority, often associated with thinkers such as Rousseau and Hocart.
8 Examples abound across the New World, most notably in the late prehistoric and colonial traditions of Mesoamerica and the Andes.
9 Also sometimes referred to as 'verticality' or 'vertical complementarity'.
10 Geertz uses 'thick description' to refer to how the work of ethnography is not only to describe, but to reveal, contextualize and make intelligible different features and practices of human cultures, which would be otherwise hidden to outsiders.

2 Region, art and society during the Early Intermediate Period

1 On 'verticality', see also Chapter 1.
2 Interestingly, one might say that this has actually served to reinforce the distinctions, with the rise of tourism and heritage economies interested in regional 'specialties'.
3 In the Spanish: *blanco sobre rojo*.
4 Gordon Willey (1948: 10–11) noted that the occurrences were likely due to independent invention (and technological convergence), rather than resulting from conquest or migration.
5 By 'elites', I mean people with great material and social capital, especially leaders, nobles and high-status families.

6 And in some cases, such as the Cajamarca ceramic tradition, over more than a millennium. The long duration and smaller extensions are fundamental differences between 'regional art traditions' and 'horizons'.

7 It is worth mentioning that many collectivities (ayllus) from Cajatambo worshipped mountains in the Cordillera Huayhuash as their ancestors and patron divinities (Salomon and Urioste 1991; Duviols 2003). Groups in Ancash proper focused on other major landforms, some in the Cordillera Blanca.

8 Many of the best Recuay collections are in European and Peruvian museums; they were made during the late nineteenthth and early twentieth centuries (see Eisleb 1987; Tello 1929). These old collections and materials from scientific excavations form the basis of this discussion.

9 This is also the case in coastal lower valleys, such as at Castillo de Huarmey (M. Giersz, personal communication 2012).

3 Familiar others

1 Broadly founded on Spanish terms, with Latin roots, of *convivir* (to live together) and *convivencia* (shared living, or life together) (see Overing and Passes 2000b).

2 I use 'art' and 'artworks' as a shorthand for finely made things with social agency (Gell 1998).

3 On the distinction between chiefship and chiefdoms, see the different perspectives provided by Lévi-Strauss (1944), Sahlins (1972), Earle (1997) and Redmond (1998a). Whitehead (1998:151) also contends that chieftaincy is 'present in any supradomestic political unit that defers to individual leadership', hence, '*Chiefdom* is then understood to be a special case of chieftaincy'.

4 This is a purposefully collapsed synoptic view over the three to four centuries of this art production. The method neither excludes the possibility of change over time, nor does it foreclose the possibility that only a subset of key actions operated at any one time or place. Put another way, the genres of action are all potential relations of Recuay chiefship; they are neither sequential nor compulsory.

5 For related discussion concerning Moche sex imagery, see Weismantel (2004: 498).

6 Ceramic forms, hollow or solid, not made to contain liquids.

7 It would be interesting to detect whether liquid offerings flowed from one vessel to another, in serial fashion, perhaps ending with the chief's.

4 Predatorial relations

1 Bellier and Hocquenghem (1991) believe the figure of the *pishtaco* goes back further in time, and argue that it/he may be associated with sacrificer figures in ancient Andean cultures.

2 See also Harrison's discussion (1993: 6–10) of war and exchange in Melanesian contexts.

3 Shamanism and exogamous marriage might be considered two others.

4 This is also true for many groups in Melanesia (see Harrison 1993).

5 There are many practical and symbolic implications that also involve commensality, eating and cannibalism, which merit further exploration elsewhere.

6 In the Tupinamba case, they were given wives, usually daughters or close relations of the captor (Viveiros de Castro 1992: 294).

7 Very often, it is impossible to discern whether the trophy item is made from a real body part or is an effigy made out of another material.

8 See also Rowe (1982).

9 In Gerald Taylor's (1987: 369) version, 'Saying' is translated as 'Of him', referring to the ancestral figure Ñamsapa (or Ñan sapa).

10 'Pampa' in Gerald Taylor's version (1987: 373), but probably referring to open air public spaces, perhaps related to *cayan* (see Doyle 1988: 111), what Arriaga (1968: 25, 178) described as 'places where huacas (or sacred idols and objects) were invoked'.

11 'Y luego, cuando en la guerra apresaban a alguien le cortaban la cara: "Esta es la prueba de que soy fuerte", diciendo, hacían que bailara. Y este hombre, el prisionero de la guerra, él mismo, solía decir: "Ya, sí, has [sic: vas] de matarme"' (Arguedas and Duviols 1966: 141).

12 'Despúes, cuando capturaban [a alguien] en la guerra, le recortaban el rostro [y, trans-formándolo en máscara] bailaban llevándolo. Decían que de esto derivaba su valentía. Y los hombres que habían sido capturados en la guerra, solían decir: "Hermano, ahora me matarás"' (Taylor 1987: 373). Such ambiguities in the translation of Quechua viewpoints have an interesting effect, even if unintentional, of mirroring the fluid relations between captives and captors.

13 The terms are *sinchi cascay* and *ancha camasca*, the latter describing 'one who received in abundance the vital force from a huaca or ancestor, and possessed shamanic powers' (Taylor 1987: 373).

14 For example, a tinku fight and engagements interested in trophy heads can be equally 'predatory'.

15 Including the well-known moustached personage known as 'Bigote' (Donnan 2004: 117–23).

16 Associated with Phase III and IV of the Larco seriation, a sequence especially pertinent to the southern Moche (of the Moche, Chicama and Virú valleys) (Donnan and McClelland 1999: 20–23).

17 Based on analysis of bone collagen.

18 I am grateful to Steve Wegner who called my attention to this.

19 Especially the spiders *Argiope argentata* and *Argiope trifasciata*, which have distinctive coloration, form and ecology (Alva Meneses 2008: 258).

20 Donnan and McClelland (1999: 135) call these 'anthropomorphized animals dressed as human warriors'.

21 Sea lions are also killed in this manner.

22 It is unclear whether Moche people practiced anthropophagy, but there is some evidence of cut marks on human bones (Verano 2008a: 208–9).

23 Christopher Donnan (1997) has suggested that deer hunting was more a high-status ritual activity, and that deer remains were destroyed during their use as sacrificial offerings.

24 The main site categories not typically associated with hilltops were for the dead (funerary sites/necropoli) and for camelids (corrals).

25 The Moche had other forms of clubs and maces (see Larco Hoyle 2001: 198 ff.).

5 The dead and the living

1 It is worthwhile to note that, for different groups, 'grandparents' are also used to describe past peoples in general or those outside generational memory (e.g., Allen 1988; Salomon 1995; Walter 2006).

2 The great Inca sovereign Topa Inca consulted with the north highland oracle divinity Catequil who would be victorious in his upcoming battle (Arriaga 1999: 32–33). With pacification under Spanish rule, predictions about the results of combat were apparently less frequent for seeing an ancestor image.

3 Mejía (1957: 101, my translation) argued that the term is based on the Quechua term (verb) *ch'ulla*, which means 'to divide, separate, isolate disintegrate'. With the suffix -pa, chullpa could be 'the division, isolation, or disintegration of an object or thing'. Mejía did not continue this interesting discussion in relation to any funerary cosmology (e.g., separation of living/dead, or corpse/soul, etc.). Although it is unclear what languages were spoken in pre-Inca Ancash, I will continue to use the term, since it provides an expedient gloss.

4 Even the places where *autos da fé* occurred became locales for veneration (Arriaga 1968: 26).
5 It is worth noting in this respect that highland women would wrap small stones in woven textiles and place them furtively next to large stones in the hope of increasing their fertility (Arriaga 1999: cap. VI).

6 Conclusions

1 Culture (also 'agriculture') it might be noted, stems from the Latin and Spanish term, *cultura* (to cultivate, grow) and *cultivar*.

BIBLIOGRAPHY

Abrams, Philip (1988) 'Notes on the difficulty of studying the state.' *Journal of Historical Sociology* 1: 58–89.

Adelaar, Willem F. H. (1988) 'Search for the Culli language.' In *Continuity and Identity in Native America: Essays in Honor of Benedikt Hartmann*, edited by Maarten Jansen, Peter van der Loo and Roswitha Manning, pp. 111–31. Brill, Leiden.

Adelaar, Willem F. H. and Pieter C. Muysken (2004) *The Languages of the Andes*. Cambridge University Press, Cambridge.

Albert, Bruce (1990) 'On Yanomami warfare: a rejoinder.' *Current Anthropology* 31: 558–63.

Alberti, Benjamin and Yvonne Marshall (2009) 'Animating archaeology: local theories and conceptually open-ended methodologies.' *Cambridge Archaeological Journal* 19: 345–57.

Aldenderfer, Mark S. (editor) (1993) *Domestic Architecture, Ethnicity and Complementarity in the South Central Andes*. University of Iowa Press, Iowa City.

Allen, Catherine J. (1981a) 'The Nasca creatures: some problems of iconography.' *Anthropology* 5(1): 43–70.

——(1981b) 'To be Quechua: the symbolism of coca chewing in highland Peru.' *American Ethnologist* 8: 157–71.

——(1982) 'Body and soul in Quechua thought.' *Journal of Latin American Lore* 8: 179–95.

——(1988) *The Hold Life Has: Coca and Cultural Identity in an Andean Community*. Smithsonian Institution Press, Washington, D.C.

——(1998) 'When utensils revolt: mind, matter and modes of being in the pre-Columbian Andes.' *Res* 33: 17–27.

——(2002) 'The Incas have gone inside: pattern and persistence in Andean iconography.' *Res* 42: 180–203.

Alva Meneses, Nestor (2008) 'Spiders and spider decapitators in Moche iconography: identification from the contexts of Sipan, antecedents and symbolism.' In *The Art and Archaeology of the Moche: An Ancient Andean Society of the Peruvian North Coast*, edited by Steve Bourget and Kimberly L. Jones, pp. 247–61. University of Texas, Austin.

Alva, Walter and Christopher B. Donnan (1993) *Royal Tombs of Sipán*. Fowler Museum of Cultural History, Los Angeles.

Amat, Hernán (2003) 'Huarás y Recuay en la secuencia cultural del Callejón de Conchucos: Valle del Mosna.' In *Arqueología de la Sierra de Ancash: Propuestas y Perspectivas*, edited by Bebel Ibarra, pp. 97–120. Instituto Cultural Runa, Lima.

Andrade Ciudad, Luis (1995) 'La lengua culle: un estado de la cuestión.' *Boletín de la Academia Peruana de la Lengua* 26: 37–130.

Antúnez, Carlos E. (1923) 'Mausoleo encontrado en Succha.' *Inca* 1(2): 557.

Appadurai, Arjun (1986) 'Introduction: commodities and politics of value.' In *The Social Life of Things*, edited by Arjun Appadurai, pp. 3–63. Cambridge University Press, Cambridge.

Ardren, Traci and Scott Hutson (2006) *The Social Experience of Childhood in Ancient Mesoamerica.* University Press of Colorado, Boulder.

Arguedas, José María and Pierre Duviols (editors) (1966) *Dioses y hombres de Huarochirí: narración quechua recogida por Francisco de Avila (¿1598?).* Instituto de Estudios Peruanos, Lima.

Århem, Kaj (1998) *Makuna, Portrait of an Amazonian People.* Smithsonian Institution Press, Washington D.C.

Arkush, Elizabeth and Charles Stanish (2005) 'Interpreting conflict in the ancient Andes: implications for the archaeology of warfare.' *Current Anthropology* 46(1): 3–28.

Arnold, Denise Y. and Christine A. Hastorf (2008) *Heads of State: Icons, Power, and Politics in the Ancient and Modern Andes.* Left Coast Press, Walnut Creek.

Arnold, Denise Y. and Juan de Dios Yapita (2006) *The Metamorphosis of Heads: Textual Struggles, Educations and Land in the Andes.* University of Pittsburgh Press, Pittburgh.

Arriaga, Pablo José de (1968) [1621] *The Extirpation of Idolatry in Peru.* Translated by Clark Keating. University of Kentucky Press, Lexington.

——(1999) *La extirpación de la idolatría en el Piru (1621).* Centro de Estudios Regionales 'Bartolomé de Las Casas', Cuzco.

Bankmann, Ulf (1979) 'Moche und Recuay.' *Baessler-Archiv, Neue Folge* 27: 253–71.

Bassie-Sweet, Karen (1991) *From the Mouth of the Dark Cave: Commemorative Sculpture of the Late Classic Maya.* University of Oklahoma Press, Norman.

Bastien, Joseph W. (1978) *Mountain of the Condor: Metaphor and Ritual in an Andean Ayllu.* West Publishing, St. Paul.

Bauer, Brian S. and Lucas C. Kellett (2010) 'Cultural transformations of the Chanka homeland (Andahuaylas, Peru) during the Late Intermediate Period (AD 1000–1400).' *Latin American Antiquity* 21: 87–111.

Bawden, Garth (1982) 'Galindo: a study in cultural transition during the Middle Horizon.' In *Chan Chan: Andean Desert City*, edited by Michael E. Moseley and Kent C. Day, pp. 285–320. University of New Mexico Press, Albuquerque.

——(1990) 'Domestic space and social structure in Pre-Columbian northern Peru.' In *Domestic Architecture and the Use of Space: An Interdisciplinary Cross-Cultural Study*, edited by Susan Kent, pp. 153–71. Cambridge University Press, Cambridge.

——(1996) *The Moche.* Blackwell Publishers, Oxford.

Baxandall, Michael (1972) *Painting and Experience in Fifteenth Century Italy: A Primer in the Social History of Pictorial Style.* Clarendon Press, Oxford.

Bazán del Campo, Francisco (2007) 'La veneración a los huancas en el Callejón de Huaylas.' *Hirka* 4: 2–6.

Bazán del Campo, Francisco and Steven Wegner (2006) 'La veneración a la huanca en el Horizonte Temprano.' *Integración: cultura ancashina* 3: 21–22.

Bellier, Irène and Anne-Marie Hocquenghem (1991) 'De los Andes a la Amazonía: una representación evolutiva del "Otro".' *Bulletin de l'Institut Français d'Etudes Andines* 20: 41–59.

Bender, Barbara, Sue Hamilton, Christopher Y. Tilley and Ed Anderson (2007) *Stone Worlds: Narrative and Reflexivity in Landscape Archaeology.* Left Coast Press, Walnut Creek.

Bennett, Wendell C. (1944) *The North Highlands of Peru: Excavations in the Callejón de Huaylas and at Chavín de Huántar.* Anthropological Papers of the American Museum of Natural History 39(1), New York.

——(1948) 'The Peruvian Co-Tradition.' In *A Reappraisal of Peruvian Archaeology*, edited by Wendell C. Bennett, pp. 1–7. Memoirs of the Society for American Archaeology 4, Menasha.

Benson, Elizabeth P. (1972) *The Mochica.* Thames & Hudson, New York.

——(1974) *A Man and a Feline in Mochica Art.* Dumbarton Oaks, Washington.

——(1997) *Birds and Beasts of Ancient Latin America*. University Press of Florida, Gainesville.
——(2008) 'Iconography meets archaeology.' In *The Art and Archaeology of the Moche: An Ancient Andean Society of the Peruvian North Coast*, edited by Steve Bourget and Kimberly L. Jones, pp. 1–21. University of Texas Press, Austin.
Bermann, Marc (1994) *Lukurmata: Household Archaeology in Prehispanic Bolivia*. Princeton University Press, Princeton.
Bernier, Hélène (2010) 'Craft specialists at Moche: organization, affiliations and identities.' *Latin American Antiquity* 21: 22–43.
Bernuy, Katiusha and Vanessa Bernal (2008) 'La tradición Cajamarca en San José de Moro: una evidencia de interacción interregional durante el Horizonte Medio.' In *Arqueología mochica: nuevos enfoques*, edited by Luis Jaime Castillo, Hélène Bernier, Gregory Lockard and Julio Rucabado, pp. 67–80. Fondo Editorial de la Pontificia Universidad Católica del Peru, Lima.
Bertonio, Ludovico (1879) [1612] *Vocabulario de la lengua aymara*. 2 vols. B.G. Teubner, Leipzig.
Bhabha, Homi (1994) *The Location of Culture*. Routledge, London.
Billman, Brian R. (1996) *The Evolution of Prehistoric Political Organizations in the Moche Valley*. Ph.D. dissertation, University of California at Santa Barbara, University Microfilms, Ann Arbor.
——(1997) 'Population pressure and the origins of warfare in the Moche Valley, Peru.' In *Integrating Archaeological Demography: Multidisciplinary Approaches to Prehistoric Population*, edited by Richard Paine, pp. 285–310. Center for Archaeological Investigations, Southern Illinois University, Carbondale.
Blackmun, Barbara (1988) 'From trader to priest in two hundred years: the transformation of a foreign figure on Benin Ivories.' *Art Journal* 47(2): 128–40.
Blier, Suzanne P. (1993) 'Imaging otherness in Ivory: African portrayals of the Portuguese ca. 1492.' *Art Bulletin* 75(3): 375–96.
Bloch, Maurice (1992) *Prey into Hunter: Politics of Religious Experience*. Cambridge University Press, Cambridge.
Bloch, Maurice and Jonathan Parry (1982) 'Introduction: death and the regeneration of life.' In *Death and the Regeneration of Life*, edited by Maurice Bloch and Jonathan Parry, pp. 1–44. Cambridge University Press, Cambridge.
Blom, Deborah E. (2005) 'Embodying borders: human body modification and diversity in Tiwanaku society.' *Journal of Anthropological Archaeology* 29: 1–24.
Boone, Elizabeth H. (2000) *Stories in Red and Black: Pictorial Histories of the Aztecs and Mixtecs*. University of Texas Press, Austin.
Borić, Dušan and John Robb (editors) (2008) *Past Bodies: Body-Centered Research in Archaeology*. Oxbow Books, Oxford.
Bourdieu, Pierre (1977) *Outline of a Theory of Practice*. Cambridge University Press, Cambridge.
Bourget, Steve (1994) *Bestiare sacré et flore magique: Écologie rituelle de l'iconographie de la culture Mochica, côte nord du Pérou*. Ph.D. dissertation, University of Montreal, Montreal.
——(2001) 'Rituals of sacrifice: its practice at Huaca de la Luna and its representation in Moche iconography.' In *Moche Art and Archaeology in Ancient Peru*, edited by Joanne Pillsbury, pp. 89–109. National Gallery of Art, Washington, D.C.
——(2006) *Sex, Death, and Sacrifice in Moche Religion and Visual Culture*. University of Texas Press, Austin.
Bourget, Steve and Kimberly L. Jones (editors) (2008) *The Art and Archaeology of the Moche: An Ancient Andean Society of the Peruvian North Coast*. 1st edn. University of Texas Press, Austin.
Boyer, Pascal (1996) 'What makes anthropomorphism natural: intuitive ontology and cultural representations.' *Journal of Royal Anthropological Institute* 2(n.s.): 83–97.
Bradley, Richard (2002) *The Past in Prehistoric Societies*. Routledge, London.
Bray, Tamara L. (2003) 'Inka pottery as culinary equipment: food, feasting, and gender in imperial design.' *Latin American Antiquity* 14(1): 3–28.

Brennan, Curtiss T. (1982) 'Cerro Arena: origins of the urban tradition on the Peruvian north coast.' *Current Anthropology* 23: 247–54.

Brown Vega, Margaret (2009) 'Conflict in the Early Horizon and Late Intermediate Period: new dates from the fortress of Acaray, Huaura valley, Perú.' *Current Anthropology* 50: 255–66.

Browne, David M., Helaine Silverman and Rubén García (1993) 'A cache of 48 Nasca trophy heads from Cerro Carapo, Peru.' *Latin American Antiquity* 4(3): 274–94.

Brush, Stephen B. (1977) *Mountain, Field, and Family: The Economy and Human Ecology of an Andean Valley.* University of Pennsylvania Press, Philadelphia.

Burger, Richard L. (1992a) *Chavín and the Origins of Andean Civilization.* Thames & Hudson, London.

——(1992b) 'Sacred center of Chavin de Huantar.' In *Ancient Americas: Art from Sacred Landscapes*, pp. 264–77. Chicago and Munich: Art Institute of Chicago/Prestel-Verlag.

——(2009) *Life and Writings of Julio C. Tello: America's First Indigenous Archaeologist.* University of Iowa Press, Iowa City.

Burger, Richard L., George F. Lau, Victor M. Ponte and Michael D. Glascock (2006) 'The history of prehispanic obsidian procurement in highland Ancash.' In *La complejidad social en la Sierra de Ancash*, edited by Alexander Herrera, Carolina Orsini and Kevin Lane, pp. 103–20. Civiche raccolte d'arte applicata del Castello Sforzesco, Milan.

Burger, Richard L., Karen L. Mohr Chávez and Sergio J. Chávez (2000) 'Through the glass darkly: prehispanic obsidian procurement and exchange in southern Peru and northern Bolivia.' *Journal of World Prehistory* 14(3): 267–362.

Burger, Richard L. and Lucy Salazar-Burger (1993) 'The place of dual organization in Early Andean ceremonialism: a comparative review.' In *El mundo ceremonial andino*, edited by Luis Millones and Yoshio Onuki, pp. 97–116. National Museum of Ethnology, Osaka.

Burgess, Jonathan S. (2001) *The Tradition of the Trojan War in Homer and the Epic Cycle.* Johns Hopkins University Press, Baltimore.

Buse, Hermann (1965) *Introducción al Peru.* Imprenta del Colegio Militar 'Leoncio Prado'. Lima.

Canessa, Andrew (2000) 'Fear and loathing on the *kharasiri* trail: alterity and identity in the Andes.' *Journal of the Royal Anthropological Institute* 6(4): 705–20.

Carey, Mark (2010) *In the Shadow of Melting Glaciers: Climate Change and Andean Society.* Oxford University Press, Oxford.

Carmichael, Patrick H. (1995) 'Nasca burial patterns: social structure and mortuary ideology.' In *Tombs for the Living: Andean Mortuary Practices*, edited by Tom Dillehay, pp. 161–87. Dumbarton Oaks, Washington, D.C.

Carneiro, Robert (1970) 'A theory on the origin of the state.' *Science* 169: 733–38.

——(1981) 'The chiefdom: precursor of the state.' In *The Transition to Statehood in the New World*, edited by Grant Jones and Robert Kautz, pp. 37–79. Cambridge University Press, Cambridge.

Carneiro da Cunha, Manuela and Eduardo Vivieros de Castro (1987) 'Vingança temporalidade: Os Tupinambá.' *Journal de la Société des Américanistes* 79: 191–208.

Carrasco, David (1999) *City of Sacrifice: The Aztec Empire and the Role of Violence in Civilization.* Beacon Press, Boston.

Carrión Cachot, Rebeca (1955) 'El culto al agua en el antiguo Peru: la paccha, elemento cultural pan-andino.' *Revista del Museo Nacional de Antropología y Arqueología* 2(2): 50–140.

——(1959) *La religión en el antiguo Peru (norte y centro de la costa, período post-clásico).* Lima.

Carsten, Janet and Stephen Hugh-Jones (editors) (1995) *About the House: Lévi-Strauss and Beyond.* Cambridge University Press, Cambridge.

Castillo, Luis Jaime (1989) *Personajes míticos, escenas y narraciones en la iconografía mochica.* Pontificia Universidad Católica del Peru, Lima.

——(1993) 'Prácticas funerarias, poder e ideología en la sociedad Moche Tardía.' *Gaceta Arqueológica Andina* 7(7): 67–73.

——(2000) 'La presencia Wari en San José de Moro.' *Boletín de Arqueología PUCP* 4: 143–80.

Castillo, Luis Jaime and Christopher B. Donnan (1994) 'Los Mochicas del norte y los Mochicas del sur.' In *Vicús*, edited by Kryszof Makowski, pp. 143–82. Banco de Crédito, Lima.

Castillo, Luis Jaime, Julio Rucabado, Martín del Carpio, Katiusha Bernuy, Carlos Rengifo, Gabriel Prieto and Carole Fraresso (2008) 'Ideología y poder en la consolidación, colapso y reconstitución del estado mochica del Jequetepeque: El Proyecto Arqueológico San José de Moro (1991–2006).' *Ñawpa Pacha* 28: 1–86.

Cerrón-Palomino, Rodolfo (1995) *La lengua de Naimlap: reconstrucción y obsolescencia del mochica*. Pontificia Universidad Católica del Peru, Lima.

Chagnon, Napoleon A. (1968) *Yanomamö, The Fierce People*. Holt, New York.

——(1988) 'Life histories, blood revenge, and warfare in a tribal population.' *Science* 239: 985–92.

Chapdelaine, Claude (2009) 'Domestic life in and around the urban sector of the Huacas de Moche site, northern Peru.' In *Domestic Life in Prehispanic Capitals: A Study of Specialization, Hierarchy and Ethnicity*, edited by Linda Manzanilla and Claude Chapdelaine, pp. 181–96. Museum of Anthropology, University of Michigan, Ann Arbor.

——(2011) 'Recent advances in Moche archaeology.' *Journal of Archaeological Research* 19: 191–231.

Chaumeil, Jean-Pierre (2007) 'Bones, flutes and the dead: memory and funerary treatments in Amazonia.' In *Time and Memory in Indigenous Amazonia: Anthropological Perspectives*, edited by Carlos Fausto and Michael Heckenberger, pp. 243–83. University Press of Florida, Gainesville.

Chicoine, David (2006) 'Early Horizon architecture at Huambacho, Nepeña Valley, Peru.' *Journal of Field Archaeology* 31: 1–22.

Church, Warren B. (1996) *Prehistoric Cultural Development and Interregional Interaction in the Tropical Montane Forests of Peru*. Ph.D. dissertation, Yale University, University Microfilms, Ann Arbor.

Classen, Constance (1993) *Inca Cosmology and the Human Body*. University of Utah Press, Salt Lake City.

Clastres, Pierre (1977) *Society against the State: The Leader as Servant and Humane Uses of Power Amongst the Indians of the Americas*. Urizen Books, New York.

——(1987) *Society against the State: Essays in Political Anthropology*. Zone Books, New York.

——(2010) *The Archeology of Violence*. Semiotext(e), Original French edition [Paris, 1980], Los Angeles.

Clendinnen, Inga (1991) *Aztecs: An Interpretation*. Cambridge University Press, Cambridge.

Clifford, James (1988) *The Predicament of Culture: Twentieth-Century Ethnography, Literature and Art*. Harvard University Press, Cambridge.

Clifford, James and George E. Marcus (1986) *Writing Culture: The Poetics and Politics of Ethnography*. University of California Press, Berkeley.

Cobo, Bernábe (1990) [1653] *Inca Religion and Customs*. Translated by Roland Hamilton. University of Texas Press, Austin.

Codere, Helen (1950) *Fighting with Property: A Study of Kwakiutl Potlatching and Warfare, 1792–1930*. University of Washington Press, Seattle.

Comaroff, John L. and Jean Comaroff (2001) 'On personhood: an anthropological perspective from Africa.' *Social Identities* 7: 267–83.

Conklin, Beth A. (2001) 'Women's blood, warriors' blood and the conquest of vitality in Amazonia.' In *Gender in Amazonia and Melanesia*, edited by Thomas Gregor and Donald Tuzin, pp. 141–74. University of California Press, Berkeley.

Conklin, William J. and Jeffrey Quilter (editors) (2008) *Chavín: Art, Architecture and Culture*. Cotsen Institute of Archaeology Monograph 61, University of California at Los Angeles, Los Angeles.

Connerton, Paul (1989) *How Societies Remember*. Cambridge University Press, Cambridge.

Cook, Anita G. (2001) 'Huari D-shaped structures, sacrificial offerings and divine rulership.' In *Ritual Sacrifice in Ancient Peru*, edited by Elizabeth P. Benson and Anita G. Cook, pp. 137–63. University of Texas Press, Austin.

Cook, Noble David (1977) 'La visita de los Conchucos por Cristóbal Ponce de León, 1543.' *Historia y Cultura* 10: 23–45.

——(1981) *Demographic Collapse: Indian Peru, 1520–1620.* Cambridge University Press, Cambridge.

Corbey, Raymond and Joep Leerssen (1991) 'Studying alterity: backgrounds and perspectives.' In *Alterity, Identity, Image: Selves and Others in Society and Scholarship*, edited by Raymond Corbey and Joseph Leerssen, pp. vi–xviii. Rodopi, Amsterdam.

Cordy-Collins, Alana (1992) 'Archaism or tradition?: the decapitation theme in Cupisnique and Moche iconography.' *Latin American Antiquity* 3(3): 206–20.

——(2001a) 'Decapitation in Cupisnique and Early Moche societies.' In *Ritual Sacrifice in Ancient Peru*, edited by Elizabeth P. Benson and Anita Cook, pp. 21–34. University of Texas Press, Austin.

——(2001b) 'Labretted ladies: foreign women in northern Moche and Lambayeque art.' In *Moche Art and Archaeology in Ancient Peru*, edited by Joanne Pillsbury, pp. 246–57. National Gallery of Art, Washington D.C.

Course, Magnus (2007) 'Death, biography and the Mapuche person.' *Ethnos* 72: 77–101.

Covey, R. Alan (2008) 'Multiregional perspectives on the archaeology of the Andes during the Late Intermediate Period (c. AD 1000–1400).' *Journal of Archaeological Research* 16: 287–338.

Cummins, Thomas B. (2008) 'The felicitous legacy of the Lanzón.' In *Chavín: Art, Architecture and Culture*, edited by William J. Conklin and Jeffrey Quilter, pp. 279–304. Cotsen Institute of Archaeology, Los Angeles.

Curatola Petrocchi, Marco and Mariusz S. Ziółkowski (editors) (2008) *Adivinación y oráculos en el mundo andino antiguo.* Instituto Francés de Estudios Andinos, Lima.

D'Altroy, Terence N. (2002) *The Incas.* Blackwell Publishers, Malden.

D'Altroy, Terence N. and Christine A. Hastorf (editors) (2001) *Empire and Domestic Economy.* Kluwer, New York.

Daggett, Richard E. (1985) 'The Early Horizon – Early Intermediate Period transition: a view from the Nepeña and Virú Valleys.' In *Recent Studies in Andean Prehistory and Protohistory*, edited by D. Peter Kvietok and Daniel H. Sandweiss, pp. 41–65. Cornell Latin American Studies Program, Ithaca (NY).

——(1986) 'The Peruvian north-central coast during the Early Intermediate Period.' In *Perspectives on Andean Prehistory and Protohistory*, edited by Daniel H. Sandweiss and D. Peter Kvietok, pp. 49–62. Cornell Latin American Studies Program, Ithaca, New York.

Davis, Whitney (1996) 'Narrativity and the Narmer Palette.' In *Replications: Archaeology, Art History, Psychoanalysis*, edited by Whitney Davis, pp. 199–231. Pennsylvania State University Press, University Park.

de Lavalle, José Antonio (editor) (1986) *Culturas precolombinas: Nazca.* Banco de Crédito del Peru, Lima.

Dean, Carolyn (2010) *A Culture of Stone: Inka Perspectives on Rock.* Duke University Press, Durham.

DeBoer, Warren R. (1991) 'The decorative burden: design, medium, and change.' In *Ceramic Ethnoarchaeology*, edited by William Longacre, pp. 144–61. University of Arizona Press, Tucson.

DeLeonardis, Lisa and George F. Lau (2004) 'Life, death and ancestors.' In *Andean Archaeology*, edited by Helaine Silverman, pp. 77–115. Blackwell Publishers, Oxford.

Deleuze, Gilles and Félix Guattari (1987) *A Thousand Plateaus: Capitalism and Schizophrenia.* University of Minnesota Press, Minneapolis.

DeMarrais, Elizabeth (2004) 'The materialization of culture.' In *Rethinking Materiality: The Engagement of Mind with the Material World*, edited by Elizabeth DeMarrais, Chris Gosden and Colin Renfrew, pp. 11–22. McDonald Institute for Archaeological Research, Cambridge.

DeMarrais, Elizabeth, Timothy Earle and Luis Jaime Castillo (1996) 'Ideology, materialization, and power strategies.' *Current Anthropology* 37: 15–31.

DeMarrais, Elizabeth, Chris Gosden and Colin Renfrew (editors) (2004) *Rethinking Materiality: The Engagement of Mind with the Material World.* McDonald Institute for Archaeological Research, Cambridge.

Descola, Philippe (1993) 'Les affinités sélectives: alliance, guerre et prédation dans l'ensemble Jívaro.' *L'Homme* 33: 171–90.
——(2001) 'Genres of gender: local models and global paradigms in the comparison of Amazonia and Melanesia.' In *Gender in Amazonia and Melanesia*, edited by Thomas A. Gregor and Donald Tuzin, pp. 91–114. University of California Press, Berkeley.
——(2005) *Par-delà nature et culture*. Gallimard, Paris.
——(2006) 'Beyond nature and culture.' *Proceedings of the British Academy* 139: 137–55.
Diamond, Jared M. (1997) *Guns, Germs, and Steel: The Fates of Human Societies*. W. W. Norton & Co., New York.
Dietler, Michael (1994) '"Our ancestors the Gauls": archaeology, ethnic nationalism, and the manipulation of Celtic identity in modern Europe.' *American Anthropologist* 96: 584–605.
Dietler, Michael and Ingrid Herbich (1998) '*Habitus*, techniques, style: an integrated approach to the social understanding of material culture and boundaries.' In *The Archaeology of Social Boundaries*, edited by Miriam Stark, pp. 232–63. Smithsonian Institution Press, Washington, D.C.
Dillehay, Tom D. (1998) 'La organización dual en los Andes: el problema y la metodología de investigación en el caso de San Luis, Zaña.' In *Perspectivas regionales del período formativo en el Perú*, pp. 37–60. Lima: Pontificia Universidad Católica del Perú.
——(2001) 'Town and country in late Moche times: a view from two northern valleys.' In *Moche Art and Archaeology in Ancient Peru*, edited by Joanne Pillsbury, pp. 259–83. National Gallery of Art, Studies in the History of Art 63, Washington, D.C.
Dillehay, Tom, Alan L. Kolata and Edward R. Swenson (2009) *Paisaje culturales en el valle del Jequetepeque: los yacimientos arqueológicos*. Ediciones SIAN, Trujillo.
Disselhoff, Hans (1967) *Daily Life in Ancient Peru*. McGraw-Hill, New York.
Domingo de Santo Tomás, Fray (1951) [1560] *Grammatica, o Arte de la lengua general de los indios de los reynos del Perú*. Instituto de Historia, Lima.
Donnan, Christopher B. (1978) *Moche Art of Peru: Pre-Columbian Symbolic Communication*. UCLA Museum of Cultural History, Los Angeles.
——(1982) 'Caza del venado en el arte mochica.' *Revista del Museo Nacional* 46: 235–51.
——(1990) 'Blowgun in Moche art.' In *Circumpacifica, Band I: Mittel-und Südamerika (Festschrift für Thomas S. Barthel)*, pp. 509–20. Peter Lang, Frankfurt am Main.
——(1992) *Ceramics of Ancient Peru*. Fowler Museum of Cultural History, Los Angeles.
——(1995) 'Moche funerary practice.' In *Tombs for the Living: Andean Mortuary Practices*, edited by Tom D. Dillehay, pp. 111–60. Dumbarton Oaks, Washington D.C.
——(1997) 'Deer hunting and combat: parallel activities in the Moche world.' In *Spirit of Ancient Peru*, edited by Kathleen Berrin, pp. 51–59. Thames & Hudson, New York.
——(2003) 'The long duration and subsequent collapse of Moche borders', paper presented at 'Objects of Contention: Boundaries, Interaction and Appropriation in the Andes', Sainsbury Research Unit (Americas symposium), University of East Anglia, Norwich (UK), 9 May 2003.
——(2004) *Moche Portraits from Ancient Peru*. University of Texas Press, Austin.
——(2007) *Moche Tombs at Dos Cabezas*. Cotsen Institute of Archaeology, University of California at Los Angeles, Los Angeles.
——(2010) 'Moche state religion: a unifying force in Moche political organization.' In *New Perspectives on Moche Political Organization*, edited by Jeffrey Quilter and Luis Jaime Castillo, pp. 47–69. Dumbarton Oaks, Washington D.C.
Donnan, Christopher B. and Donna McClelland (1999) *Moche Fineline Painting: Its Evolution and its Artists*. Fowler Museum of Cultural History, University of California, Los Angeles.
Douglas, Mary (1976) *Purity and Danger: An Analysis of Concepts of Pollution and Taboo*. Routledge & Kegan Paul, London.
Doyle, Mary Eileen (1988) *Ancestor Cult and Burial Ritual in Seventeenth and Eighteenth Century Central Peru*. Ph.D. dissertation, University of California at Los Angeles, University Microfilms, Ann Arbor.

Dransart, Penny (2002) *Earth, Water, Fleece and Fabric: A Long-Term Ethnography of Camelid Herding in the Andes.* Routledge, London.

Drennan, Robert D. and Carlos Uribe (1987) 'Introduction.' In *Chiefdoms in the Americas*, edited by Robert D. Drennan and Carlos Uribe, pp. vii–xii. University Press of America, Lanham.

Drew, Leslie and Doug Wilson (1980) *Argillite, Art of the Haida.* Hancock House, North Vancouver.

Druc, Isabelle C. (1998) *Ceramic Production and Distribution in the Chavín Sphere of Influence (North Central Andes).* BAR International Series 731, Oxford.

——(2009) 'Tradiciones alfareras, identidad social y el concepto de etnias tardías en Conchucos, Ancash, Perú.' *Boletín del Instituto Francés de Estudios Andinos* 38: 87–106.

Dunbar, Robin I. M. (2004) *The Human Story.* Faber & Faber, London.

Duviols, Pierre (1971) *La lutte contre les religions autochtones dans le Pérou colonial: 'l'extirpation de l'idolâtrie,' entre 1532 et 1660.* Institut français d'études andines, Lima.

——(1973) 'Huari y llacuaz, agricultores y pastores: un dualismo prehispánico de oposición y complementaridad.' *Revista del Museo Nacional* 39: 153–91.

——(1977) 'Un symbolisme andin du double: la lithomorphose de l'ancêtre.' *Actes du XLIIe Congrès International des Américanistes (Paris)* 4: 359–64.

——(1979) 'Un symbolisme de l'occupation, de l'aménagement et de l'exploitation de l'espace: la monolithe "huanca" et sa fonction dans les Andes préhispaniques.' *L'Homme* 19: 7–31.

——(2003) *Procesos y visitas de idolatrías: Cajatambo, siglo XVII.* Instituto Francés de Estudios Andinos, Lima.

Earle, Timothy K. (1997) *How Chiefs Come to Power: The Political Economy in Prehistory.* Stanford University Press, Palo Alto.

Ehrenreich, Barbara (1997) *Blood Rites: Origins and History of the Passions of War.* Holt, New York.

Eisleb, Dieter (1987) *Altperuanische Kulturen IV: Recuay.* Staatlische Museen Preussischer Kulturbesitz, Museum für Völkerkunde, Berlin.

Eliade, Mircea (1959) *The Myth of the Eternal Return, or, Cosmos and History.* Harper, New York.

Emberling, Geoffrey (1997) 'Ethnicity in complex societies: archaeological perspectives.' *Journal of Archaeological Research* 5: 295–344.

Espinoza Soriano, Waldemar (1964) 'El curacazgo de Conchucos y la visita de 1543.' *Bulletin de l'Institut Français d'Études andines* 3: 9–31.

——(1978) *Huaraz: poder, sociedad y economía en los siglos XV y XVI – reflexiones en torno a las visitas de 1558, 1594 y 1712.* Seminario de Historia Rural Andina, Universidad Nacional Mayor de San Marcos, Lima.

Falcón, Victor (2004) 'Los orígenes del huanca como objeto de culto en la época precolonial.' *Allpanchis* 64: 35–54.

Fausto, Carlos (2000) 'Of enemies and pets: warfare and shamanism in Amazonia.' *American Ethnologist* 26: 933–56.

——(2001) *Inimigos fiéis: história, guerra e xamanismo na Amazônia.* EDUSP, Universidade de São Paolo, São Paulo.

——(2007) 'Feasting on people: cannibalism and commensality in Amazonia.' *Current Anthropology* 48: 497–530.

Fausto, Carlos and Michael Heckenberger (editors) (2007) *Time and Memory in Indigenous Amazonia: Anthropological Perspectives.* University Press of Florida, Gainesville.

Ferguson, R. Brian and Neil L. Whitehead (editors) (2000) *War in the Tribal Zone: Expanding States and Indigenous Warfare.* School of American Research, Albuquerque.

Fitzsimmons, James (2011) 'Perspectives on death and transformation in ancient Maya society: human remains as a means to an end.' In *Living with the Dead: Mortuary Ritual in Mesoamerica*, edited by James Fitzsimmons and Izumi Shimada, pp. 53–77. University of Arizona Press, Tucson.

Fitzsimmons, James L. (2009) *Death and the Classic Maya Kings*. University of Texas Press, Austin.

Fonseca, César (1974) 'Modalidades de la *minka*.' In *Reciprocidad e intercambio en los Andes peruanos*, edited by Giorgio Alberti and Enrique Mayer, pp. 86–109. Instituto de Estudios Andinos, Lima.

Fortune, Reo (1963) *Sorcerers of Dobu: The Social Anthropology of the Dobu Islanders of the Western Pacific*. Routledge & Kegan Paul, London.

Foucault, Michel (1977) *Discipline and Punish: The Birth of the Prison*. Pantheon Books, New York.

Fowler, Chris (2004) *The Archaeology of Personhood: An Anthropological Approach*. Routledge, London.

Franco Jordán, Régulo (2010) 'La dame de Cao.' *Pour la science* 390: 36–42.

Franco Jordán, Régulo G., Cesar Galvez M. and Segundo Vásquez Sánchez (2005) *El Brujo: pasado milenario*. Ediciones SIAN, Trujillo, Perú.

Gade, Daniel W. (1999) *Nature and Culture in the Andes*. University of Wisconsin Press, Madison.

Gambini, Wilfredo (1984) *Santa y Nepeña: dos valles, dos culturas*. Imprenta M. Castillo, Lima.

Gamboa, Jorge A. (2010) *Proyecto de inventariado y análisis de materiales del Proyecto Obras de Emergencia Chavín 2003 (PIAM-POECH), Valle de Mosna, Departamento de Ancash*. Reported presented to Ministerio de Cultura del Perú.

Geertz, Clifford (1973) 'Thick description.' In *The Interpretation of Cultures*, edited by Clifford Geertz, pp. 3–30. Basic Books, New York.

Gell, Alfred (1998) *Art and Agency: An Anthropological Theory*. Clarendon Press, Oxford.

Gelles, Paul H. (1995) 'Equilibrium and extraction: dual organization in the Andes.' *American Ethnologist* 22: 710–42.

Gero, Joan and Margaret Conkey (editors) (1990) *Engendering Archaeology*. Blackwell, Oxford.

Gero, Joan M. (1990) 'Pottery, power, and … parties!' *Archaeology* 43(2, Mar/Apr): 52–56.

——(1991) 'Who experienced what in prehistory?: A narrative explanation from Queyash, Peru.' In *Processual and Postprocessual Archaeologies: Multiple Ways of Knowing the Past*, edited by Robert W. Preucel, pp. 126–39. Center for Archaeological Investigations, Southern Illinois University, Occasional Paper 10, Carbondale.

——(1992) 'Feasts and females: gender ideology and political meals in the Andes.' *Norwegian Archaeological Review* 25(1): 15–30.

——(1999) 'La iconografía Recuay y el estudio de género.' *Gaceta Arqueológica Andina* 25: 23–44.

——(2001) 'Field knots and ceramic beaus: interpreting gender in the Peruvian Early Intermediate Period.' In *Gender in Pre-Hispanic America*, edited by Cecelia Klein, pp. 15–55. Dumbarton Oaks, Washington, D.C.

——(2004) 'Sex pots of ancient Peru: post-gender reflections.' In *Combining the Past and the Present: Archaeological Perspectives on Society*, edited by Terje Oestigaard, Nils Anfinset and Tore Saetersdal, pp. 3–22. BAR International Series 1210, Oxford.

Ghezzi, Ivan (2006) 'Religious warfare at Chankillo.' In *Andean Archaeology III: North and South*, edited by William H. Isbell and Helaine Silverman, pp. 67–84. Springer, New York.

Gillespie, Susan D. (2001) 'Personhood, agency and mortuary ritual: a case study from the ancient Maya.' *Journal of Anthropological Archaeology* 20: 73–112.

Gillespie, Susan and Rosemary Joyce (editors) (2000) *Beyond Kinship: Social and Material Reproduction in House Societies*. University of Pennsylvania Press, Philadelphia.

Gnecco, Cristóbal (1999) 'Archaeology and historical multivocality: a reflection from the Colombian multicultural context.' In *Archaeology in Latin America*, edited by Gustavo Politis and Benjamin Alberti, pp. 258–70. Taylor & Francis, London.

Goffman, Erving (1967) *Interaction Ritual: Essays on Face-to Face Behavior*. Doubleday, Garden City.

Goldhausen, Marco (2001) 'Avances en el estudio de iconografía Lima.' *Arqueológicas* 25: 223–63.

Goldstein, Paul S. (1993) 'House, community, and state in the earliest Tiwanaku colony: domestic patterns and state integration at Omo M12, Moquegua.' In *Domestic Architecture, Ethnicity, and Complementarity in the South-Central Andes*, edited by Mark S. Aldenderfer, pp. 25–41. University of Iowa, Iowa City.

——(2005) *Andean Diaspora: The Tiwanaku Colonies and the Origins of South American Empire.* University Press of Florida, Gainesville.

Golte, Jürgen (2009) *Moche, cosmología y sociedad: una interpretación iconográfica.* Instituto de Estudios Peruanos and Centro Bartolomé de Las Casas, Lima.

González Holguin, Diego (1989) [1608] *Vocabulario de la lengua general de todo el Peru llamada lengua Qquichua o del Inca.* UNMSM, Lima.

Gosden, Chris (2001) 'Postcolonial archaeology: issues of culture, identity, and knowledge.' In *Archaeological Theory Today*, edited by Ian Hodder, pp. 241–61. Polity Press, Oxford.

——(2004) 'The past and foreign countries: colonial and postcolonial archaeology and anthropology.' In *A Companion to Social Archaeology*, edited by Lynn Meskell and Robert W. Preucel, pp. 161–78. Blackwell, Malden.

Gosden, Chris and Chantal Knowles (2001) *Collecting Colonialism: Material Culture and Colonial Change.* Berg, Oxford; New York.

Gose, Peter (1994) *Deathly Waters and Hungry Mountains: Agrarian Ritual and Class Formation in an Andean Town.* University of Toronto Press, Toronto.

——(2008) *Invaders as Ancestors: On the Intercultural Making and Unmaking of Spanish Colonialism in the Andes.* University of Toronto Press, Toronto.

Gosselain, Olivier P. (2002) *Poteries du Cameroun méridional: styles techniques et rapports à l'identité.* CNRS éditions, Paris.

Gow, Peter (1991) *Of Mixed Blood: Kinship and History in Peruvian Amazonia.* Clarendon Press, Oxford.

——(1999) 'Piro designs: paintings as meaningful action in an Amazonian lived world.' *Journal of the Royal Anthropological Institute* 5: 229–46.

Graeber, David (2001) *Toward an Anthropological Theory of Value: The False Coin of Our Own Dreams.* Palgrave, New York.

Grieder, Terence (1978) *The Art and Archaeology of Pashash.* University of Texas Press, Austin.

——(1992) 'Signs of an ideology of authority in Ancash.' In *Ancient Images, Ancient Thought: The Archaeology of Ideology*, edited by A. S. Goldsmith, S. Garvie, D. Selin and J. Smith, pp. 181–85. Archaeological Association of the University of Calgary, Calgary.

Griffiths, Nicholas (1996) *The Cross and the Serpent: Religious Repression and Resurgence in Colonial Peru.* University of Oklahoma Press, Norman.

Gross, Daniel (1975) 'Protein capture and cultural development in the Amazon basin.' *American Anthropologist* 77: 526–49.

Gruzinski, Serge (1992) *Painting the Conquest: The Mexican Indians and the European Renaissance.* Flammarion, Paris.

——(1993) *The Conquest of Mexico: The Incorporation of Indian Societies into the Western World, 16th–18th Centuries.* Polity Press, Cambridge.

Guaman Poma de Ayala, Felipe (1980) [1615] *Nueva corónica y buen gobierno.* Translated by Jorge L. Urioste. Siglo Veintiuno, Mexico (DF).

Guenther, Mathias (1988) 'Animals in Bushman thought, myth and art.' In *Hunters and Gatherers 2: Property, Power and Ideology*, edited by Tim Ingold, David Riches and James Woodburn, pp. 192–202. Berg, Oxford.

Guthrie, Stewart (1993) *Faces in the Clouds: A New Theory of Religion.* Oxford University Press, New York.

Hall, Stuart (1997) 'The spectacle of the "Other".' In *Representation: Cultural Representations and Signifying Practices*, edited by Stuart Hall, pp. 223–90. Sage, London.

Harris, Olivia (1981) 'Households as natural units.' In *Of Marriage and the Market: Women's Subordination in International Perspective*, edited by K. Young, C. Wolkowitz and R. McCullogh, pp. 136–55. Committee of Socialist Economists Books, London.

——(1982) 'The dead and the devils among the Bolivian Laymi.' In *Death and the Regeneration of Life*, edited by Maurice Bloch and Jonathan Parry, pp. 45–73. Cambridge University Press, Cambridge.

Harrison, Simon (1993) *The Mask of War: Violence, Ritual and the Self in Melanesia*. Manchester University Press, Manchester.

Hassig, Ross (1988) *Aztec Warfare*. University of Oklahoma Press, Norman.

Hay, Jonathan (2010) 'Seeing through dead eyes: how early Tang tombs staged the afterlife.' *RES* 57/58: 16–54.

Heckenberger, Michael (2005) *The Ecology of Power: Culture, Place and Personhood in the Southern Amazon, AD 1000–2000*. Routledge, New York.

——(2007) 'Xinguano heroes, ancestors, and others: materializing the past in chiefly bodies, ritual space and landscape.' In *Time and Memory in Indigenous Amazonia: Anthropological Perspectives*, edited by Carlos Fausto and Michael Heckenberger, pp. 284–311. University Press of Florida, Gainesville.

Heggarty, Paul and David Beresford-Jones (2012) *Archaeology and Language in the Andes: A Cross-Disciplinary Exploration of Prehistory*. Proceedings of the British Academy, London.

Helms, Mary W. (1993) *Craft and the Kingly Ideal*. University of Texas Press, Austin.

——(1998) *Access to Origins: Affines, Ancestors and Aristocrats*. University of Texas Press, Austin.

Hernández Príncipe, Rodrigo (1923) 'Mitología andina – idolatrías en Recuay.' *Inca* 1: 25–78.

Herrera, Alexander (2008) 'Las *kanchas* circulares: espacios de interacción sociales en la sierra norte del Peru.' *Boletín de arqueología PUCP (2005)* 9: 233–55.

Herrera, Alexander, Carolina Orsini and Kevin Lane (editors) (2006) *La complejidad social en la Sierra de Ancash: ensayos sobre paisaje, economía y continuidades culturales*. Civiche Raccolte d'Arte Aplicada del Castello Sforzesco, Milan.

Hertz, Robert (1960) *Death and the Right Hand*. Translated by R. Needham and C. Needham. Free Press, New York.

Herzfeld, Michael (1991) *A Place in History: Social and Monumental Time in a Cretan Town*. Princeton University Press, Princeton, N.J.

Heyden, Doris (1981) 'Caves, gods and myths: world-view and planning in Teotihuacan.' In *Mesoamerican Sites and World-Views*, edited by Elizabeth Benson, pp. 1–39. Dumbarton Oaks, Washington, D.C.

Hill, Erica (2000) 'The embodied sacrifice.' *Cambridge Archaeological Journal* 10: 317–26.

Hobsbawm, Eric J. (1990) *Nations and Nationalism since 1780: Programme, Myth and Reality*. Cambridge University Press, Cambridge.

Hocquenghem, Anne Marie (1983) *Hanan y Hurin*. Amerindia 9 (supplement), Paris.

——(1987) *Iconografía Mochica*. Pontificia Universidad de Católica de Peru, Lima.

Hodder, Ian (1986) *Reading the Past: Current Approaches to Interpretation in Archaeology*. Cambridge University Press, Cambridge.

——(1999) *The Archaeological Process: An Introduction*. Blackwell, Malden.

——(2000) *Towards Reflexive Method in Archaeology: The Example at Çatalhöyük*. McDonald Institute for Archaeological Research, Cambridge.

Hohmann, Carolina (2003) 'El rostro circular frontal de boca dentada en la iconografía Recuay.' *Arqueológicas* 26: 131–52.

——(2010) *Das Spiel mit den Welten: Die Ikonographie von Recuay*. PhD dissertation, Freien Universität Berlin, Berlin.

Houston, Stephen D. and David Stuart (1996) 'Of gods, glyphs and kings: divinity and rulership among the Classic Maya.' *Antiquity* 70: 289–312.

Houston, Stephen D., David Stuart and Karl Taube (2006) *The Memory of Bones: Body, Being and Experience among the Classic Maya*. University of Texas Press, Austin.

Howard, Rosaleen (2006) 'Rumi: an ethnolinguistic approach to the symbolism of stone(s) in the Andes.' In *Kay Pacha: Cultivating Earth and Water in the Andes*, edited by Penelope Dransart, pp. 233–45. BAR International Series 1478, Oxford.

Hu, Hsien Chin (1944) 'The Chinese concept of "face".' *American Anthropologist* 46: 45–64.

Hugh-Jones, Stephen (1995) 'Inside-out and back-to-front: the androgynous house in northwest Amazonia.' In *About the House: Lévi-Strauss and Beyond*, edited by Janet Carsten and Stephen Hugh-Jones, pp. 226–52. Cambridge University Press, Cambridge.

Huntington, Richard and Peter Metcalf (1979) *Celebrations of Death: The Anthropology of Mortuary Ritual*. Cambridge University Press, Cambridge.

Hwang, Kwang-kuo (1987) 'Face and favor: the Chinese power game.' *American Journal of Sociology* 92: 944–74.

Ibarra, Bebel (editor) (2003a) *Arqueología de la sierra de Ancash: propuestas y perspectivas*. Instituto Cultural Runa, Lima.

——(2003b) 'Arqueología del Valle del Puchca: economía, cosmovisión y secuencia estilística.' In *Arqueología de la sierra de Ancash: propuestas y perspectivas*, edited by Bebel Ibarra, pp. 251–330. Instituto Cultural Runa, Lima.

——(2009) *Historia prehispánica de Huari: 3000 años de historia desde Chavín hasta los Inkas*. Instituto de Estudios Huarinos, Huari.

Insoll, Timothy (editor) (2006) *Archaeology of Identities*. Routledge, London.

Isbell, William H. (1977) 'Cosmological order expressed in prehistoric ceremonial centers.' *Proceedings of the 42nd International Congress of Americanists* 4: 269–97.

——(1991) 'Honcopampa: monumental ruins in Peru's North Highlands.' *Expedition* 33(3): 27–36.

——(1997) *Mummies and Mortuary Monuments: A Postprocessual Prehistory of Central Andean Social Organization*. University of Texas Press, Austin.

Jackson, Margaret A. (2008) *Moche Art and Visual Culture in Ancient Peru*. University of New Mexico Press, Albuquerque.

Janusek, John W. (2002) 'Out of many, one: style and social boundaries at Tiwanaku.' *Latin American Antiquity* 13: 35–61.

——(2004) *Identity and Power in the Ancient Andes: Tiwanaku Cities through Time*. Routledge, New York.

Jennings, Justin (2011) *Globalizations and the Ancient World*. Cambridge University Press, Cambridge.

Jones, Sian (1997) *The Archaeology of Ethnicity: Constructing Identities in the Past and Present*. Routledge, London.

Joyce, Rosemary A. (2001a) 'Burying the dead at Tlatilco: social memory and social identities.' In *Social Memory, Identity and Death: Anthropological Perspectives on Mortuary Rituals*, edited by Meredith S. Chesson, pp. 12–26. Archeological Papers of the American Anthropological Association 10, Washington D.C.

——(2001b) *Gender and Power in Prehispanic Mesoamerica*. University of Texas Press, Austin.

Joyce, Rosemary and Susan D. Gillespie (editors) (2000) *Beyond Kinship: Social and Material Reproduction in House Societies*. University of Pennsylvania Press, Philadelphia.

Julien, Daniel G. (1988) *Ancient Cuismancu: Settlement and Cultural Dynamics in the Cajamarca Region of the North Highlands of Peru, 200 BC–AD 1532*. Ph.D. dissertation, University of Texas, Austin.

——(1993) 'Late pre-Inkaic ethnic groups in highland Peru: an archaeological–ethnohistorical model of the political geography of the Cajamarca region.' *Latin American Antiquity* 4(3): 246–73.

Kato, Yasutake (1993) 'Resultados de las excavaciones en Kuntur Wasi, Cajamarca.' In *El mundo ceremonial andino*, edited by Luis Millones and Yoshio Onuki, pp. 203–28. National Museum of Ethnology, Senri Ethnological Studies 37, Osaka.

Kaulicke, Peter (2001) *Memoria y muerte en el Perú antiguo*. Pontificia Universidad Católica del Perú, Lima.

Knudson, Kelly J., Sloan R. Williams, Rebecca Osborn, Kathleen Forgey and P. Ryan Williams (2009) 'The geographic origins of Nasca trophy heads using strontium, oxygen, and carbon isotope data.' *Journal of Anthropological Archaeology* 28: 244–57

Koepcke, Maria (1983) *The Birds of the Department of Lima, Peru*. Harrowood, Newtown Square.

Korpisaari, Antti (2006) *Death in the Bolivian High Plateau: Burials and Tiwanaku Society*. Archaeopress, BAR International Series 1536, Oxford.

Kosok, Paul (1965) *Life, Land, and Water in Ancient Peru*. Long Island University Press, New York.

Kroeber, A. L. (1944) *Peruvian Archeology in 1942*. Viking Fund Publications in Anthropology 4, New York.

Kroeber, A. L., Donald Collier and Patrick H. Carmichael (1998) *The Archaeology and Pottery of Nazca, Peru: Alfred L. Kroeber's 1926 Expedition*. AltaMira Press, Walnut Creek.

Krzanowski, Andrzej (1986) 'Cultural chronology of northern Andes of Peru (the Huamachuco-Quiruvilca-Otuzco region).' *Acta archaeologica carpathica* 25: 231–64.

Krzanowski, Andrzej and Maciej Pawlikowski (1980) 'North Peruvian ceramics in the aspect of petrographic analysis.' In *Polish Contributions to New World Archaeology, Part II*, edited by Janusz Koslowski, pp. 63–101. Prace Komisji Archeologicznej 19, Polska Academia Nauk, Warsaw.

Küchler, Susanne (2002) *Malanggan: Art, Memory, and Sacrifice*. Berg, Oxford.

Kutscher, Gerdt (1950) *Chimu: Eine Altindianische Hochkultur*. Gebr. Mann, Berlin.

——(1983) *Nordperuanische Gefässmalereien des Moche-Stils*. C. H. Beck, Materialien zur allgemeinen und vergleichenden Archäologie 18, München.

Lagrou, Els (2009) 'The crystallized memory of artifacts: a reflection on agency and alterity in Cashinahua image-making.' In *The Occult Life of Things: Native Amazonian Theories of Materiality and Personhood*, edited by Fernando Santos-Granero, pp. 192–213. University of Arizona Press, Tucson.

Lanning, Edward P. (1967) *Peru before the Incas*. Prentice-Hall, Englewood Cliffs.

Larco Hoyle, Rafael (1938) *Los mochicas*. Casa Editora 'La Crónica' y 'Variedades', Lima.

——(1941) *Los cupisniques*. Casa Editora 'La Crónica' y 'Variedades', Lima.

——(2001) *Los mochicas*. 2 vols. Museo Arqueológico Rafael Larco Hoyle, Lima.

Lathrap, Donald W. (1973a) 'The antiquity and importance of long-distance trade relationships in the moist tropics of Pre-Columbian South America.' *World Archaeology* 5(2): 171–86.

——(1973b) 'Gifts of the cayman: some thoughts on the subsistence basis of Chavin.' In *Variation in Anthropology: Essays in Honor of John C. McGregor*, edited by Donald W. Lathrap and Jody Douglas, pp. 91–103. Illinois Archaeological Survey, Urbana.

——(1974) 'The moist tropics, the arid lands, and the appearance of Great Art styles in the New World.' In *Art and Environment in Native North America*, edited by M. E. King and I. Traylor, pp. 115–58. Special Publications 7, The Museum, Texas Tech University, Lubbock.

——(1985) 'Jaws: the control of power in the early nuclear American ceremonial center.' In *Early Ceremonial Architecture in the Andes*, edited by Christopher B. Donnan, pp. 241–67. Dumbarton Oaks, Washington, D.C.

Lau, George F. (2000) 'Espacio ceremonial Recuay.' In *Los Dioses del Antiguo Peru*, edited by Krzysztof Makowski, pp. 178–97. Banco de Crédito, Lima.

——(2002) 'Feasting and ancestor veneration at Chinchawas, north highlands of Ancash, Peru.' *Latin American Antiquity* 13: 279–304.

——(2004a) 'Object of contention: an examination of Recuay–Moche combat imagery.' *Cambridge Archaeological Journal* 14: 163–84.

——(2004b) 'The Recuay culture of Peru's north-central highlands: a reappraisal of chronology and its implications.' *Journal of Field Archaeology* 29: 177–202.

——(2005) 'Core-periphery relations in the Recuay hinterlands: economic interaction at Chinchawas, Peru.' *Antiquity* 79: 78–99.

——(2006a) 'Northern exposures: Recuay–Cajamarca boundaries and interaction.' In *Andean Archaeology III: North and South*, edited by William H. Isbell and Helaine Silverman, pp. 143–70. Plenum/Kluwer Publishers, New York.

——(2006b) 'Recuay tradition sculptures of Chinchawas, north highlands of Ancash, Peru.' *Zeitschrift für Archäologie Aussereuropäischer Kulturen* 1: 183–250.

——(2007) 'Animal resources and Recuay cultural transformations at Chinchawas (Ancash, Peru).' *Andean Past* 8: 449–76.

——(2008) 'Ancestor images in the Andes.' In *Handbook of South American Archaeology*, edited by Helaine Silverman and William H. Isbell, pp. 1025–43. Springer Science, New York.

——(2010a) *Ancient Community and Economy at Chinchawas (Ancash, Peru)*. Peabody Museum of Natural History & Yale University Publications in Anthropology 90, New Haven.

——(2010b) 'Fortifications as warfare culture: the hilltop center of Yayno (Ancash, Peru), AD 400–800.' *Cambridge Archaeological Journal* 20: 420–49.

——(2010c) 'House forms and Recuay culture: residential compounds at Yayno (Ancash, Peru), a fortified hilltop town, AD 400–800.' *Journal of Anthropological Archaeology* 29: 327–51.

——(2010d) 'The work of surfaces: object worlds and techniques of enhancement in the ancient Andes.' *Journal of Material Culture* 15(3): 259–86.

——(2011) *Andean Expressions: Art and Archaeology of the Recuay Culture*. University of Iowa Press, Iowa City.

——(2012) 'Culturas y lenguas antiguas de la sierra norcentral del Peru: una investigación arqueolingüística.' *Boletín de Arqueología PUCP* 14: 141–64.

Lavallée, Danièle (1970) *Les représentations animales dans la céramique Mochica*. Institut d'ethnologie, Paris.

Lechtman, Heather N. (1984) 'Andean value systems and the development of prehistoric metallurgy.' *Technology and Culture* 25(1): 1–36.

——(1996) 'El bronce y el Horizonte Medio.' *Boletín Museo del Oro* 41: 3–25.

León Gomez, Miguel A. (2003) 'Espacio geográfico y organización social de los grupos étnicos del Callejón de Conchucos durante los siglos XVI y XVII.' In *Arqueología de la sierra de Ancash: propuestas y perspectivas*, edited by Bebel Ibarra, pp. 457–66. Instituto Runa, Lima.

Leroi-Gourhan, André (1964) *Le geste et la parole*. A. Michel, Paris.

Lévi-Strauss, Claude (1944) 'The social and psychological aspects of chieftainship in a primitive tribe: the Nambikuara.' *Transactions of the New York Academy of Sciences* 7: 16–32.

——(1963a) 'Do dual organizations exist?' In *Structural Anthropology*, edited by Claude Lévi-Strauss, pp. 132–63. Basic Books, New York.

——(1963b) *Totemism*. Beacon Press, Boston.

——(1966) *The Savage Mind*. University of Chicago Press, Chicago.

——(1969) *The Elementary Structures of Kinship*. Beacon Press, Boston.

——(1983) *The Way of the Masks*. Translated by Sylvia Modelski. Jonathan Cape, London.

Lizot, Jacques (1994) 'On warfare: an answer to N. A. Chagnon.' *American Ethnologist* 21: 845–62.

Lockard, Gregory (2005) *Political Power and Economy at the Archaeological Site of Galindo, Moche Valley, Peru*. Ph.D. dissertation, University Microfilms, Ann Arbor.

López Austin, Alfredo (1988) *The Human Body and Ideology: Concepts of the Ancient Nahuas*. 2 vols. University of Utah Press, Salt Lake City.

Lumbreras, Luis G. (1974a) 'Informe de labores del proyecto Chavín.' *Arqueológicas* 15: 37–55.

——(1974b) *The Peoples and Cultures of Ancient Peru*. Smithsonian Institution Press, Washington, D.C.

——(1977) 'Excavaciones en el templo antiguo de Chavín (sector R); informe de la sexta campaña.' *Ñawpa Pacha* 15: 1–38.

Lynch, Thomas F. (1980) 'Guitarrero cave in its Andean context.' In *Guitarrero Cave: Early Man in the Andes*, edited by Thomas F. Lynch, pp. 293–320. Academic Press, New York.

Lyon, Patricia Jean (1978) 'Female supernaturals in ancient Peru.' *Ñawpa Pacha* 16: 95–137.

MacCormack, Sabine (1991) *Religion in the Andes: Vision and Imagination in Early Colonial Peru*. Princeton University Press, Princeton.

Makowski, Krzysztof (2000) 'Dos cántaros en estilo Recuay: guerreros y ancestros de la sierra de Ancash.' *Iconos* 4: 60–61.

——(2004) *Primeras civilizaciones (tomo IX)*. El Comercio Enciclopedia Temática del Perú, Lima.

——(2008) 'Poder e identidad étnica en el mundo moche.' In *Señores de los reinos de la luna*, edited by Krzysztof Makowski, pp. 55–76. Banco de Crédito, Lima.

——(2009) 'Virú–Moche relations: technological identity, stylistic preferences, and the ethnic identity of ceramic manufacturers and users.' In *Gallinazo: An Early Cultural Tradition on the Peruvian North Coast*, edited by Jean-François Millaire and Magali Morlion, pp. 33–60. Cotsen Institute of Archaeology Press, Los Angeles.

Makowski, Krzysztof, Christopher B. Donnan, Luis Jaime Castillo, Magdalena Diez Canseco, Iván Amaro, Otto Eléspuru and Juan Antonio Murro (editors) (1994) *Vicús*. Banco de Crédito del Perú, Lima.

Makowski, Krzysztof and Julio Rucabado Yong (2000) 'Hombres y deidades en la iconografía Recuay.' In *Los Dioses del Antiguo Peru*, edited by K. Makowski, pp. 199–235. Banco de Crédito, Lima.

Mamani, Mauricio (1981) 'El chuño: preparación, uso, almacenamiento.' In *La tecnología en el mundo andino*, edited by Heather Lechtman and Ana María Soldi, pp. 235–46. Universidad Autónoma de México, México D.F.

Mantha, Alexis (2009) 'Territoriality, social boundaries and ancestor veneration in the central Andes of Peru.' *Journal of Anthropological Anthropology* 28: 158–76.

Marcus, George E. and Michael M. Fischer (1986) *Anthropology as Cultural Critique: An Experimental Moment in the Human Sciences*. University of Chicago, Chicago.

Martin, Simon (2006) 'On Pre-Columbian narrative: representation across the word-image divide.' In *A Pre-Columbian World*, edited by Jeffrey Quilter and Mary Miller, pp. 55–106. Dumbarton Oaks, Washington D.C.

Martin, Simon and Nikolai Grube (2000) *Chronicle of the Maya Kings and Queens*. Thames & Hudson, London.

Masferrer Kan, Elio R. (1984) 'Criterios de organización andina: Recuay siglo XVII.' *Bulletin – Institut français d'études andines* 13(1): 47–61.

Masuda, Shozo, Izumi Shimada and Craig Morris (editors) (1985) *Andean Ecology and Civilization: An Interdisciplinary Perspective on Andean Ecological Complementarity*. University of Tokyo Press, Tokyo.

Masur, Louis P. (1989) *Rites of Execution: Capital Punishment and the Transformation of American Culture, 1776–1865*. Oxford University Press, New York.

Matsumoto, Ryozo (1988) 'The Cajamarca culture: its evolution and interaction with coastal peer polities.' Paper presented at 1988 SAA Meeting, Phoenix.

——(1994) 'Dos modos de proceso sociocultural: el Horizonte Temprano y el Período Intermedio Temprano en el valle de Cajamarca.' In *El Mundo Ceremonial Andino*, edited by Luis Millones and Yoshio Onuki, pp. 167–97. Editorial Horizonte, Lima.

——(2006) 'Arqueología de Llanganuco: resumen de las excavaciones desde el año 2002 al 2004.' Paper presented at the II Conversatorio Internacional de Arqueología de Ancash, Instituto Nacional de Cultura – Ancash (18–21 Agosto 2006), Huaraz.

Mauss, Marcel (1967) [1925] *The Gift: Forms and Functions of Exchange in Archaic Societies*. Norton, New York.

Mayer, Enrique (1985) 'Production zones.' In *Andean Ecology and Civilization*, edited by Shozo Masuda, Izumi Shimada and Craig Morris, pp. 45–84. University of Tokyo Press, Tokyo.

——(2002) *The Articulated Peasant: Household Economies in the Andes*. Westview Press, Boulder.

McEwan, Colin and Maarten van de Guchte (1992) 'Ancestral time and sacred space in Inca state ritual.' In *Ancient Americas: Art from Sacred Landscapes*, edited by Richard F. Townsend, pp. 358–71. Art Institute of Chicago, Chicago.

McEwan, Gordon F. (2005) *Pikillacta: The Wari Empire in Cuzco*. University of Iowa Press, Iowa City.

Meddens, Frank M. and Anita G. Cook (2001) 'La administración Wari y el culto a los muertos: Yako, los edificios en forma "D" en la sierra sur-central del Peru.' In *Wari: arte precolombino peruano*, edited by Pedro Bazán, pp. 213–28. Fundación El Monte, Lima.

Mejía Xesspe, Toribio (1948) 'Los soterrados de Katak.' In *El Comercio*, p. 9 (7 January), Lima.

——(1957) 'Chullpas precolombinas en el área andina.' *Revista de la Universidad Nacional de la Plata 2*: 101–8.

Menzel, Dorothy (1964) 'Style and time in the Middle Horizon.' *Ñawpa Pacha* 2: 1–105.

Menzel, Dorothy, John Howland Rowe and Lawrence E. Dawson (1964) *The Paracas Pottery of Ica: A Study in Style and Time*. University of California Publications in American Archaeology and Ethnology 50, Berkeley.

Meskell, Lynn (2002) 'The intersections of identity and politics in archaeology.' *Annual Review of Anthropology* 31: 279–301.

Meskell, Lynn and Rosemary A. Joyce (2003) *Embodied Lives: Figuring Ancient Maya and Egyptian Experience*. Routledge, London.

Meskell, Lynn and Robert W. Preucel (2004) 'Identities.' In *A Companion to Social Archaeology*, edited by Lynn Meskell and Robert W. Preucel, pp. 121–41. Blackwell, Malden.

Métraux, Alfred (1949) 'Warfare, cannibalism, and human trophies.' In *Handbook of South American Indians, Volume 5: The Comparative Ethnology of South American Indians*, edited by Julian H. Steward, pp. 383–410. Bureau of American Ethnology Bulletin 143, Smithsonian Institution, Washington, D.C.

Millaire, Jean-François (2002) *Moche Burial Patterns: An Investigation into Prehispanic Social Structure*. Archaeopress, BAR International Series 1066, Oxford.

——(2004) 'The manipulation of human remains in Moche society: delayed burials, grave reopening, and secondary offerings of human bones on the Peruvian north coast.' *Latin American Antiquity* 15: 371–88.

——(2008) 'Beware of highlanders: coast–highland interactions in the Virú Valley, Peru.' Paper presented at the 73rd Annual Meeting of the Society for American Archaeology, Vancouver.

——(2009) *Gallinazo: An Early Cultural Tradition on the Peruvian North Coast*. Cotsen Institute of Archaeology, Los Angeles.

——(2010) 'Primary state formation in the Virú Valley, north coast of Peru.' *Proceedings of the National Academy of Sciences* 107: 6186–91.

Miller, George R. and Richard L. Burger (1995) 'Our father the cayman, our dinner the llama: animal utilization at Chavín de Huántar, Peru.' *American Antiquity* 60: 421–58.

Miller, Mary E. and Simon Martin (editors) (2004) *Courtly Art of the Ancient Maya*. Thames & Hudson, New York.

Millones, Luis (1979) 'Religion and power in the Andes: idolatrous curacas of the Central Sierra.' *Ethnohistory* 26: 243–63.

Mills, Barbara J. and William H. Walker (2008) *Memory Work: Archaeologies of Material Practices*. School for Advanced Research Press, Santa Fe.

Mills, Kenneth (1994) 'Especialistas en rituales y resistencia cultural en la región norcentral del Peru, 1642–72.' In *En el nombre del Señor: shamanes, demonios y curanderos del norte del Peru*, edited by Luis Millones and Moises Lemlij, pp. 148–83. Biblioteca Peruana de Psicoanálisis, Lima.

——(1997) *Idolatry and Its Enemies: Colonial Andean Religion and Extirpation, 1640–1750*. Princeton University Press, Princeton.

Mithen, Steven J. (2005) *The Singing Neanderthals: The Origins of Music, Language, Mind and Body*. Weidenfeld & Nicolson, London.

Monaghan, John (1995) *The Covenants with Earth and Rain: Exchange, Sacrifice and Revelation in Mixtec Sociality*. University of Oklahoma Press, Oklahoma City.

Montenegro, Jorge (1993) 'El estilo Cajamarca Costeño: una aproximación.' In *IX Congreso Peruano del Hombre y la Cultura Andina*, edited by S. Arréstegui, pp. 137–50. Universidad Nacional de Cajamarca, Cajamarca.

Moore, Jerry D. (1995) 'Archaeology of dual organization in Andean South America: a theoretical review and case study.' *Latin American Antiquity* 6(2): 165–81.

——(2005) *Cultural Landscapes in the Ancient Andes: Archaeologies of Place*. University Press of Florida, Gainesville.

Morris, Craig (1985) 'From principles of ecological complementarity to the organization and administration of Tawantinsuyu.' In *Andean Ecology and Civilization*, edited by Shozo Masuda, Izumi Shimada and Craig Morris, pp. 477–90. University of Tokyo, Tokyo.

Moseley, Michael E. (1975) *The Maritime Foundations of Andean Civilization*. Cummings Publishing, Menlo Park, California.

——(1983) 'Good old days were better: agrarian collapse and tectonics.' *American Anthropologist* 85: 773–99.

——(1992) *The Incas and Their Ancestors: The Archaeology of Peru*. Thames & Hudson, New York.

——(1999) 'Preposterism: oxymorons of post-modern prehistory.' *Review of Archaeology* 20: 1–11.

Mullins, Paul R. and Robert Paynter (2000) 'Representing colonizers: an archaeology of creolization, ethnogenesis, and indigenous material culture among the Haida.' *Historical Archaeology* 34: 73–84.

Murra, John V. (1972) 'El "control vertical" de un máximo de pisos ecológicos en la economia de las sociedades andinas.' In *Visita de la Provincia de Leon de Huánuco en 1562, por Iñigo Ortiz de Zuñiga (tomo 2)*, edited by John V. Murra, pp. 427–76. Universidad Nacional Hermilio Valdizán, Huánuco.

Murúa, Martín de (2004) [ca.1598] *Códice Murúa: historia y genealogía de los reyes Incas del Perú del Padre Mercedario Fray Martín de Murúa : códice Galvin.* 2 vols. Testimonio Compañía Editorial, Madrid.

Nash, Donna (2009) 'Household archaeology in the Andes.' *Journal of Archaeological Research* 17: 205–61.

Netherly, Patricia J. (1977) *Local Level Lords on the North Coast of Peru.* Ph.D. dissertation, Cornell University, University Microfilms, Ann Arbor.

——(1993) 'The nature of the Andean state.' In *Configurations of Power: Holistic Anthropology in Theory and Practice*, edited by John S. Henderson and Patricia J. Netherly, pp. 11–35. Cornell University Press, Ithaca.

Nicholson, Henry B. (1971) 'Pre-hispanic central Mexican historiography.' In *Investigaciones contemporáneas sobre la historia de México: memorias de la tercera reunión de historiadores Mexicanos y Norteamericanos* (Oaxtepec, 1969), pp. 38–81. Universidad Nacional Autónoma de Mexico, México D.F.

O'Hanlon, Michael and Robert Louis Welsch (2000) *Hunting the gatherers: ethnographic collectors, agents and agency in Melanesia, 1870s–1930s.* Berghahn Books, New York.

Oakland Rodman, Amy and Arabel Fernández (2001) 'Tejidos de Huari y Tiwanaku: comparaciones y contextos.' *Boletín de Arqueología PUCP (2000)* 4: 119–30.

Oliver, José R. (2009) *Caciques and Cemí Idols: The Web Spun by Taíno Rulers between Hispaniola and Puerto Rico.* University of Alabama Press, Tuscaloosa.

Onuki, Yoshio (1997) 'Ocho tumbas especiales de Kuntur Wasi.' In *La muerte en el antiguo Peru: contextos y conceptos funerarios*, edited by Peter Kaulicke, pp. 79–114. Boletín de Arqueología PUCP 1, Lima.

Orsini, Carolina (2007) *Pastori e Guerrieri: I Recuay, un popolo preispanico delle Ande del Peru.* Jaca Books, Milan.

Overing, Joanna (1989) 'The aesthetics of production: the sense of community among the Cubeo and Piaroa.' *Dialectical Anthropology* 14: 159–75.

Overing, Joanna and Alan Passes (2000a) *The Anthropology of Love and Anger: The Aesthetics of Conviviality in Native Amazonia.* Routledge, London.

——(2000b) 'Introduction: conviviality and the opening up of Amazonian anthropology.' In *The Anthropology of Love and Anger: The Aesthetics of Conviviality in Native Amazonia*, edited by Joanna Overing and Alan Passes, pp. 1–30. Routledge, London.

Owen, Bruce (2007) 'The Wari heartland on the Arequipa coast: Huamanga ceramics from Beringa, Majes Valley, Peru.' *Andean Past* 8: 287–373.

Paredes, Juan (2005) 'Redescubriendo Willkawaín e Ichic Willkawaín.' *Integración: Cultura Ancashina (INC-Huaraz)* 2: 7–8.

Paredes, Juan, Berenice Quintana and Moisés Linares (2001) 'Tumbas de la época Wari en el Callejón de Huaylas.' In *Huari y Tiwanaku: modelos vs. evidencias, primera parte*, edited by Peter Kaulicke and William H. Isbell, pp. 253–88. Boletín de Arqueología PUCP 4, Lima.

Parsons, Jeffrey R., Charles M. Hastings and Ramiro Matos M. (2000) *Prehispanic Settlement Patterns in the Upper Mantaro and Tarma Drainages, Junín, Peru: The Tarama–Chinchaycocha Region (2 vols.).* Memoirs of the University of Michigan Museum of Anthropology 34, Ann Arbor.

Patterson, Thomas C. (1987) 'Tribes, chiefdoms, and kingdoms in the Inca empire.' In *Power Relations and State Formation*, edited by Thomas C. Patterson and Christine W. Gailey, pp. 117–27. American Anthropological Association, Washington.

Pauketat, Timothy R. (2007) *Chiefdoms and Other Archaeological Delusions*. AltaMira Press, Lanham.

Paul, Anne (1990) *Paracas Ritual Attire: Symbols of Authority in Ancient Peru*. University of Oklahoma Press, Norman.

——(1991) *Paracas Art and Architecture: Object and Context in South Coastal Peru*. University of Iowa Press, Iowa City.

——(1992) 'Paracas necropolis textiles: symbolic visions of coastal Peru.' In *Ancient Americas: Art from Sacred Landscapes*, edited by Richard F. Townsend, pp. 278–89. Art Institute of Chicago, Chicago.

Pérez Calderón, Ismael (1988) 'Monumentos arqueológicos de Santiago de Chuco, La Libertad.' *Boletín de Lima* 60: 33–44.

——(1994) 'Monumentos arqueológicos de Santiago de Chuco, La Libertad.' *Boletín de Lima* 91–96: 225–74.

Peters, Ann (1991) 'Ecology and society in embroidered images from the Paracas necrópolis.' In *Paracas Art and Architecture: Object and Context in South Coastal Peru*, edited by Anne Paul, pp. 240–314. University of Iowa Press, Iowa City.

Phillips, Ruth B. (1998) *Trading Identities: The Souvenir in Native North American Art from the Northeast, 1700–1900*. University of Washington Press, Seattle.

Pillsbury, Joanne (editor) (2001) *Moche Art and Archaeology in Ancient Peru*. National Gallery of Art, Studies in the History of Art 63, Washington, D.C.

Platt, Tristan (1986) 'Mirrors and maize: the concept of yanantin among the Macha of Bolivia.' In *Anthropological History of Andean Polities*, edited by John Murra, Jacques Revel and Nathan Wachtel, pp. 228–59. Cambridge University Press, New York.

——(2002) 'El feto agresivo. Parto, formación de la persona y mito-historia en los Andes.' *Estudios atacameños* 22: 127–55.

Polia, Mario (1999) *La cosmovisión religiosa andina en documentos inéditos del Archivo Romano de la Compañia de Jesus 1581–1752*. Pontificia Universidad Católica del Perú, Lima.

Politis, Gustavo (2007) *Nukak: Ethnoarchaeology of an Endangered Amazonian People*. Left Coast Press, Walnut Creek.

Pollitt, J. J. (1979) *Art and Experience in Classical Greece*. Cambridge University Press, Cambridge.

Ponte, Victor M. (2001) 'Transformación social y política en el Callejón de Huaylas, siglos III–X d.C.' In *Huari y Tiwanaku: modelos vs. evidencias, primera parte*, edited by Peter Kaulicke and William H. Isbell, pp. 219–52. Boletín de Arqueología PUCP 4 (2000), Lima.

——(2006) 'Recuay burial practices: rank differentiation and ceremonies beyond death.' *Arkeos, Revista Electrónica de Arqueología* 1(2): 47–55.

——(2009) 'An analysis of the Isabelita Rock engraving and its archaeological context, Callejón de Huaylas, Peru.' *Andean Past* 9: 131–75.

Pozorski, Shelia and Thomas Pozorski (2002) 'The Sechín Alto complex and its place within Casma Valley Initial Period development.' In *Andean Archaeology I: Variations in Socio-political Organization*, edited by William H. Isbell and Helaine Silverman, pp. 21–51. Kluwer Academic/Plenum, New York.

Prieto, Gabriel (2008) 'Rituales de enterramiento arquitectónico en el núcleo urbano moche: una aproximación desde una residencia de elite en el valle de Moche.' In *Arqueología mochica: nuevos enfoques*, edited by Luis Jaime Castillo, Hélène Bernier, Greg Lockard and Julio Rucabado, pp. 307–23. Pontificia Universidad Católica del Peru, Lima.

Proulx, Donald A. (1982) 'Territoriality in the Early Intermediate Period: the case of Moche and Recuay.' *Ñawpa Pacha* 20: 83–96.

——(1989) 'Nasca trophy heads: victims of warfare or ritual sacrifice?' In *Cultures in Conflict: Current Archaeological Perspectives*, edited by Diana C. Tkaczuk and Brian C. Vivian, pp. 73–85. Proceedings of the Twentieth Annual Chacmool Conference, University of Calgary, Calgary.

——(1994) 'Stylistic variation in proliferous Nasca pottery.' *Andean Past* 4: 91–107.

——(2001) 'Ritual uses of trophy heads in Nasca society.' In *Ritual Sacrifice in Ancient Peru*, edited by Elizabeth Benson and Anita Cook, pp. 137–63. University of Texas Press, Austin.

——(2006) *A Sourcebook of Nasca Ceramic Iconography: Reading a Culture through Its Art*. University of Iowa Press, Iowa City.

——(2007) *Settlement Patterns and Society in South Coastal Peru: Report on a Survey of the Lower Rio Nasca and Rio Grande, 1998*. University of Massachusetts at Amherst (online resource: http://people.umass.edu/~proulx/online_pubs/1998_Nasca_Survey_Report.pdf).

——(2008) 'Paracas and Nasca: regional cultures on the south coast of Peru.' In *Handbook of South American Archaeology*, edited by Helaine Silverman and William H. Isbell, pp. 563–85. Springer, New York.

Prufer, Keith M. and James Edward Brady (2005) *Stone Houses and Earth Lords: Maya Religion in the Cave Context*. University Press of Colorado, Boulder.

Pugh, Timothy W. (2009) 'Contagion and alterity: Kowoj Maya appropriations of European objects.' *American Anthropologist* 111: 373–86.

Pulgar Vidal, Javier (1972) *Los ocho regiones naturales del Peru*. Editorial Universo, Lima.

Quilter, Jeffrey (1990) 'Moche revolt of the objects.' *Latin American Antiquity* 1(1): 42–65.

——(2002) 'Moche politics, religion, and warfare.' *Journal of World Prehistory* 16: 145–95.

——(2008) 'Art and Moche martial arts.' In *The Art and Archaeology of the Moche: An Ancient Andean Society of the Peruvian North Coast*, edited by Steve Bourget and Kimberly Jones, pp. 215–28. University of Texas Press, Austin.

——(2010) 'Moche: archaeology, ethnicity, identity.' *Bulletin de l'Institut Français d'Études Andines* 39: 225–41.

Quilter, Jeffrey and Luis Jaime Castillo (editors) (2010) *New Perspectives on Moche Political Organization*. Dumbarton Oaks, Washington, D.C.

Quilter, Jeffrey, Marc Zender, Karen Spalding, Régulo G. Franco Jordán, César Gálvez Mora and Juan Castañeda Murga (2010) 'Traces of a lost language and number system discovered on the north coast of Peru.' *American Anthropologist* 112: 357–69.

Ramírez, Susan E. (1996) *The World Upside Down: Cross-Cultural Contact and Conflict in Sixteenth Century Peru*. Stanford University Press, Stanford.

——(2005) *To Feed and Be Fed: The Cosmological Bases of Authority and Identity in the Andes*. Stanford University Press, Palo Alto.

——(2006) 'From people to place and back again: back translation as decentering – an Andean case study.' *Ethnohistory* 53: 355–81.

Ramón, Gabriel (2008) *Potters of the Northern Peruvian Andes: A Palimpsest of Technical Styles in Motion*. Ph.D. dissertation, University of East Anglia, Norwich.

Ramos, Gabriela (2010) *Death and Conversion in the Andes: Lima and Cuzco, 1532–1670*. University of Notre Dame Press, South Bend.

Rea, Amadeo M. (1986) 'Black vultures and human victims: archaeological evidence from Pacatnamú.' In *The Pacatnamú Papers, Volume 1*, edited by Christopher B. Donnan and Guillermo A. Cock, pp. 139–44. UCLA Museum of Cultural History, Los Angeles.

Redmond, Elsa (1994) *Tribal and Chiefly Warfare in South America*. Memoirs of the Museum of Anthropology 28, University of Michigan, Ann Arbor.

Redmond, Elsa M. (editor) (1998a) *Chiefdoms and Chieftaincy in the Americas*. University Press of Florida, Gainesville.

——(1998b) 'In war and peace: alternative paths to centralized leadership.' In *Chiefdoms and Chieftaincy in the Americas*, edited by Elsa M. Redmond, pp. 68–103. University Press of Florida, Gainesville.

Reichert, Raphael X. (1977) *The Recuay Ceramic Style: A Reevaluation*. Ph.D. dissertation, University of California, Los Angeles.

——(1978) 'Ceramic sculpture of ancient Peru.' *Pacific Discovery* 31(4): 28–32.

——(1982) 'Moche iconography – the highland connection.' In *Pre-Columbian Art History: Selected Readings*, edited by Alana Cordy-Collins, pp. 279–91. Peek Publications, Palo Alto (CA).

——(1989) 'A Moche battle and the question of identity.' In *Cultures in Conflict: Current Archaeological Perspectives*, edited by Diana C. Tkaczuk and Brian C. Vivian, pp. 86–89. Proceedings of the Twentieth Annual Chacmool Conference, University of Calgary, Calgary.

Reichlen, Henry and Paule Reichlen (1949) 'Recherches archéologiques dans les Andes de Cajamarca: Premier rapport de la Mission Ethnologique Française au Perou Septentrional.' *Journal de la Société des Américanistes* 38: 137–74.

Reinhard, Johan (1985) 'Chavín and Tiahuanaco: a new look at two Andean ceremonial centers.' *National Geographic Research* 1: 345–422.

——(2005) *The Ice Maiden: Inca Mummies, Mountain Gods, and Sacred Sites in the Andes*. National Geographic Society, Washington, D.C.

Renfrew, Colin and Ezra Zubrow (1994) *The Ancient Mind: Elements of Cognitive Archaeology*. Cambridge University Press, London.

Rice, Don S. (editor) (1993) *Latin American Horizons*. Dumbarton Oaks, Washington, D.C.

Richter, Daniel (1992) *Ordeal of the Longhouse: The Peoples of the Iroquois League in the Era of European Colonization*. University of North Carolina Press, Chapel Hill.

Rick, John W. (2008) 'Context, construction and ritual in the development of authority at Chavín de Huántar.' In *Chavín: Art, Architecture and Culture*, edited by William J. Conklin and Jeffrey Quilter, pp. 3–34. Cotsen Institute of Archaeology Monograph 61, Los Angeles.

Ringberg, Jennifer (2008) 'Figurines, household rituals, and the use of domestic space in a middle Moche rural community.' In *Arqueología mochica: nuevos enfoques*, edited by Luis Jaime Castillo, Hélène Bernier, Greg Lockard and Julio Rucabado, pp. 341–57. Pontificia Universidad Católica del Peru, Lima.

Rival, Laura M. (2001) 'Seed and clone: the symbolic and social significance of bitter manioc cultivation.' In *Beyond the Visible and the Material*, edited by Laura M. Rival and Neil L. Whitehead, pp. 57–79. Oxford University Press, Oxford.

Roark, Richard Paul (1965) 'From monumental to proliferous in Nasca pottery.' *Ñawpa Pacha* 3: 1–92.

Rostworowski, María (1988) *Conflicts over Coca Fields in XVIth-Century Peru*. Memoirs of the Museum of Anthropology, University of Michigan 21, Ann Arbor.

Rowe, Ann Pollard (1990) 'Nasca figurines and costume.' *Textile Museum Journal* 29–30: 93–128.

Rowe, John Howland (1946) 'Inca culture at the time of the Spanish conquest.' In *Handbook of South American Indians, Volume 2: The Andean Civilizations*, edited by Julian Steward, pp. 183–330. Bureau of American Ethnology Bulletin 143, Washington, D.C.

——(1962) *Chavín Art: An Inquiry into Its Form and Meaning*. Museum of Primitive Art, New York.

——(1971) 'The influence of Chavín art on later styles.' In *Dumbarton Oaks Conference on Chavín*, edited by Elizabeth P. Benson, pp. 101–24. Dumbarton Oaks, Washington, D.C.

——(1982) 'Inca policies and institutions relating to the cultural unification of the empire.' In *Inca and Aztec States, 1400–1800: Anthropology and History*, edited by George Collier, Renato Rosaldo and John Wirth, pp. 93–118. Academic Press, New York.

Rowe, John Howland and Dorothy Menzel (editors) (1967) *Peruvian Archaeology: Selected Readings*. Peek Publications, Palo Alto.

Rowlands, Michael (1993) 'The role of memory in the transmission of culture.' *World Archaeology* 25: 141–51.

Russell, Glenn S. and Margaret A. Jackson (2011) 'Political economy and patronage at Cerro Mayal, Peru.' In *Moche Art and Archaeology in Ancient Peru*, edited by Joanne Pillsbury, pp. 158–75. National Gallery of Art, Washington D.C.

Sahlins, Marshall (1972) *Stone Age Economics*. Aldine Publishing, New York.

——(1985) *Islands of History*. University of Chicago Press, Chicago.

——(2011) 'What kinship is (part one).' *Journal of Royal Anthropological Institute* 17: 2–19.

Said, Edward W. (1978) *Orientalism*. Pantheon Books, New York.

Salazar-Burger, Lucy and Richard L. Burger (1982) 'La araña en la iconografía del Horizonte Temprano en la costa norte del Peru.' *Beiträge zur allgemeinen und vergleichenden Archäologie* 4: 213–53.

Salazar, Lucy and Richard L. Burger (2000) 'Las divinidades del universo religioso Cupisnique y Chavín.' In *Señores de los reinos de la Luna*, edited by Krzysztof Makowski, pp. 29–69. Banco de Crédito del Perú, Lima.

Salomon, Frank (1986). *Native Lords of Quito in the Age of the Incas*. Cambridge University Press, Cambridge.

——(1991) 'Introductory essay: the Huarochirí Manuscript.' In *The Huarochirí Manuscript: A Testament of Ancient and Colonial Religion*, edited by Frank Salomon and George Urioste, pp. 1–38. University of Texas Press, Austin.

——(1995) '"Beautiful grandparents": Andean ancestor shrines and mortuary ritual as seen through colonial records.' In *Tombs for the Living: Andean Mortuary Practices*, edited by Tom D. Dillehay, pp. 315–53. Dumbarton Oaks, Washington, D.C.

——(1998) 'How the huacas were: the language of substance and transformation in the Huarochiri Quechua manuscript.' *Res* 33: 7–17.

——(2004) 'Andean opulence: indigenous ideas about wealth in colonial Peru.' In *The Colonial Andes: Tapestries and Silverwork, 1530–1830*, edited by Elena Phipps, Johanna Hecht and Cristina Esteras Martín, pp. 114–24. Metropolitan Museum of Art, New York.

Salomon, Frank and George Urioste (editors) (1991) *The Huarochirí Manuscript: A Testament of Ancient and Colonial Religion*. University of Texas Press, Austin.

Sandweiss, Daniel H. (1992) *The Archaeology of Chincha Fishermen: Specialization and Status in Inka Peru*. Carnegie Museum of Natural History, Pittsburgh.

Santos-Granero, Fernando (1986) 'Power, ideology and the ritual of production in lowland South American.' *Man* 21: 657–79.

——(2007) 'Of fear and friendship: Amazonian sociality beyond kinship and affinity.' *Journal of the Royal Anthropological Institute* 13: 1–18.

——(2009a) 'Introduction: Amerindian constructional views of the world.' In *The Occult Life of Things: Native Amazonian Theories of Materiality and Personhood*, edited by Fernando Santos-Granero, pp. 1–29. University of Arizona Press, Tucson.

——(2009b) *The Occult Life of Things: Native Amazonian Theories of Materiality and Personhood*. University of Arizona Press, Tucson.

——(2009c) *Vital Enemies: Slavery, Predation, and the Amerindian Political Economy of Life*. University of Texas Press, Austin.

Saunders, Nicholas J. (1999) 'Biographies of brilliance: pearls, transformations of matter and being, c. AD 1492.' *World Archaeology* 31: 243–57.

Sawyer, Alan R. (1997) *Early Nasca Needlework*. Laurence King, London.

Schaedel, Richard P. (1948) 'Stone sculpture in the Callejón de Huaylas.' In *A Reappraisal of Peruvian Archaeology*, edited by Wendell C. Bennett, pp. 66–79. Memoirs of the Society for American Archaeology 4, Menasha.

——(1952) *An Analysis of Central Andean Stone Sculpture*. Ph.D. dissertation, Yale University, University Microfilms, Ann Arbor.

——(1985) 'Coast–highland interrelationships and ethnic groups in Northern Peru (500 BC–AD 1980).' In *Andean Ecology and Civilization: An Interdisciplinary Perspective in Ecological Complementarity*, edited by Shozo Masuda, Izumi Shimada and Craig Morris, pp. 443 – 474. University of Tokyo Press, Tokyo.

Schele, Linda and David A. Freidel (1990) *A Forest of Kings: The Untold Story of the Ancient Maya*. Morrow, New York.

Schele, Linda and Mary Ellen Miller (1986) *The Blood of Kings: Dynasty and Ritual in Maya Art*. George Braziller, New York.

Schiffer, Michael B. (1995) *Behavioral Archaeology: First Principles*. University of Utah Press, Salt Lake City.

Schreiber, Katharina J. and Josué Lancho Rojas (1995) 'Puquios of Nasca.' *Latin American Antiquity* 6(3): 229–54.

——(2003) *Irrigation and Society in the Peruvian Desert: The Puquios of Nasca*. Lexington Books, Lanham.

Schuler-Schömig, Immina von (1979) 'Die "Fremdkrieger" in Darstellungen der Moche-Keramik. Eine ikonographische Studie.' *Baessler Archiv, Neue Folge* 27: 135–213.

——(1981) 'Die sogenannten Fremdkrieger und ihre weiteren ikonographischen Bezuge in der Moche-Keramik.' *Baessler Archiv, Neue Folge* 29: 207–39.

Scott, David A. (1998) 'Technical examination of ancient South American metals: some examples from Colombia, Peru and Argentina.' *Boletín, Museo del Oro* 44: 79–105.

Seabright, Paul (2004) *The Company of Strangers: A Natural History of Economic Life*. Princeton University Press, Princeton.

Segura Llanos, Rafael (2006) 'La cerámica lima en las albores del Horizonte Medio y algunas notas para el debate.' In *Puruchuco y la sociedad de Lima: un homenaje a Arturo Jiménez Borja*, edited by Luis Felipe Villacorta, pp. 97–117. CONCYTEC, Lima.

Service, Elman R. (1962) *Primitive Social Organization*. Random House, New York.

Shady, Ruth (1988) 'La época Huari como interacción de las sociedades regionales.' *Revista Andina* 6(1): 67–99.

Shady, Ruth and Hermilio Rosas (1977) *El Horizonte Medio en Chota: prestigio de la cultura Cajamarca y su relación con el 'Imperio Huari'*. Arqueológicas 16, Instituto Nacional de Cultura Museo Nacional de Antropología y Arqueología, Lima.

Shanks, Michael and Christopher Y. Tilley (1987) *Re-constructing Archaeology: Theory and Practice*. Cambridge University Press, Cambridge.

Sherbondy, Jeannette (1988) '*Mallki*: ancestros y cultivo de árboles en los Andes.' In *Sociedad andina: pasado y presente*, edited by Ramiro Matos, pp. 101–36. Fomciencias, Lima.

Shimada, Izumi (1994) *Pampa Grande and the Mochica Culture*. University of Texas Press, Austin.

——(2001) 'Late Moche urban craft production: a first approximation.' In *Moche Art and Archaeology in Ancient Peru*, edited by Joanne Pillsbury, pp. 177–206. National Gallery of Art, Washington, D.C.

Shimada, Izumi, Ken-Ichi Shinoda, Walter Alva, Steve Bourget, Claude Chapdelaine and Santiago Uceda (2008) 'The Moche people: genetic perspectives on their sociopolitical composition and organization.' In *The Art and Archaeology of the Moche: An Ancient Andean Society of the Peruvian North Coast*, edited by Steve Bourget and Kimberly Jones, pp. 179–93. University of Texas Press, Austin.

Shimada, Izumi, Ken-Ichi Shinoda, Steve Bourget, Walter Alva and Santiago Uceda (2005) 'MtDNA analysis of Moche and Sicán populations of pre-Hispanic Peru.' In *Biomolecular Archaeology: Genetic Approaches to the Past*, edited by D. Reed, pp. 61–92. Southern Illinois University Press, Carbondale.

Shinoda, Ken-Ichi, Izumi Shimada, Walter Alva and Santiago Uceda (2002) 'DNA analysis of Moche and Sicán populations: results and implications.' Poster presented at the 67th Meeting of the Society for American Archaeology, Denver.

Sillar, Bill (1996) 'The dead and the drying: techniques for transforming people and things in the Andes.' *Journal of Material Culture* 1: 259–89.

——(2000) *Shaping Culture: Making Pots and Constructing Households: An Ethnoarchaeological Study of Pottery Production, Trade and Use in the Andes*. BAR International Series 883, Oxford.

Silverblatt, Irene Marsha (2004) *Modern Inquisitions: Peru and the Colonial Origins of the Civilized World*. Duke University Press, Durham.

Silverman, Helaine (1993) *Cahuachi in the Ancient Nasca World*. University of Iowa Press, Iowa City.

——(1996) *Ancient Peruvian Art: An Annotated Bibliography*. G. K. Hall, New York.

——(2002a) *Ancient Nasca Settlement and Society*. University of Iowa Press, Iowa City.

——(2002b) 'Touring ancient times: the present and presented past in contemporary Peru.' *American Anthropologist* 104(3): 881–902.

Silverman, Helaine and Donald A. Proulx (2002) *The Nasca*. Blackwell Publishers, Malden.

Silverman, Helaine and David B. Small (editors) (2002) *The Space and Place of Death*. Archeological Papers of the American Anthropological Association 11, Washington, D.C.

Skar, Harald O. (1982) *The Warm Valley People: Duality and Land Reform among the Quechua Indians of Highland Peru*. Universitetsforlaget, Oslo.

Smith, John W., Jr. (1978) *The Recuay Culture: A Reconstruction Based on Artistic Motifs*. Ph.D. dissertation, University of Texas, Austin.

Spalding, Karen (1984) *Huarochirí: An Andean Society under Inca and Spanish Rule*. Stanford University Press, Stanford.

Spencer, Charles S. (1998) 'Investigating the development of Venezuelan chiefdoms.' In *Chiefdoms and Chieftaincy in the Americas*, edited by Elsa M. Redmond, pp. 104–37. University Press of Florida, Gainesville.

Stanish, Charles (1989) 'Household archaeology: testing models of zonal complementarity in the south central Andes.' *American Anthropologist* 91(1): 7–24.

——(1992) *Ancient Andean Political Economy*. University of Texas Press, Austin.

——(2003) *Ancient Titicaca: The Evolution of Complex Society in Southern Peru and Northern Bolivia*. University of California Press, Berkeley.

Stark, Miriam T. (editor) (1998) *The Archaeology of Social Boundaries*. Smithsonian Institution Press, Washington, D.C.

Steward, Julian H. (editor) (1946) *Handbook of South American Indians, Volume 2: The Andean Civilizations*. Bureau of American Ethnology Bulletin 143, Washington, D.C.

Steward, Julian H. and Louis C. Faron (1959) *Native Peoples of South America*. McGraw-Hill, New York.

Strathern, Marilyn (1988) *Gender of the Gift: Problems with Women and Problems with Society in Melanesia*. University of California Press, Berkeley.

Strickland, Debra Higgs (2003) *Saracens, Demons & Jews: Making Monsters in Medieval Art*. Princeton University Press, Princeton.

Sturtevant, William C. (1998) 'Tupinambá chiefdoms.' In *Chiefdoms and Chieftaincy in the Americas*, edited by Elsa M. Redmond, pp. 138–49. University Press of Florida, Gaineville.

Sutter, Richard C. and Rosa Cortez (2005) 'The nature of Moche human sacrifice: a bio-archaeological perspective.' *Current Anthropology* 46: 521–49.

Sutter, Richard C. and John W. Verano (2007) 'Biodistance analysis of the Moche sacrificial victims from Huaca de la Luna Plaza 3C: matrix method test of their origins.' *American Journal of Physical Anthropology* 132: 193–206.

Swenson, Edward R. (2003) 'Cities of violence: sacrifice, power and urbanization in the Andes.' *Journal of Social Archaeology* 3(2): 256–96.

Sztutman, Renato (2009) 'Religião nômade ou germe do estado? Pierre e Hélène Clastres ea vertigem tupi.' *Novos Estudos-CEBRAP* 83: 129–57.

Taussig, Michael (1993) *Mimesis and Alterity: A Particular History of the Senses*. Routledge, London.

Taylor, Anne-Christine (1996) 'The soul's body and its states: an Amazonian perspective on the nature of being human.' *Journal of the Royal Anthropological Institute* 2: 201–15.

Taylor, Gerald (1987) *Ritos y tradiciones de Huarochirí: manuscrito quechua de comienzos del siglo XVII*. Instituto de Estudios Peruanos y Instituto Francés de Estudios Andinos, Lima.

Tello, Julio C. (1923) 'Wira Kocha.' *Inca* 1(1): 93–320; 1(3): 583–606.

——(1929) *Antiguo Perú: primera época*. Comisión Organizadora del Segundo Congreso de Turismo, Lima.

——(1930) 'Andean civilization: some problems of Peruvian archaeology.' In *Proceedings of the 23rd International Congress of Americanists (New York, 1928)*, pp. 259–90.

——(1942) *Origen y desarrollo de las civilizaciones prehistoricas andinas*. Librería e Imprenta Gil, Lima.

——(1960) *Chavín: cultura matriz de la civilización andina*. Universidad Nacional Mayor de San Marcos, Lima.

Terada, Kazuo and Ryozo Matsumoto (1985) 'Sobre la cronología de la tradición Cajamarca.' In *Historia del Cajamarca: Tomo 1 (Arqueología)*, edited by Fernando Silva S., Waldemar Espinoza S. and Rogger Ravines, pp. 67–89. Instituto Nacional de Cultura, Cajamarca.

Thatcher, John P. (1972) *Continuity and Change in the Ceramics of Huamachuco*. Ph.D. dissertation, University of Pennsylvania, Philadelphia.

Thomas, Julian (1996) *Time, Culture, and Identity: An Interpretative Archaeology*. Routledge, London.

Thomas, Nicholas (1991) *Entangled Objects: Exchange, Material Culture, and Colonialism in the Pacific.* Harvard University Press, Cambridge.

Todorov, Tzvetan (1984) *The Conquest of America: The Question of the Other.* Harper & Row, New York.

Topic, John R. (1998) 'Ethnogenesis in Huamachuco.' *Andean Past* 5: 109–27.

Topic, John R. and Theresa L. Topic (1983) 'Coast–highland relations in northern Peru: some observations on routes, networks, and scales of interaction.' In *Civilization in the Ancient Americas: Essays in Honor of Gordon R. Willey,* edited by Richard Leventhal and Alan Kolata, pp. 237–59. University of New Mexico Press, Albuquerque.

——(1987) 'The archaeological investigation of Andean militarism: some cautionary observations.' In *The Origins and Development of the Andean State,* edited by J. Haas, S. Pozorski and T. Pozorski, pp. 47–55. Cambridge University Press, Cambridge.

——(1997a) 'Hacia una comprensión conceptual de la guerra andina.' In *Arqueología, antropología e historia en los Andes: homenaje a Maria Rostworowski,* edited by Rafael Varon Gabai and Javier Flores Espinoza, pp. 567–95. Instituto de Estudios Peruanos, Lima.

——(1997b) 'La guerra mochica.' *Revista Arqueológica 'SIAN'* 4: 10–12.

——(2001) 'Hacia la comprensión del fenómeno Huari: una perspectiva norteña.' *Boletín de Arqueología PUCP* 4: 181–217.

Topic, Theresa L. (1977) *Excavations at Moche.* Unpublished Ph.D. dissertation, Harvard University, Cambridge.

——(1982) 'The Early Intermediate Period and its legacy.' In *Chan Chan: Andean Desert City,* edited by Michael E. Moseley and Kent C. Day, pp. 255–84. School of American Research, University of New Mexico, Albuquerque.

——(1985) 'The kaolin ceramic tradition in northern Peru.' Paper for the 4th Annual Northeast Conference on Andean Archaeology and Ethnohistory, SUNY Albany.

——(1991) 'The Middle Horizon in northern Peru.' In *Huari Administrative Structure: Prehistoric Monumental Architecture and State Government,* edited by William H. Isbell and Gordon F. McEwan, pp. 233–46. Dumbarton Oaks, Washington, D.C.

Topic, Theresa L. and John R. Topic (1982) *Prehistoric Fortifications of Northern Peru: Preliminary Report on the Final Season, January–December, 1980.* Trent University Department of Anthropology, Peterborough.

——(1984) *Huamachuco Archaeological Project: Preliminary Report of the Third Season, June–August 1983.* Trent University Occasional Papers in Anthropology 1, Peterborough, Ontario.

——(1987) *Huamachuco Archaeological Report: Preliminary Report on the 1986 Field Season.* Trent University Occasional Papers in Anthropology 4, Peterborough, Ontario.

Torrence, Robin and Anne Clarke (editors) (2000) *The Archaeology of Difference: Negotiating Cross-Cultural Engagements in Oceania.* Routledge, London.

Tosi, Jr., Joseph A. (1960) *Zonas de vida natural en el Peru.* Boletín Técnico 5, Instituto de Ciencias Agrícolas de la OEA, Zona Andina, Lima.

Townsend, Richard F. (1985) 'Deciphering the Nazca world: ceramic images from Peru.' *Art Institute of Chicago Museum Studies* 11(2): 117–39.

Trexler, Richard (1999) *Sex and Conquest: Gendered Violence, Political Order, and the European Conquest of the Americas.* Cornell University Press, Ithaca.

Trimborn, Hermann (1949) *Señorío y barbarie en el valle del Cauca, estudio sobre la antigua civilización quimbaya y grupos afines del oeste de Colombia.* Consejo Superior de Investigaciones Científicas, Instituto Gonzalo Fernández de Oviedo, Madrid.

Tschauner, Hartmut (2003) 'Honco Pampa: arquitectura de élite del Horizonte Medio del Callejón de Huaylas.' In *Arqueología de la sierra de Ancash: propuestas y perspectivas,* edited by Bebel Ibarra, pp. 193–220. Instituto Cultural Runa, Lima.

Tung, Tiffiny A. (2008) 'Dismembering bodies for display: a bioarchaeological study of trophy heads from the Wari site of Conchopata, Peru.' *American Journal of Physical Anthropology* 136: 294–308.

Tung, Tiffiny A. and Kelly J. Knudson (2008) 'Social identities and geographical origins of Wari trophy heads from Conchopata, Peru.' *Current Anthropology* 49: 915–25.

Turner, Terence (1980) 'The social skin.' In *Not Work Alone: A Cross-Cultural View of Activities Superfluous to Survival*, edited by Jeremy Cherfas and Roger Lewin, pp. 112–40. Temple Smith, London.

——(1995) 'Social body and embodied subject: the production of bodies, actors and society among the Kayapo.' *Cultural Anthropology* 10: 143–70.

——(1996) 'Social complexity and recursive hierarchy in indigenous South American societies.' *Journal of the Steward Anthropological Society* 24: 37–60.

Uceda, Santiago (2001) 'Investigations at Huaca de la Luna, Moche Valley: an example of Moche religious architecture.' In *Moche Art and Architecture*, edited by Joanne Pillsbury, pp. 47–68. National Gallery of Art, Washington, D.C.

Uceda, Santiago and Carlos E. Rengifo (2006) 'La especialización del trabajo: teoría y arqueología. El caso de los orfebres Mochicas.' *Bulletin de l'Institut Français d'Études Andines* 35: 149–85.

Uceda, Santiago and Elias Mujica (editors) (1994) *Moche: propuestas y perspectivas*. Instituto Francés de Estudios Andinos, Trujillo.

——(2003) *Moche: hacia el final del milenio*. Pontificia Universidad Católica del Peru, Lima.

Uceda, Santiago and Moisés Tufinio (2003) 'El complejo arquitectónico religioso moche de Huaca de la Luna: una aproximación a su dinámica ocupacional.' In *Moche: hacia el final del milenio (tomo 2)*, edited by Santiago Uceda and Elías Mujica, pp. 179–228. Universidad Nacional de Trujillo y Pontificia Universidad Catolica del Peru, Lima.

Urioste, George (1981) 'Sickness and death in Pre-Conquest Andean cosmology.' In *Health in the Andes*, edited by J. Bastien and J. Donahue, pp. 9–18. American Anthropological Association, Washington, D.C.

Urton, Gary (1993) 'Actividad ceremonial y división de mitades en el mundo andino: las batallas rituales en los carnavales del Sur del Peru.' In *El Mundo Ceremonial Andino*, edited by Luis Millones and Yoshio Onuki, pp. 117–42. Editorial Horizonte, Lima.

——(1996) 'The body of meaning in Chavín art.' *Res* 29: 237–55.

——(1999) *Inca Myths*. University of Texas Press, Austin.

Van Buren, Mary (1996) 'Rethinking the vertical archipelago: ethnicity, exchange, and history in the south central Andes.' *American Anthropologist* 98: 338–51.

Van de Guchte, Maarten (1996) 'Sculpture and the concept of the double among the Inca kings.' *Res* 29/30: 257–68.

——(1999) 'The Inca cognition of landscape: archaeology, ethnohistory, and the aesthetic of alterity.' In *Archaeologies of Landscape: Contemporary Perspectives*, edited by Wendy Ashmore and A. Bernard Knapp, pp. 149–69. Blackwell, Malden.

Van Dyke, Ruth M. and Susan E. Alcock (editors) (2003) *Archaeologies of Memory*. Blackwell Publishers, Malden.

Van Gijseghem, Hendrik (2001) 'Household and family at Moche, Peru: an analysis of building and residence patterns in a prehispanic urban center.' *Latin American Antiquity* 12(3): 257–73.

Van Gijseghem, Hendrik and Kevin J. Vaughn (2008) 'Regional integration and the built environment in middle-range societies: Paracas and early Nasca houses and communities.' *Journal of Anthropological Archaeology* 27: 111–30.

Varón Gabai, Rafael (1980) *Curacas y encomenderos: acomodamiento nativo en Huaraz, siglos XVI–XVII*. P. L. Villanueva, Lima.

Vaughn, Kevin J. (2004) 'Households, crafts, and feasting in the ancient Andes: the village context of early Nasca craft consumption.' *Latin American Antiquity* 15: 61–88.

——(2005) 'Crafts and the materialization of chiefly power.' In *Foundations of Power in the Ancient Andes*, edited by Kevin J. Vaughn, Dennis E. Ogburn and Christina A. Conlee, pp. 113–30. Archaeological Papers of the American Anthropological Association 14, Washington D.C.

——(2009) *The Ancient Andean Village: Marcaya in Prehispanic Nasca*. University of Arizona Press, Tucson.

Velarde, María Inés, and Pamela Castro de la Mata (2011) 'Análisis e interpretación de los ornamentos de metal de un personaje de élite Recuay: Pashash'. *Arqueológicas* 28: 33–86.

Venturoli, Sofia (2006) 'Construcción y organización spacial de la ciudad de Huari: entre mito e historia.' In *La complejidad social en la Sierra de Ancash: ensayos sobre paisaje, economía y continuidades culturales*, edited by Alexander Herrera, Carolina Orsini and Kevin Lane, pp. 165–75. Civiche raccolte d'arte applicata del Castello Sforzesco, Milan.

Verano, John and Michael J. DeNiro (1993) 'Locals or foreigners? Morphological, biometric and isotopic approaches to the question of group affinity in human skeletal remains recovered from unusual archaeological contexts.' In *Investigations of Ancient Human Tissue: Chemical Analysis in Anthropology*, edited by Mary K. Sandford, pp. 361–86. Gordon & Breach, New York.

Verano, John W. (1986) 'A mass burial of mutilated individuals at Pacatnamu.' In *The Pacatnamú Papers, Volume 1*, edited by Christopher B. Donnan and Guillermo A. Cock, pp. 117–38. UCLA Museum of Cultural History, Los Angeles.

——(1995) 'Where do they rest? The treatment of human offerings and trophies in ancient Peru.' In *Tombs for the Living: Andean Mortuary Practices*, edited by Tom D. Dillehay, pp. 189–227. Dumbarton Oaks, Washington, D.C.

——(2001) 'War and death in the Moche world: osteological evidence and visual discourse.' In *Moche Art and Archaeology in Ancient Peru*, edited by Joanne Pillsbury, pp. 111–25. National Gallery of Art, Studies in the History of Art 63, Washington, D.C.

——(2008a) 'Communality and diversity in Moche human sacrifice.' In *The Art and Archaeology of the Moche: An Ancient Andean Society of the Peruvian North Coast*, edited by Steve Bourget and Kimberly Jones, pp. 195–213. University of Austin Press, Austin.

——(2008b) 'Trophy-head taking and human sacrifice in Andean South America.' In *Handbook of South American Archaeology*, edited by Helaine Silverman and William H. Isbell, pp. 1047–60. Kluwer, New York.

Vilaça, Aparecida (2002) 'Making kin out of others in Amazonia.' *Journal of the Royal Anthropological Institute* 8: 347–65.

——(2005) 'Chronically unstable bodies: reflections on Amazonian corporalities.' *Journal of the Royal Anthropological Institute* 11: 445–64.

——(2010) *Strange Enemies: Indigenous Agency and Scenes of Encounters in Amazonia*. Duke University Press, Durham.

Viveiros de Castro, Eduardo (1992) *From the Enemy's Point of View: Humanity and Divinity in an Amazonian Society*. University of Chicago Press, Chicago.

——(1996) 'Images of nature and society in Amazonian ethnology.' *Annual Review of Anthropology* 25: 179–200.

——(1998) 'Cosmological deixis and Amerindian perspectivism.' *Journal of the Royal Anthropological Institute* 4(n.s.): 469–88.

——(2001) 'GUT feelings about Amazonia: potential affinity and the construction of sociality.' In *Beyond the Visible and the Material*, edited by Laura M. Rival and Neil L. Whitehead, pp. 19–43. Oxford University Press, Oxford.

——(2004) 'Exchanging perspectives: the transformation of objects into subjects in Amerindian ontologies.' *Common Knowledge* 10: 463–84.

——(2010) 'The untimely, again.' In *The Archeology of Violence*, edited by Pierre Clastres, pp. 9–51. Semiotexte, Los Angeles.

Wagner, Roy (1991) 'The fractal person.' In *Big Men and Great Men: Personifications of Power in Melanesia*, edited by Marilyn Strathern and Maurice Godelier, pp. 159–73. Cambridge University Press, Cambridge.

Walens, Stanley (1981) *Feasting with Cannibals: An Essay on Kwakiutl Cosmology*. Princeton University Press, Princeton.

Wallerstein, Immanuel (1974–80) *The Modern World System I–II*. Academic Press, New York.

Walter, Doris (1997) 'Comment meurent les pumas: du mythe au rite à Huaraz (centre-nord du Pérou).' *Bulletin de l'Institut Français d'Études Andines* 26(3): 447–71.

——(2002) *La domestication de la nature dans les Andes Péruviennes*. L'Harmattan, Paris.

——(2006) 'Los sitios arqueológicos en el imaginario de los campesinos de la Cordillera Blanca (Sierra de Ancash).' In *Complejidad social en la arqueología y antropología de la sierra de*

Ancash, Peru, edited by Alexander Herrera, Carolina Orsini and Kevin Lane, pp. 177–90. Comune di Milano-Raccolte Extra Europee del Castello Sforzesco, Milan.

Watanabe, Shinya (2009) 'La cerámica caolín en la cultura Cajamarca (sierra norte del Perú): el caso de la fase Cajamarca Medio.' *Bulletin de l'Institut Français d'Ètudes Andines* 38(3): 205–35.

Wegner, Steven A. (1988) *Cultura Recuay*. Exhibit pamphlet. Banco Continental and Museo Arqueológico de Ancash, Lima, September–October.

——(2000) *Arqueología y arte antiguo de Chacas*. Instituto Cultural Ancashwain, Huaraz.

——(2011) *Iconografías prehispánicos de Ancash (tomo II): cultura Recuay*. Asociación Ancash, Lima.

Weiner, Annette B. (1992) *Inalienable Possessions: The Paradox of Keeping-while-Giving*. University of California Press, Berkeley.

Weismantel, Mary J. (1988) *Food, Gender, and Poverty in the Ecuadorian Andes*. University of Pennsylvania Press, Philadelphia.

——(1989) 'Making breakfast and raising babies: the Zumbagua household as constituted process.' In *Household Economy: Reconsidering the Domestic Mode of Production*, edited by Richard Wilk, pp. 55–72. Westview Press, Boulder.

——(2001) *Cholas and Pishtacos: Stories of Race and Sex in the Andes*. University of Chicago Press, Chicago.

——(2004) 'Moche sex pots: reproduction and temporality in ancient South America.' *American Anthropologist* 106: 495–505.

Wengrow, David (2011) 'Cognition, materiality and monsters: the cultural transmission of counter-intuitive forms in Bronze Age societies.' *Journal of Material Culture* 16: 131–49.

White, Christine D., T. Douglas Price and Fred J. Longstaffe (2007) 'Residential histories of the human sacrifices at the Moon Pyramid, Teotihuacan: evidence from oxygen and strontium isotopes.' *Ancient Mesoamerica* 18: 159–72.

White, Christine D., Michael W. Spence, Fred J. Longstaffe, Hilary Stuart-Williams and Kimberly R. Law (2002) 'Geographic identities of the sacrificial victims from the Feathered Serpent Pyramid, Teotihuacan: implications for the nature of state power.' *Latin American Antiquity* 13: 217–36.

Whitehead, Neil L. (1998) 'Colonial chieftains of the Lower Orinoco and Guyana coast.' In *Chiefdoms and Chieftaincy in the Americas*, edited by Elsa M. Redmond, pp. 150–63. University Press of Florida, Gainesville.

Willey, Gordon R. (1945) 'Horizon styles and pottery traditions in Peruvian archaeology.' *American Antiquity* 11: 49–56.

——(1948) 'A functional analysis of "horizon styles" in Peruvian archaeology.' In *A Reappraisal of Peruvian Archaeology*, edited by Wendell C. Bennett, pp. 8–15. Society for American Archaeology Memoir 4, Menasha.

Williams, Sloan R. (2005) 'Ethnicity, kinship and ancient DNA.' In *Us and Them: Archaeology and Ethnicity in the Andes*, edited by Richard Martin Reycraft, pp. 134–52. Cotsen Institute of Archaeology, UCLA, Los Angeles.

Wilson, David J. (1987) 'Reconstructing patterns of early warfare in the Lower Santa Valley: new data on the role of conflict in the origins of north coast complexity.' In *The Origins and Development of the Andean State*, edited by Jonathan Haas, Shelia Pozorski and Thomas Pozorski, pp. 56–69. Cambridge University Press, Cambridge.

——(1988) *Prehispanic Settlement Patterns in the Lower Santa Valley, Peru: A Regional Perspective on the Origins and Development of Complex North Coast Society*. Smithsonian Institution Press, Washington, D.C.

Woloszyn, Janusz Z. (2008) *Los rostros silenciosos: los huacos retrato de la cultura moche*. Pontificia Universidad Católica del Perú, Lima.

Woodford, Susan (1993) *The Trojan War in Ancient Art*. Duckworth, London.

Yacovleff, Eugenio (1932) 'Las falcónidas en el arte y en las creencias de los antiguos peruanos.' *Revista del Museo Nacional* 1(1): 33–111.

Yoffee, Norman (2005) *Myths of the Archaic State*. Cambridge University Press, Cambridge.

Young, Kenneth R. and Blanca León (1999) *Peru's Humid Eastern Montane Forests: An Overview of Their Physical Settings, Biological Diversity, Human Use and Settlement, and Conservation Needs*.

Centre for Research on the Cultural and Biological Diversity of Andean Rainforests, Oyacachi.

Zuidema, R. Tom (1973) 'Kinship and ancestor cult in three Peruvian communities: Hernández Príncipe's account of 1622.' *Bulletin de l'Institut Français d'Ètudes Andines* 2(1): 16–33.

——(1978) 'Shaft-tombs and the Inca empire.' *Journal of the Steward Anthropological Society* 9: 133–78.

——(1985) 'Lion in the city: royal symbols of transition in Cuzco.' In *Animal Myths and Metaphors in South America*, edited by Gary Urton, pp. 183–250. University of Utah Press, Salt Lake City.

——(1990) 'Dynastic structures in Andean culture.' In *Northern Dynasties: Kingship and Statecraft in Chimor*, edited by Michael E. Moseley and Alana Cordy-Collins, pp. 489–505. Dumbarton Oaks, Washington, D.C.

INDEX

Note: Figures are shown in *italics,* with the page number after the prefix *fig.* Plates are shown in **bold,** with the plate number after the prefix **pl.**

www.routledge.com/archaeology

Also from Routledge ...

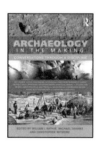

Archaeology in the Making

Conversations Through a Discipline

William L Rathje, Michael Shanks, Christopher Witmore

Archaeology in the Making is a collection of bold statements about archaeology, its history, how it works, and why it is more important than ever. Comprised of conversations between notable contemporary figures in the field, the book delves into questions concerning major events in human history such as the origins of agriculture and the state, and about the way archaeologists go about their work.

This is a unique document detailing the history of archaeology in the second half of the twentieth century to the present day. It will be invaluable for anybody who wants to understand the theory and practice of this ever-developing discipline.

HB: 978-0-415-63480-9

For more information and to order a copy visit www.routledge.com/9780415630489

Available from all good bookshops

www.routledge.com/archaeology

Also from Routledge ...

An Archaeology of the Cosmos

Rethinking Religion and Agency in Ancient America

Timothy Pauketat

This volume seeks answers to two fundamental questions of humanity and human history: why do so many people believe in supreme beings and holy spirits? What causes beliefs to change?

Using evidence gathered from ancient America and drawing on and adapting theories of agency and religion, the author examines the intimate association of agency and religion by studying how relationships between people, places, and things were bundled together and positioned in ways that constituted the fields of human experience.

The work provides readers with thought-provoking conclusions that will lead them to reassess the way they approach the study of ancient religion.

PB: 978-0-415-52129-1
HB: 978-0-415-52128-4

For more information and to order a copy visit
www.routledge.com/9780415521291

Available from all good bookshops